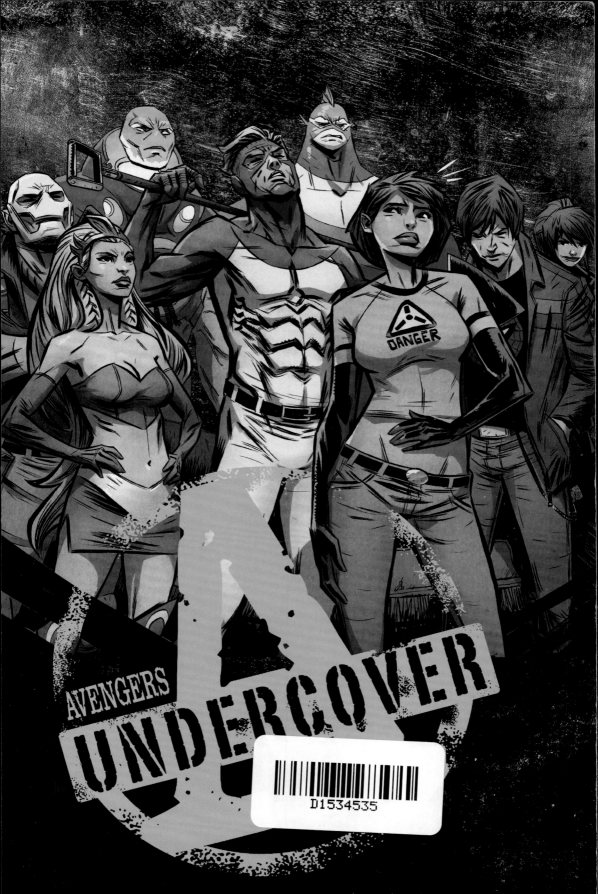

AVENGERS
UNDERCOVER

GOING NATIVE

HAZMAT CHASE NICO DEATH LOCKET

CAMMI ANACHRONISM BLOODSTONE

COLLECTION EDITOR: **JENNIFER GRÜNWALD**
ASSISTANT EDITOR: **SARAH BRUNSTAD**   ASSOCIATE MANAGING EDITOR: **ALEX STARBUCK**
EDITOR, SPECIAL PROJECTS: **MARK D. BEAZLEY**   SENIOR EDITOR, SPECIAL PROJECTS: **JEFF YOUNGQU**
SVP PRINT, SALES & MARKETING: **DAVID GABRIEL**   BOOK DESIGNER: **RODOLFO MURAGUCHI**

EDITOR IN CHIEF: **AXEL ALONSO**   CHIEF CREATIVE OFFICER: **JOE QUESADA**
PUBLISHER: **DAN BUCKLEY**   EXECUTIVE PRODUCER: **ALAN FINE**

AVENGERS UNDERCOVER VOL. 2: GOING NATIVE. Contains material originally published in magazine form as AVENGERS UNDERCOVER #6-10. First printing 2014. ISBN# 978-0-7851-8
Published by MARVEL WORLDWIDE, INC., a subsidiary of MARVEL ENTERTAINMENT, LLC. OFFICE OF PUBLICATION: 135 West 50th Street, New York, NY 10020. Copyright © 2014 Marvel Char
Inc. All rights reserved. All characters featured in this issue and the distinctive names and likenesses thereof, and all related indicia are trademarks of Marvel Characters, Inc. No similarity betwe
of the names, characters, persons, and/or institutions in this magazine with those of any living or dead person or institution is intended, and any such similarity which may exist is purely coinci
Printed in Canada. ALAN FINE, EVP - Office of the President, Marvel Worldwide, Inc. and EVP & CMO Marvel Characters B.V.; DAN BUCKLEY, Publisher & President - Print, Animation & Digital Div
JOE QUESADA, Chief Creative Officer; TOM BREVOORT, SVP of Publishing; DAVID BOGART, SVP of Operations & Procurement, Publishing; C.B. CEBULSKI, SVP of Creator & Content Develo
DAVID GABRIEL, SVP Print, Sales & Marketing; JIM O'KEEFE, VP of Operations & Logistics; DAN CARR, Executive Director of Publishing Technology; SUSAN CRESPI, Editorial Operations Manage
MORALES, Publishing Operations Manager; STAN LEE, Chairman Emeritus. For information regarding advertising in Marvel Comics or on Marvel.com, please contact Niza Disla, Director of
Partnerships, at ndisla@marvel.com. For Marvel subscription inquiries, please call 800-217-9158. **Manufactured between 9/19/2014 and 10/27/2014 by SOLISCO PRINTERS, SCOTT, QC, CA**

10 9 8 7 6 5 4 3 2 1

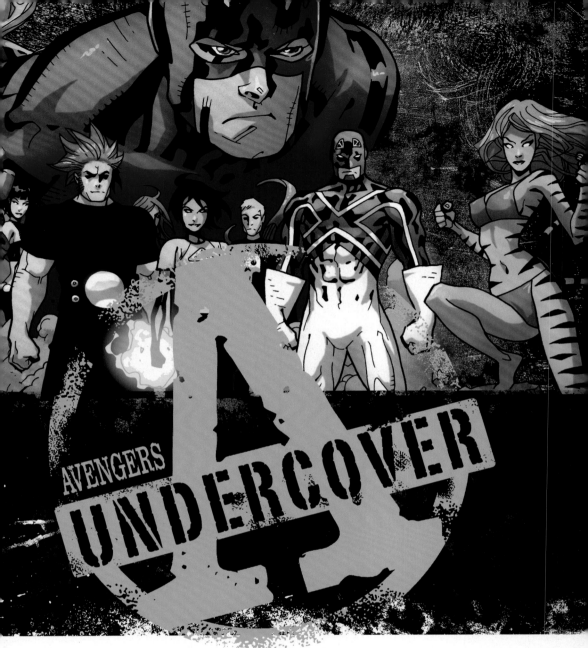

AVENGERS UNDERCOVER

GOING NATIVE

WRITER:
DENNIS HOPELESS

ARTISTS:
TIMOTHY GREEN II (#6 & #9),
KEV WALKER & JASON GORDER (#7)
AND **TIGH WALKER** (#8 & #10)

COLOR ARTIST: JEAN-FRANCOIS BEAULIEU
LETTERER: VC'S JOE CARAMAGNA
COVER ART: FRANCESCO MATTINA
ASSISTANT EDITOR: JON MOISAN
EDITOR: BILL ROSEMANN

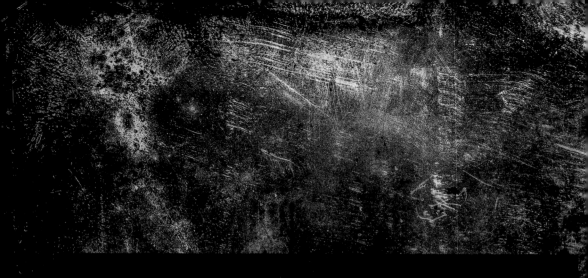

P R E V I O U S L Y

Three months after the demented Arcade kidnapped
16 super-powered teens and made them fight each
other to the death on Murder World, the survivors of his
savage game found their tormentor and killed him.

With the attack caught on video, the teens were incarcerated
by S.H.I.E.L.D....until Daimon Hellstrom, the literal son of Satan,
teleported them all back to the capital city of Bagalia, where
Baron Zemo offered them a chance to join his Masters of Evil.

After being given a night to explore the city and see what the
Masters had to offer, they accepted Zemo's offer, but only for
the purpose of taking him and the entire city of villains down
from within. Cammi, the only member of the group who decided
not to join, soon discovered that leaving wasn't really an option
when she was brutally attacked and captured by Constrictor.

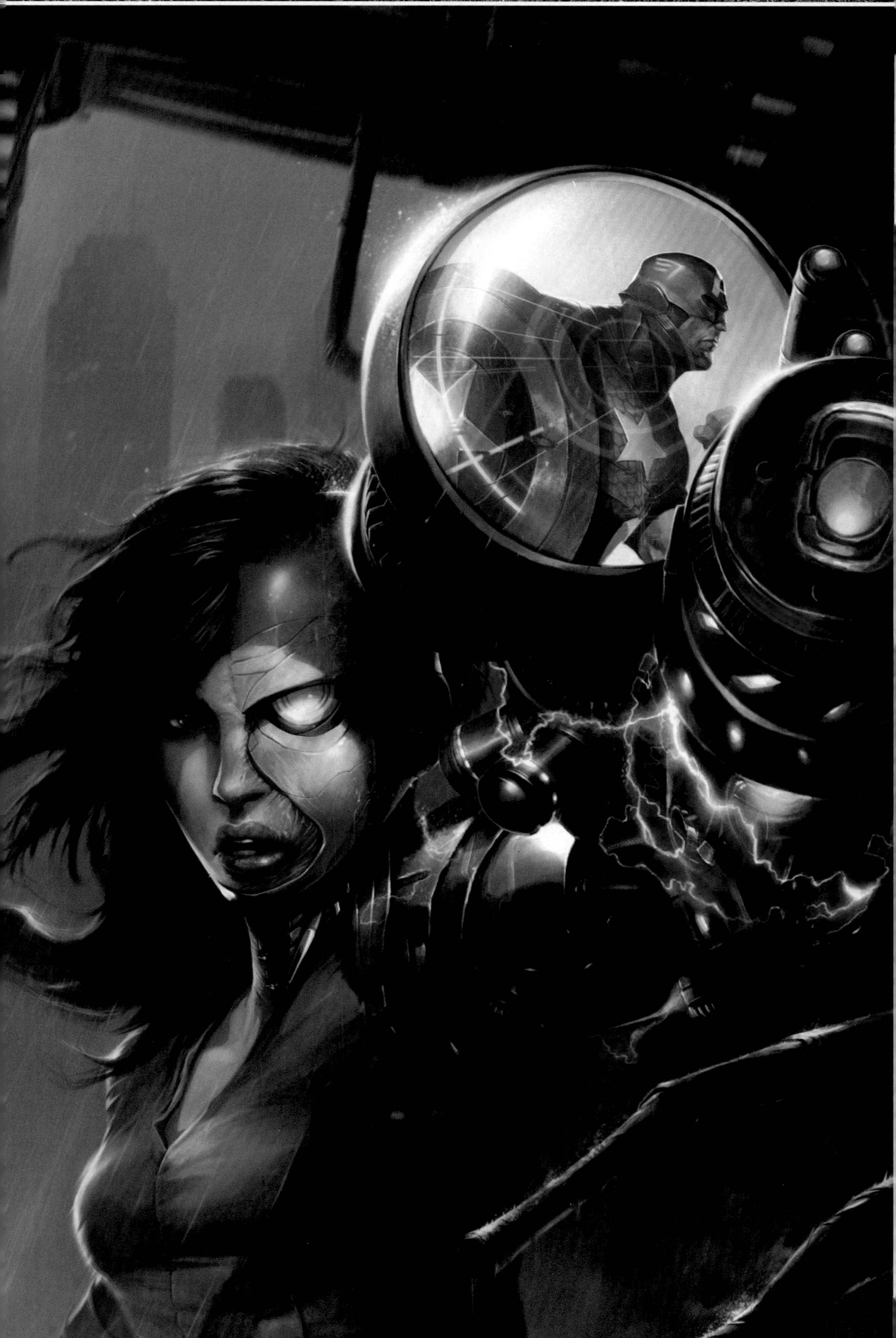

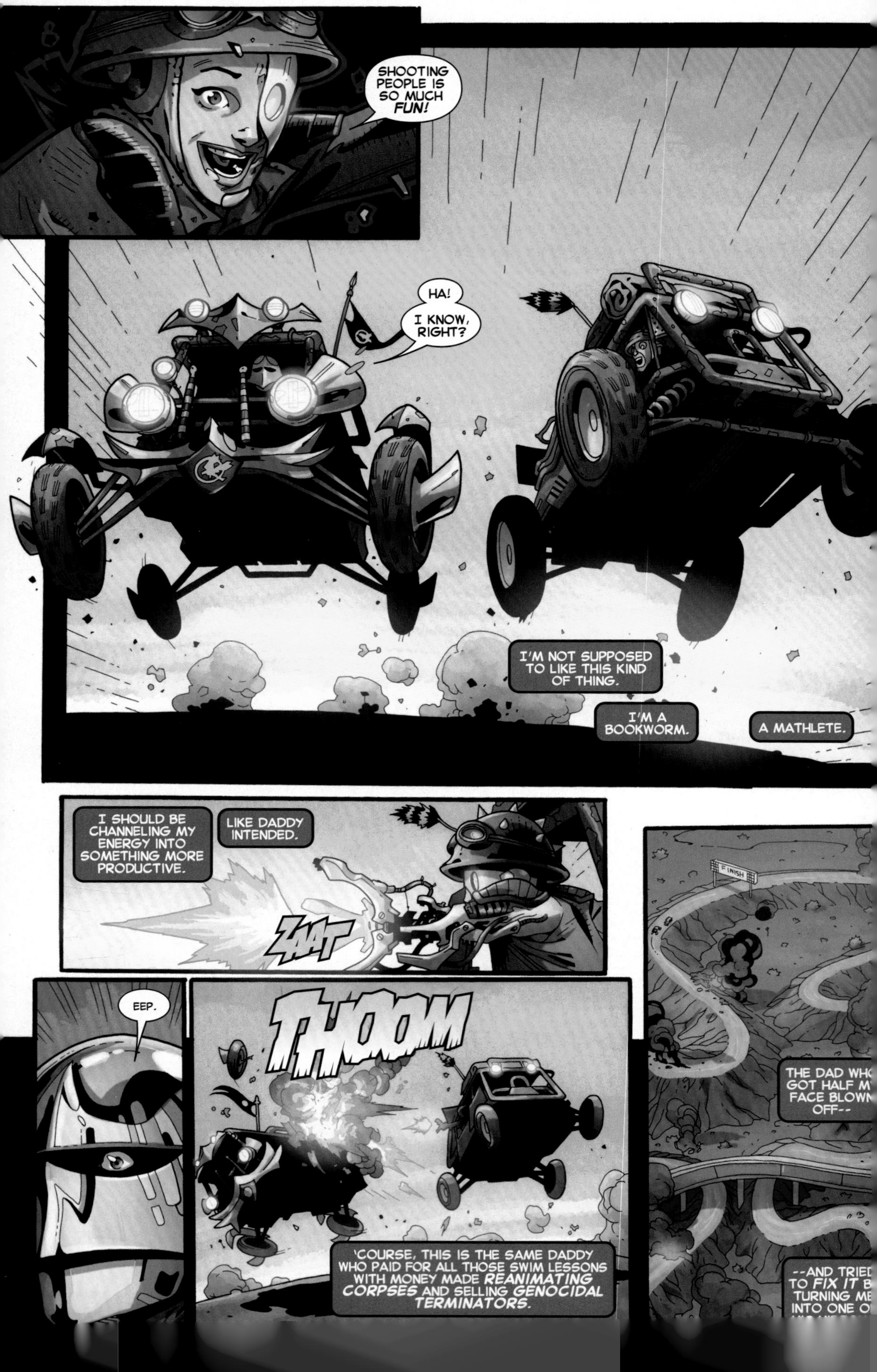
SHOOTING PEOPLE IS SO MUCH *FUN!*
HA!
I KNOW, RIGHT?
I'M NOT SUPPOSED TO LIKE THIS KIND OF THING.
I'M A BOOKWORM.
A MATHLETE.
I SHOULD BE CHANNELING MY ENERGY INTO SOMETHING MORE PRODUCTIVE.
LIKE DADDY INTENDED.
ZAAT
EEP.
THOOM
'COURSE, THIS IS THE SAME DADDY WHO PAID FOR ALL THOSE SWIM LESSONS WITH MONEY MADE *REANIMATING CORPSES* AND SELLING *GENOCIDAL TERMINATORS.*
FINISH
THE DAD WHO GOT HALF MY FACE BLOWN OFF--
--AND TRIED TO *FIX IT* BY TURNING ME INTO ONE OF

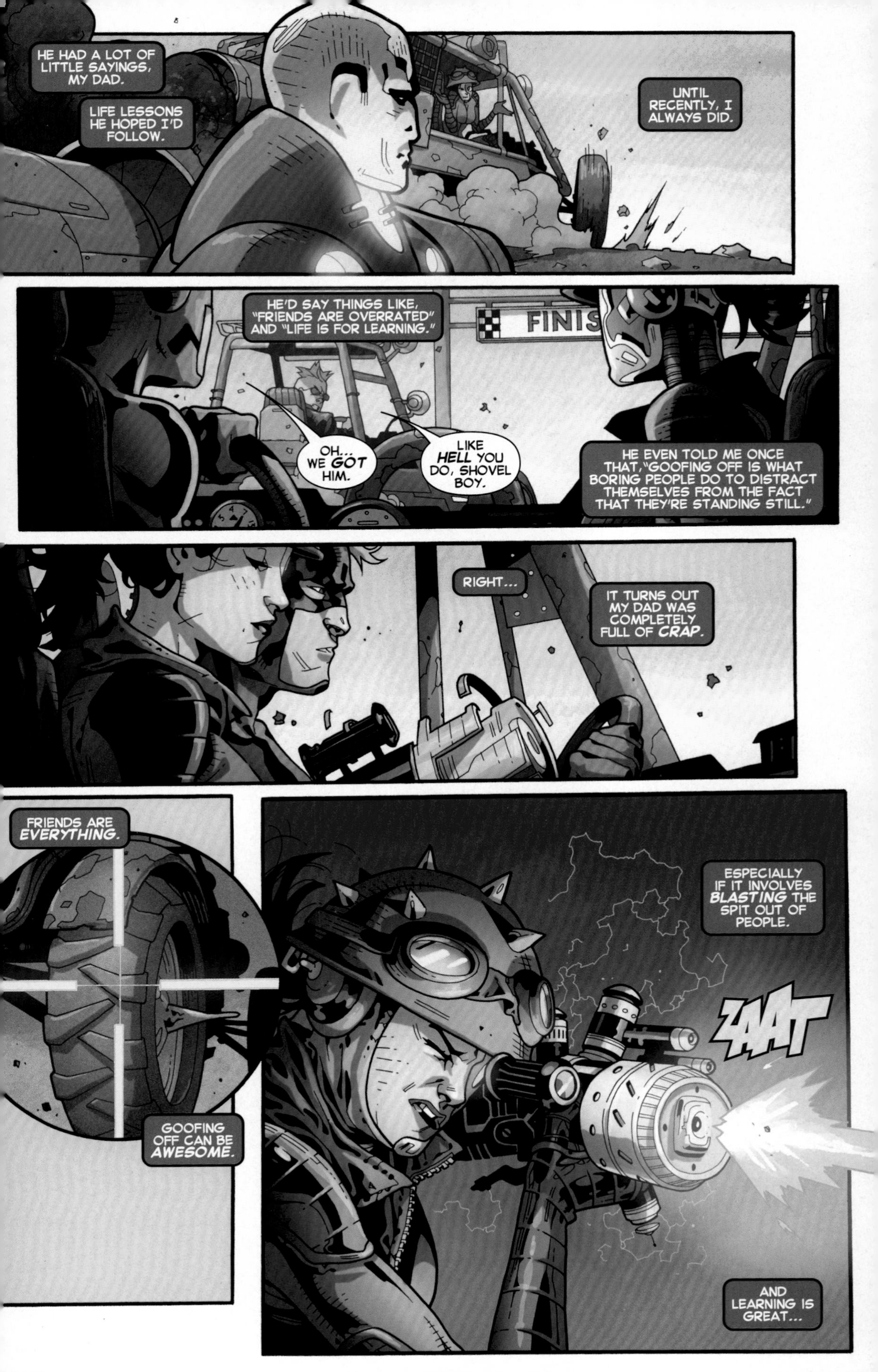
HE HAD A LOT OF LITTLE SAYINGS, MY DAD.
LIFE LESSONS HE HOPED I'D FOLLOW.
UNTIL RECENTLY, I ALWAYS DID.
HE'D SAY THINGS LIKE, "FRIENDS ARE OVERRATED" AND "LIFE IS FOR LEARNING."
FINIS
OH... WE **GOT** HIM.
LIKE **HELL** YOU DO, SHOVEL BOY.
HE EVEN TOLD ME ONCE THAT, "GOOFING OFF IS WHAT BORING PEOPLE DO TO DISTRACT THEMSELVES FROM THE FACT THAT THEY'RE STANDING STILL."
RIGHT...
IT TURNS OUT MY DAD WAS COMPLETELY FULL OF ***CRAP***.
FRIENDS ARE ***EVERYTHING***.
GOOFING OFF CAN BE ***AWESOME***.
ESPECIALLY IF IT INVOLVES ***BLASTING*** THE SPIT OUT OF PEOPLE.
ZAAT
AND LEARNING IS GREAT...

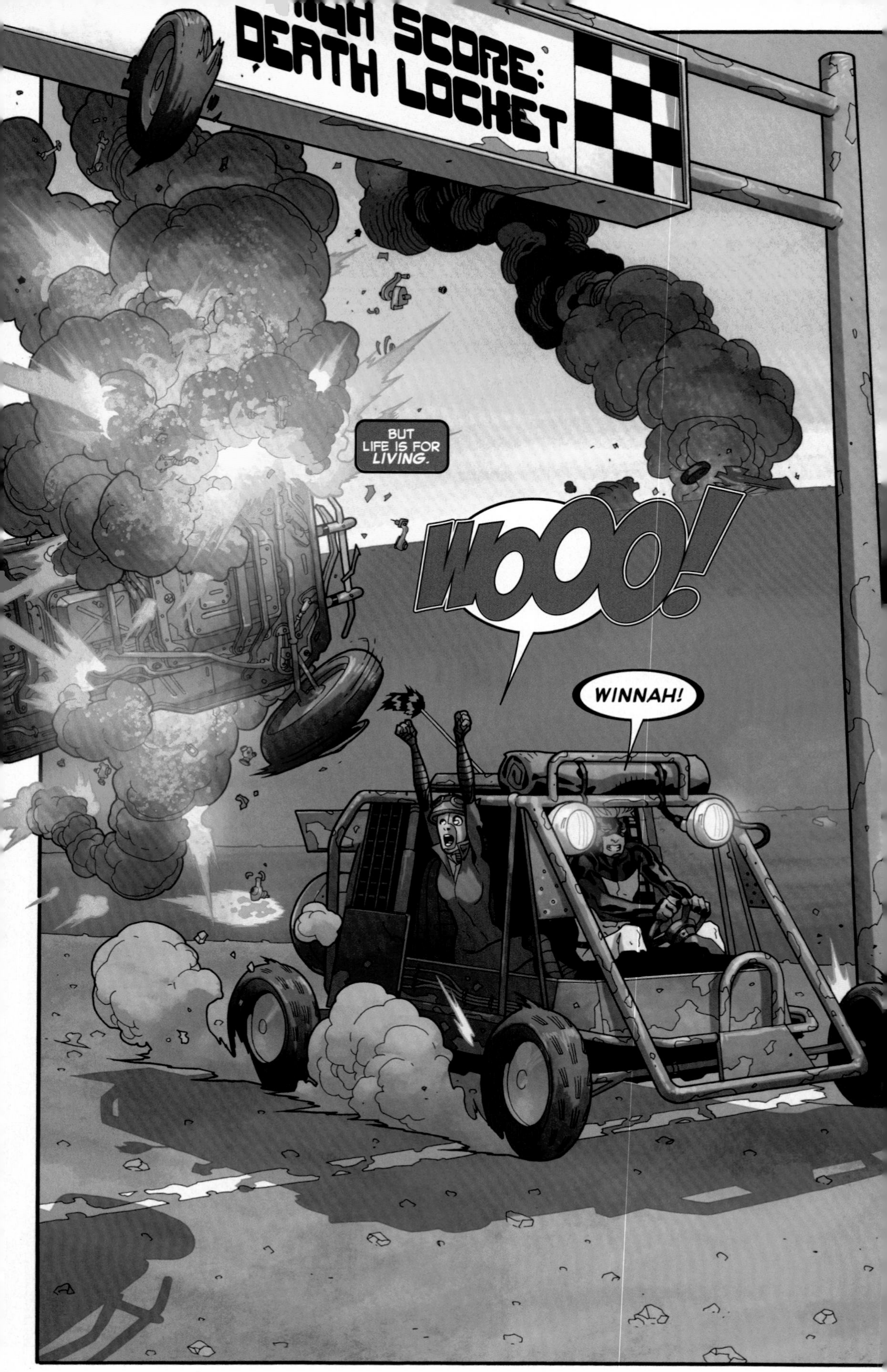
HIGH SCORE:
DEATH LOCKET
BUT LIFE IS FOR LIVING.
WOOO!
WINNAH!

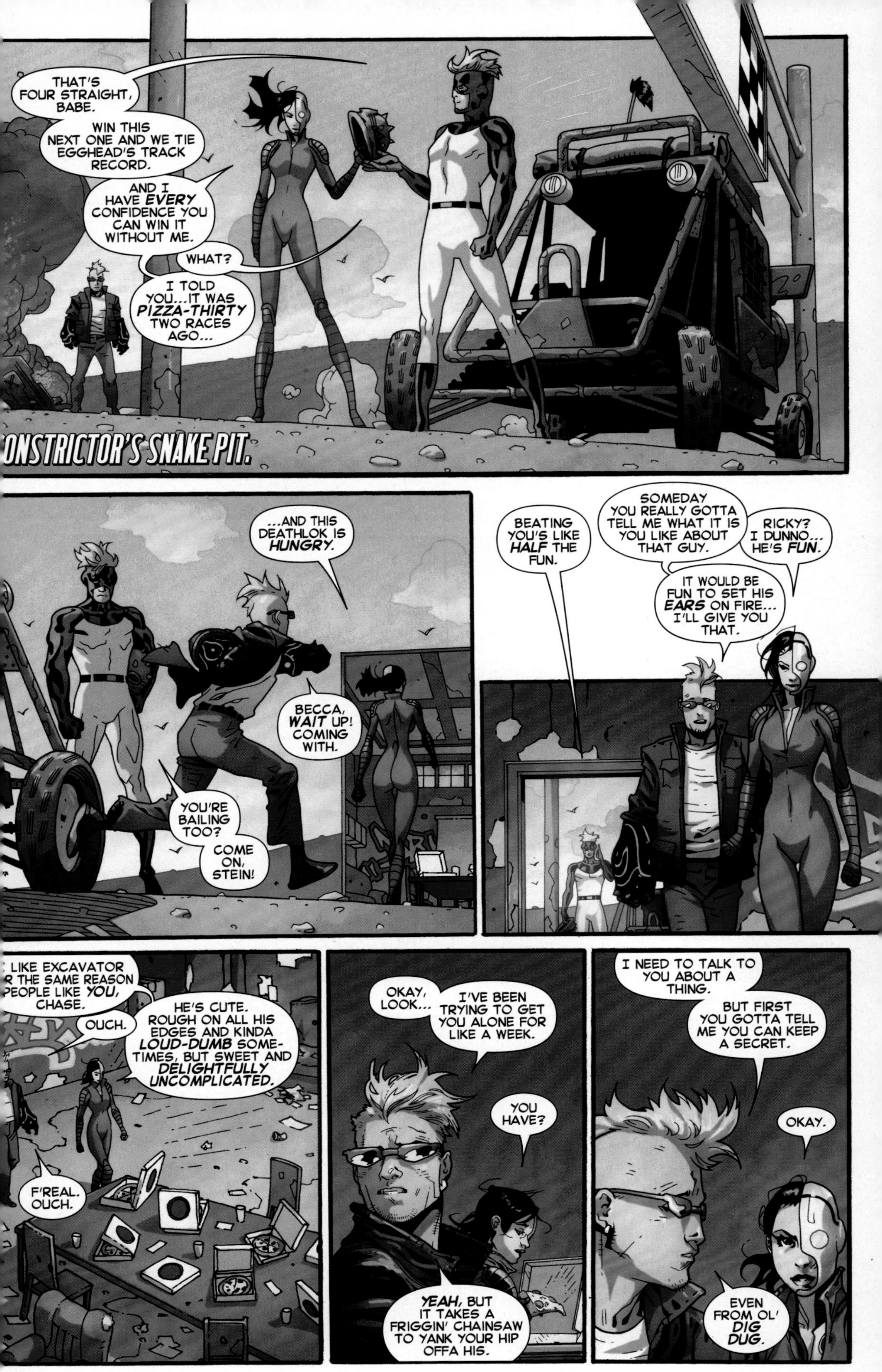
THAT'S FOUR STRAIGHT, BABE.
WIN THIS NEXT ONE AND WE TIE EGGHEAD'S TRACK RECORD.
AND I HAVE EVERY CONFIDENCE YOU CAN WIN IT WITHOUT ME.
WHAT?
I TOLD YOU...IT WAS PIZZA-THIRTY TWO RACES AGO...
ONSTRICTOR'S SNAKE PIT.
...AND THIS DEATHLOK IS HUNGRY.
BECCA, WAIT UP! COMING WITH.
YOU'RE BAILING TOO?
COME ON, STEIN!
BEATING YOU'S LIKE HALF THE FUN.
SOMEDAY YOU REALLY GOTTA TELL ME WHAT IT IS YOU LIKE ABOUT THAT GUY.
RICKY? I DUNNO... HE'S FUN.
IT WOULD BE FUN TO SET HIS EARS ON FIRE... I'LL GIVE YOU THAT.
LIKE EXCAVATOR R THE SAME REASON PEOPLE LIKE YOU, CHASE.
OUCH.
HE'S CUTE. ROUGH ON ALL HIS EDGES AND KINDA LOUD-DUMB SOMETIMES, BUT SWEET AND DELIGHTFULLY UNCOMPLICATED.
F'REAL. OUCH.
OKAY, LOOK...
I'VE BEEN TRYING TO GET YOU ALONE FOR LIKE A WEEK.
YOU HAVE?
YEAH, BUT IT TAKES A FRIGGIN' CHAINSAW TO YANK YOUR HIP OFFA HIS.
I NEED TO TALK TO YOU ABOUT A THING.
BUT FIRST YOU GOTTA TELL ME YOU CAN KEEP A SECRET.
OKAY.
EVEN FROM OL' DIG DUG.

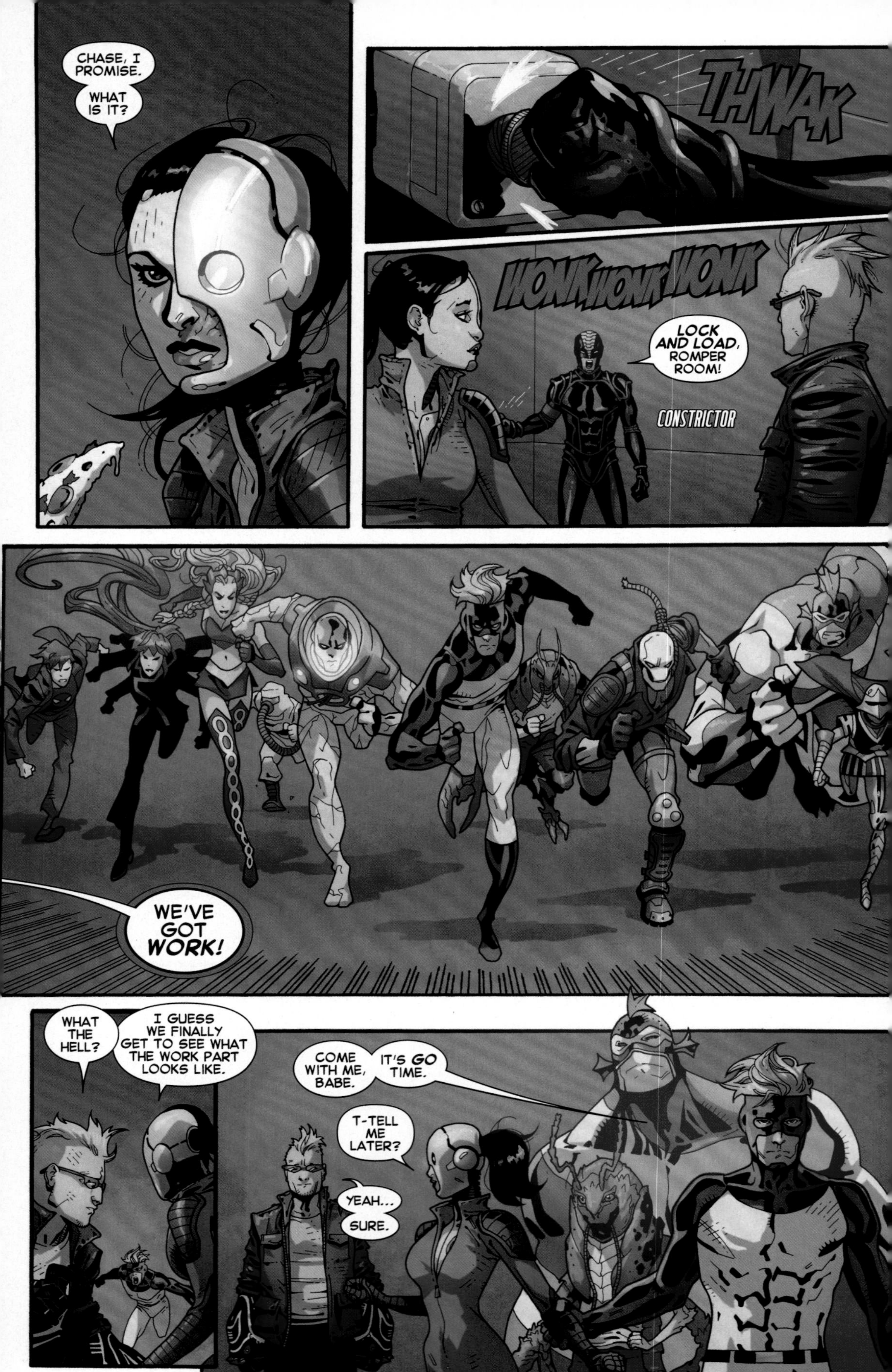
CHASE, I PROMISE.
WHAT IS IT?
THWAK
WONK WONK WONK
LOCK AND LOAD, ROMPER ROOM!
CONSTRICTOR
WE'VE GOT WORK!
WHAT THE HELL?
I GUESS WE FINALLY GET TO SEE WHAT THE WORK PART LOOKS LIKE.
COME WITH ME, BABE.
IT'S GO TIME.
T-TELL ME LATER?
YEAH...
SURE.

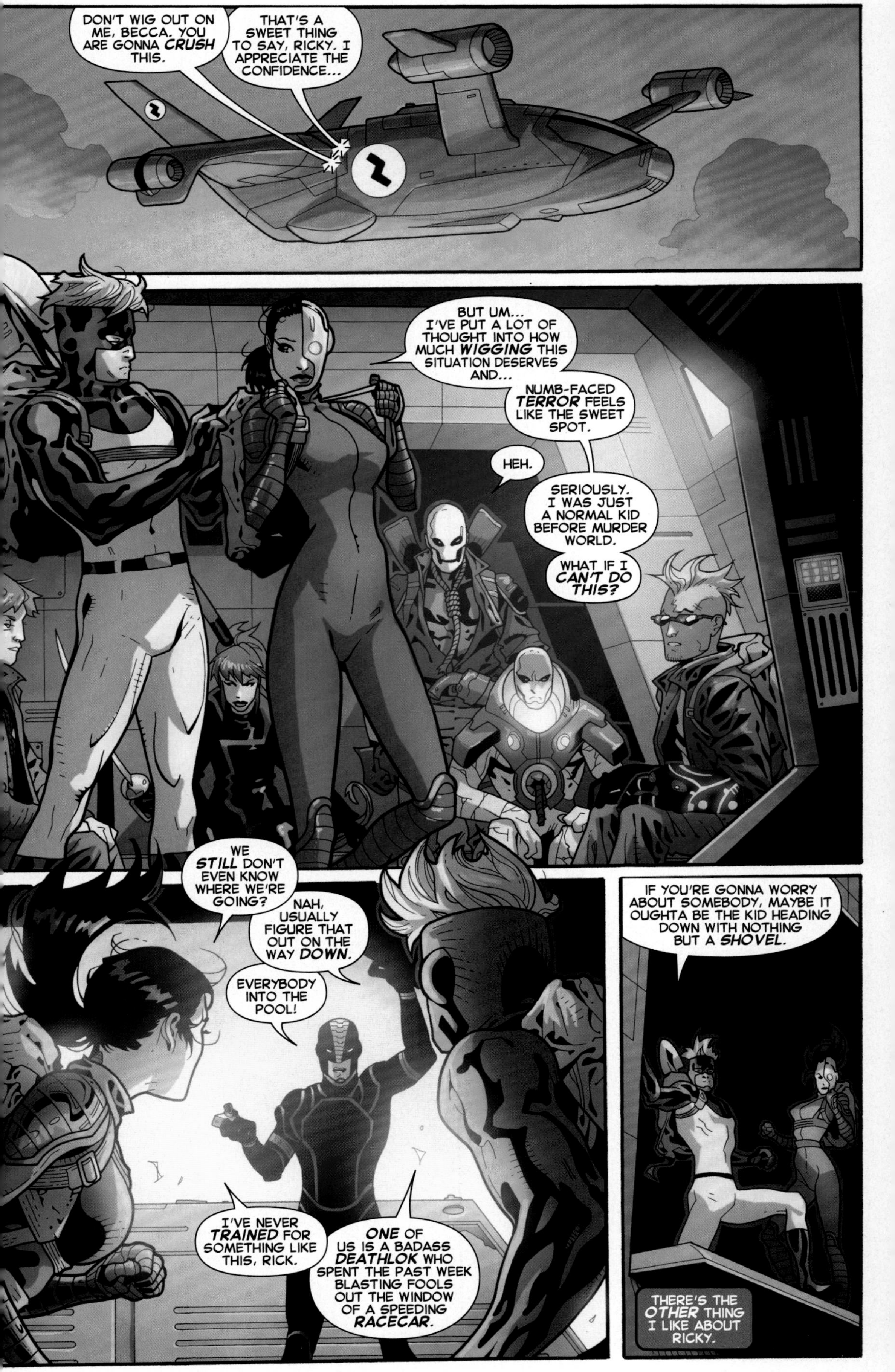
DON'T WIG OUT ON ME, BECCA. YOU ARE GONNA CRUSH THIS.
THAT'S A SWEET THING TO SAY, RICKY. I APPRECIATE THE CONFIDENCE...
BUT UM... I'VE PUT A LOT OF THOUGHT INTO HOW MUCH WIGGING THIS SITUATION DESERVES AND...
NUMB-FACED TERROR FEELS LIKE THE SWEET SPOT.
HEH.
SERIOUSLY. I WAS JUST A NORMAL KID BEFORE MURDER WORLD.
WHAT IF I CAN'T DO THIS?
WE STILL DON'T EVEN KNOW WHERE WE'RE GOING?
NAH, USUALLY FIGURE THAT OUT ON THE WAY DOWN.
EVERYBODY INTO THE POOL!
I'VE NEVER TRAINED FOR SOMETHING LIKE THIS, RICK.
ONE OF US IS A BADASS DEATHLOK WHO SPENT THE PAST WEEK BLASTING FOOLS OUT THE WINDOW OF A SPEEDING RACECAR.
IF YOU'RE GONNA WORRY ABOUT SOMEBODY, MAYBE IT OUGHTA BE THE KID HEADING DOWN WITH NOTHING BUT A SHOVEL.
THERE'S THE OTHER THING I LIKE ABOUT RICKY.

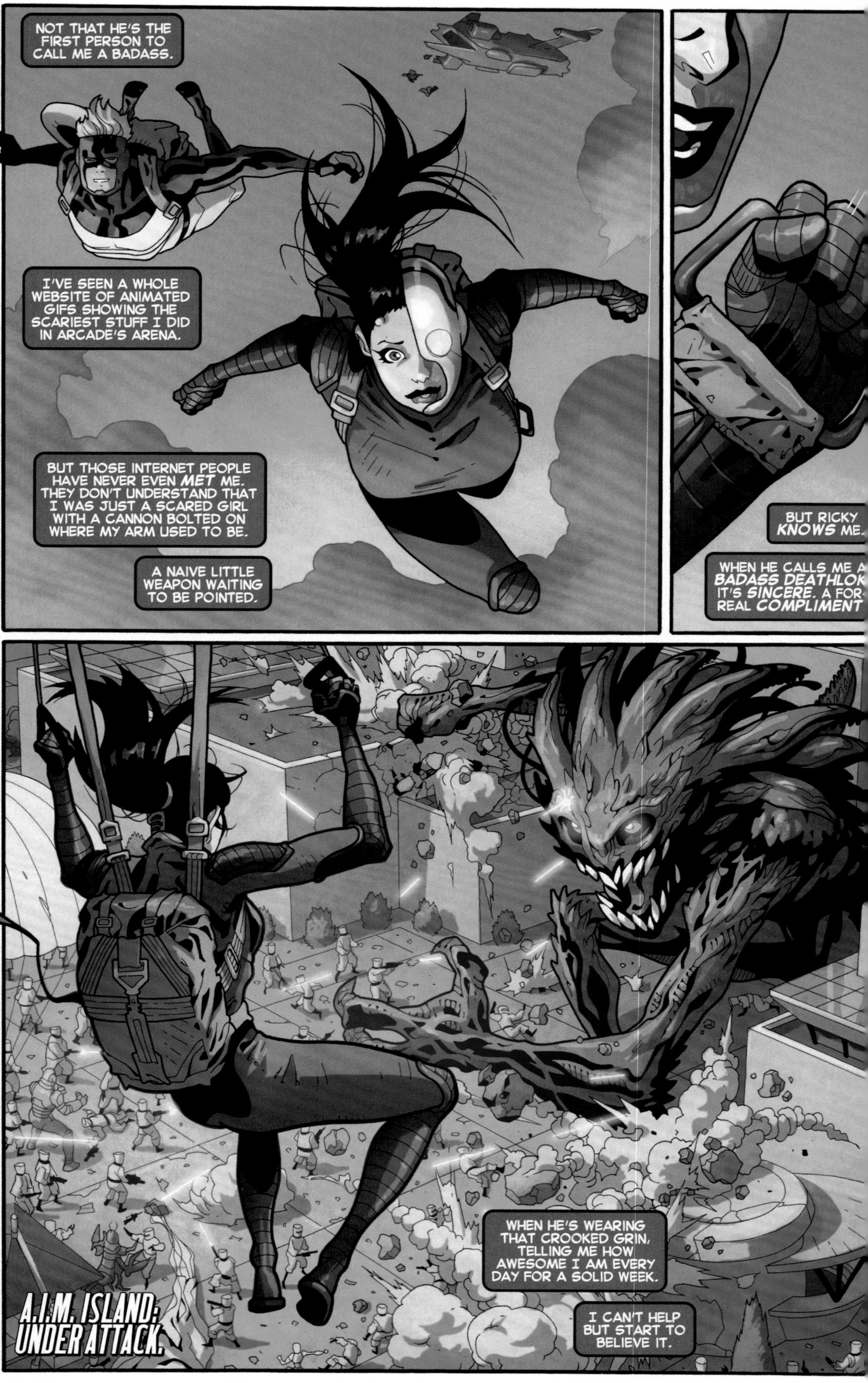
NOT THAT HE'S THE FIRST PERSON TO CALL ME A BADASS.
I'VE SEEN A WHOLE WEBSITE OF ANIMATED GIFS SHOWING THE SCARIEST STUFF I DID IN ARCADE'S ARENA.
BUT THOSE INTERNET PEOPLE HAVE NEVER EVEN MET ME. THEY DON'T UNDERSTAND THAT I WAS JUST A SCARED GIRL WITH A CANNON BOLTED ON WHERE MY ARM USED TO BE.
A NAIVE LITTLE WEAPON WAITING TO BE POINTED.
BUT RICKY KNOWS ME.
WHEN HE CALLS ME A BADASS DEATHLOK IT'S SINCERE. A FOR-REAL COMPLIMENT
A.I.M. ISLAND: UNDER ATTACK.
WHEN HE'S WEARING THAT CROOKED GRIN, TELLING ME HOW AWESOME I AM EVERY DAY FOR A SOLID WEEK.
I CAN'T HELP BUT START TO BELIEVE IT.

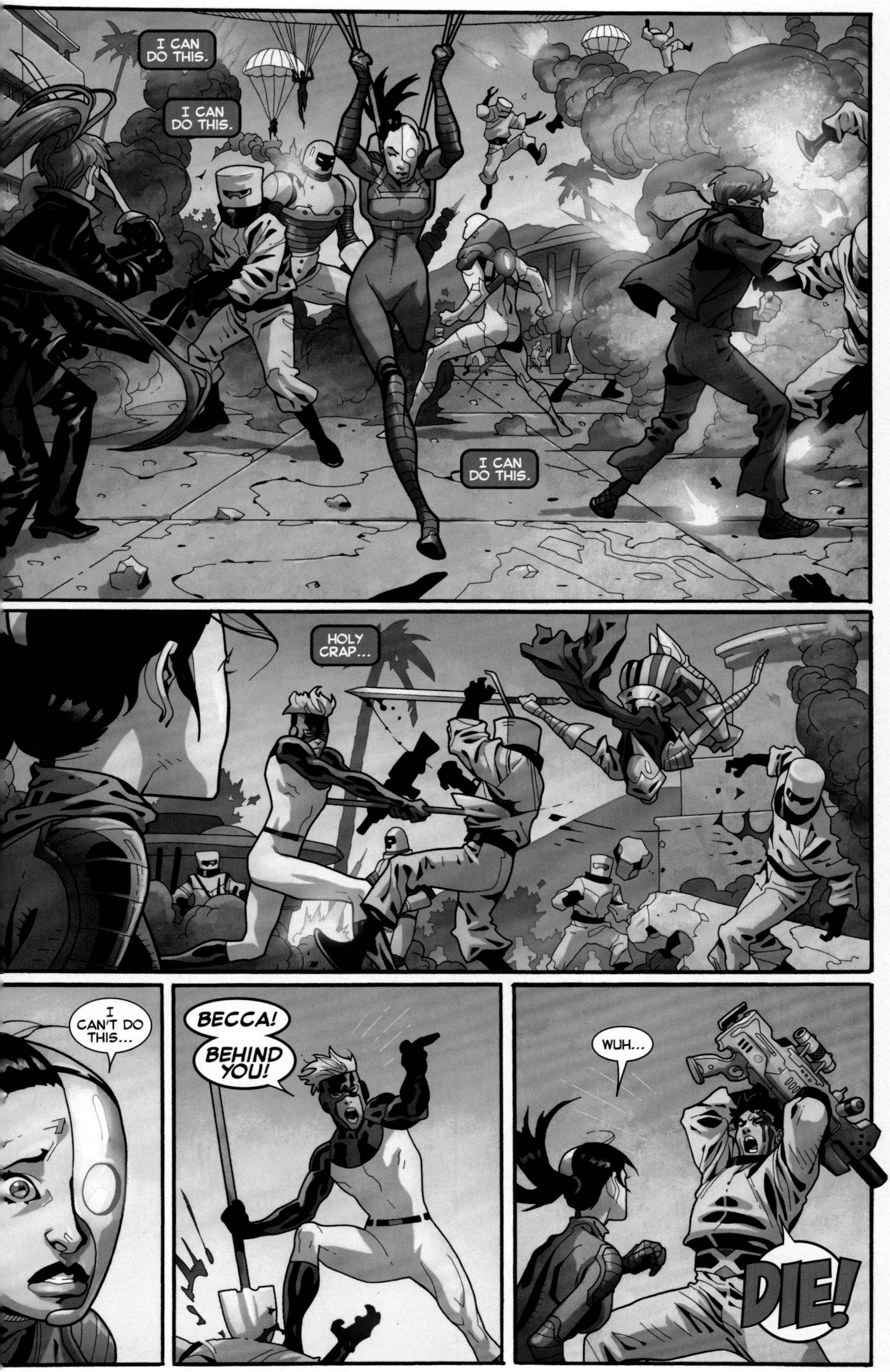
I CAN DO THIS.
I CAN DO THIS.
I CAN DO THIS.
HOLY CRAP...
I CAN'T DO THIS...
BECCA!
BEHIND YOU!
WUH...
DIE!

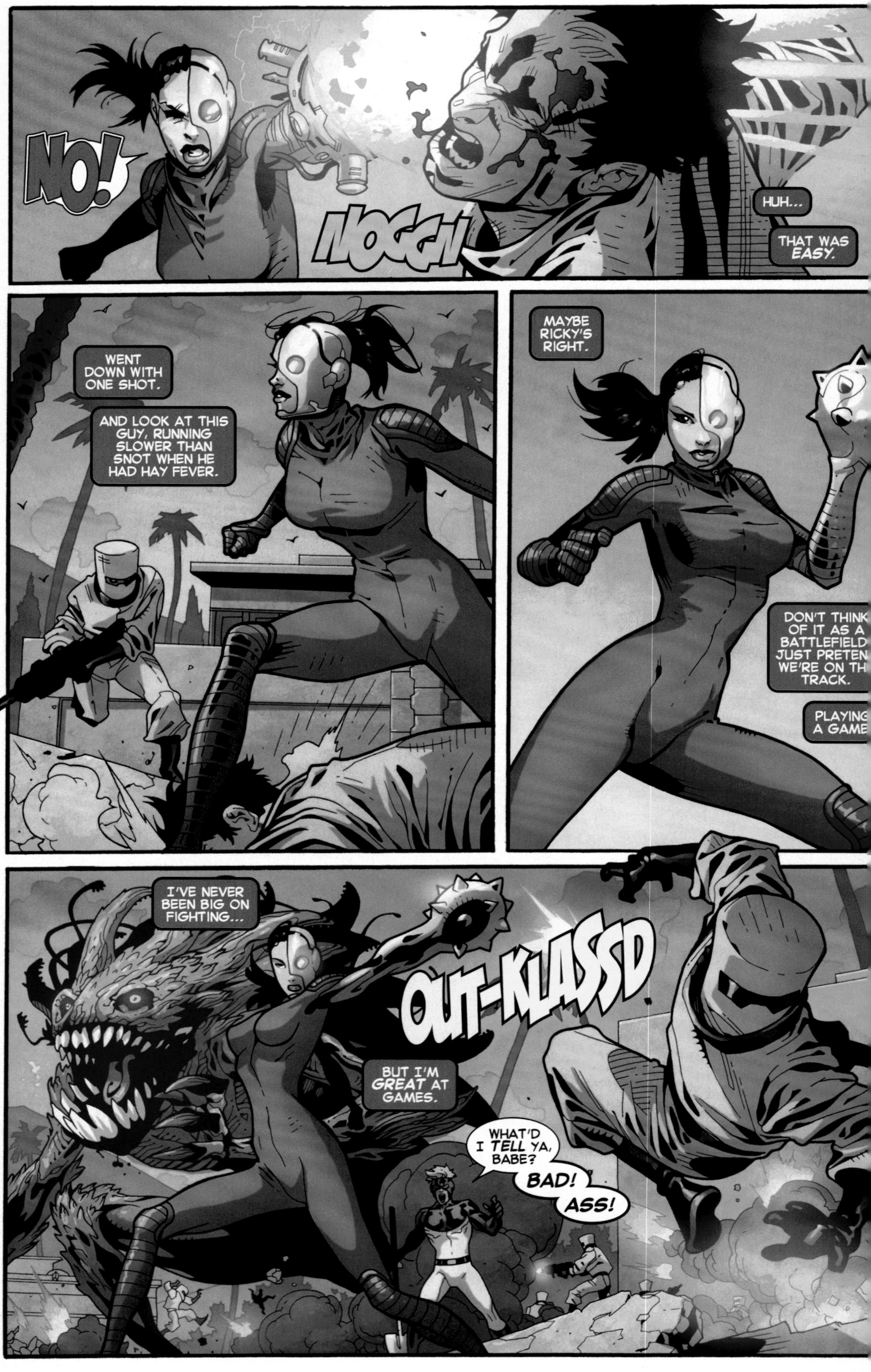
NO!
NOGGN
HUH...
THAT WAS EASY.
WENT DOWN WITH ONE SHOT.
AND LOOK AT THIS GUY, RUNNING SLOWER THAN SNOT WHEN HE HAD HAY FEVER.
MAYBE RICKY'S RIGHT.
DON'T THINK OF IT AS A BATTLEFIELD JUST PRETEN WE'RE ON TH TRACK.
PLAYING A GAME
I'VE NEVER BEEN BIG ON FIGHTING...
OUT-KLASSD
BUT I'M GREAT AT GAMES.
WHAT'D I TELL YA, BABE?
BAD!
ASS!

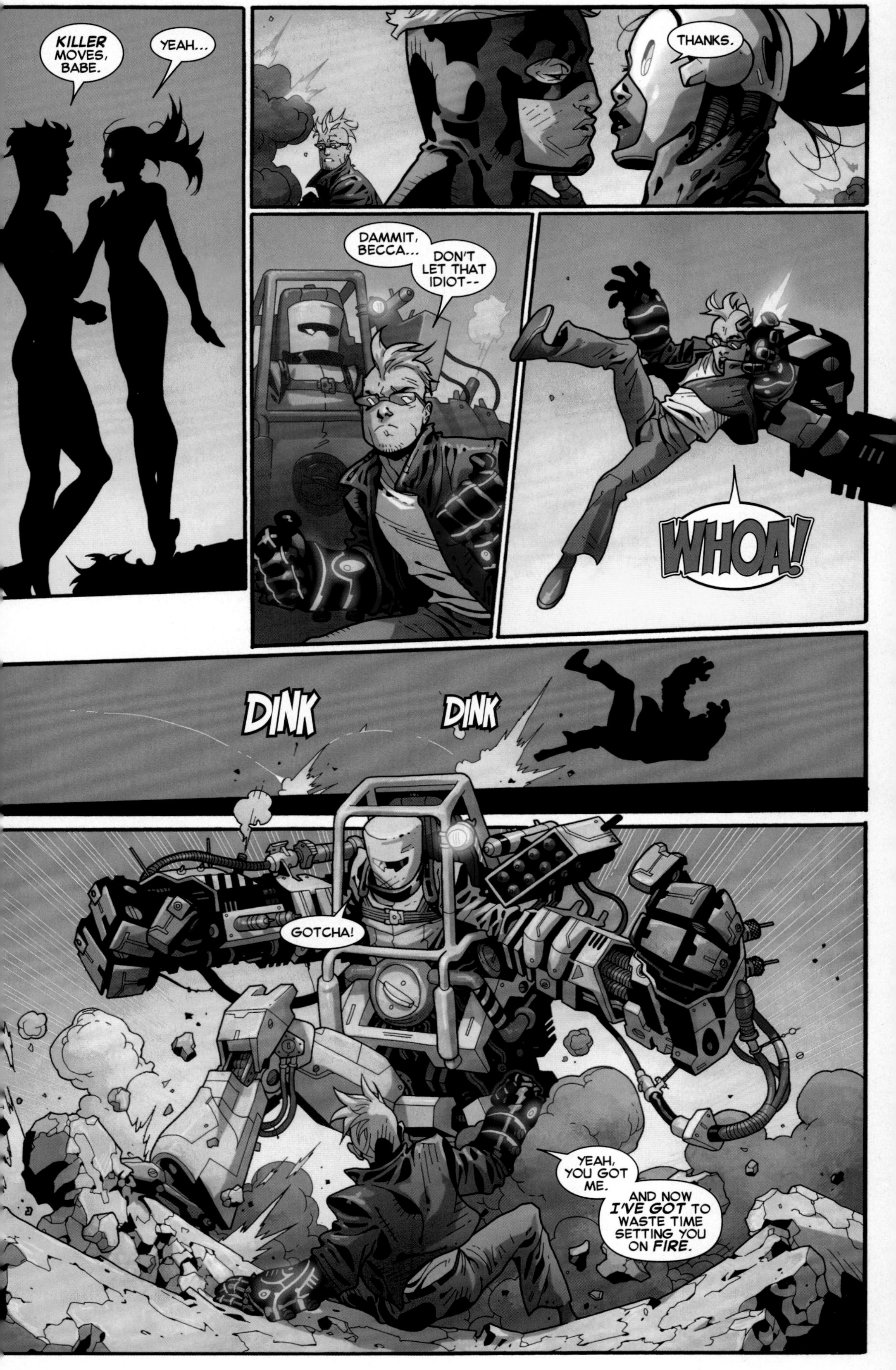
KILLER MOVES, BABE.
YEAH...
THANKS.
DAMMIT, BECCA...
DON'T LET THAT IDIOT--
WHOA!
DINK
DINK
GOTCHA!
YEAH, YOU GOT ME.
AND NOW I'VE GOT TO WASTE TIME SETTING YOU ON FIRE.

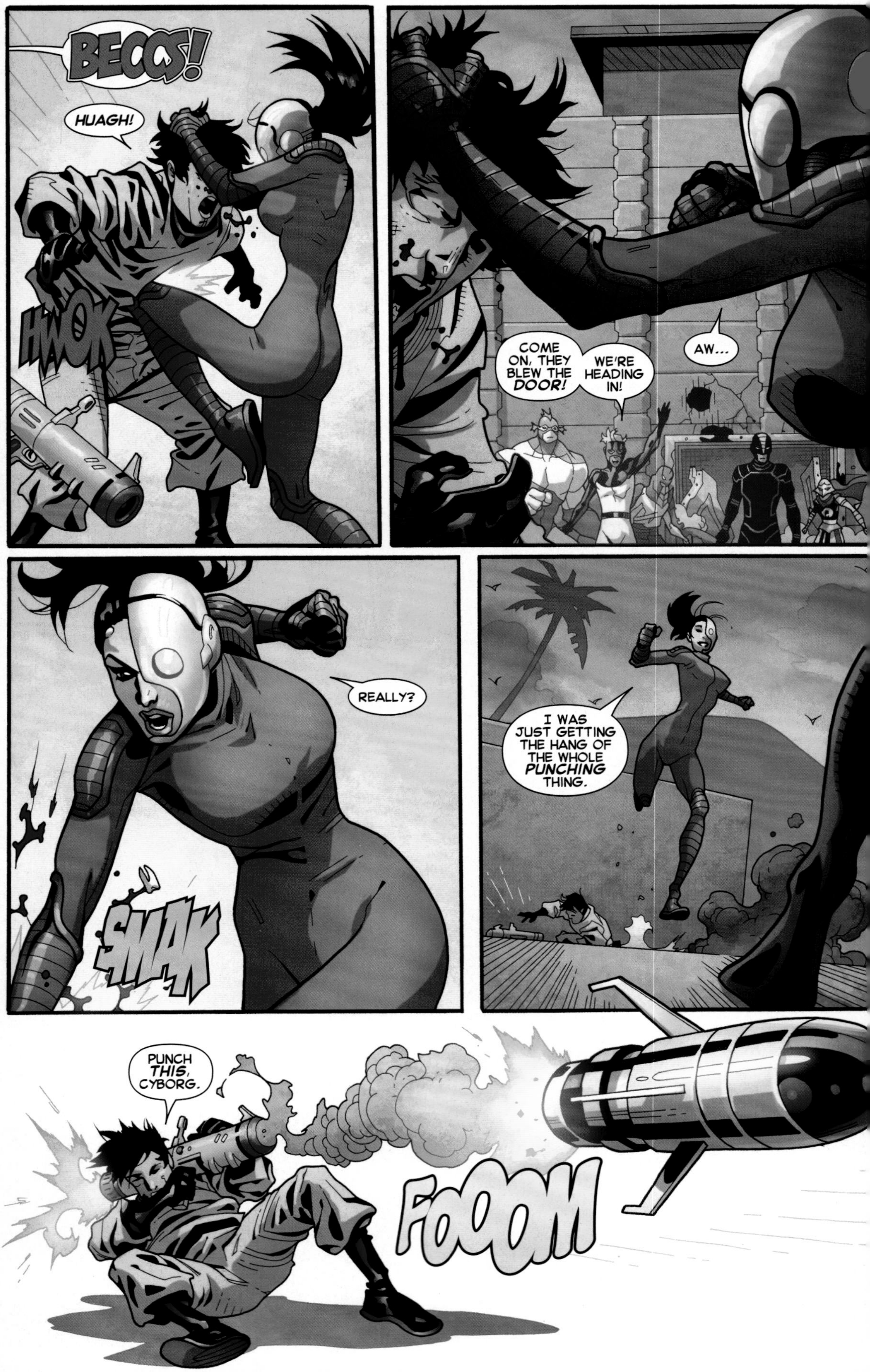
BECCS!
HUAGH!
HWOK
COME ON, THEY BLEW THE DOOR!
WE'RE HEADING IN!
AW...
REALLY?
SMAK
I WAS JUST GETTING THE HANG OF THE WHOLE PUNCHING THING.
PUNCH THIS, CYBORG.
FOOOM

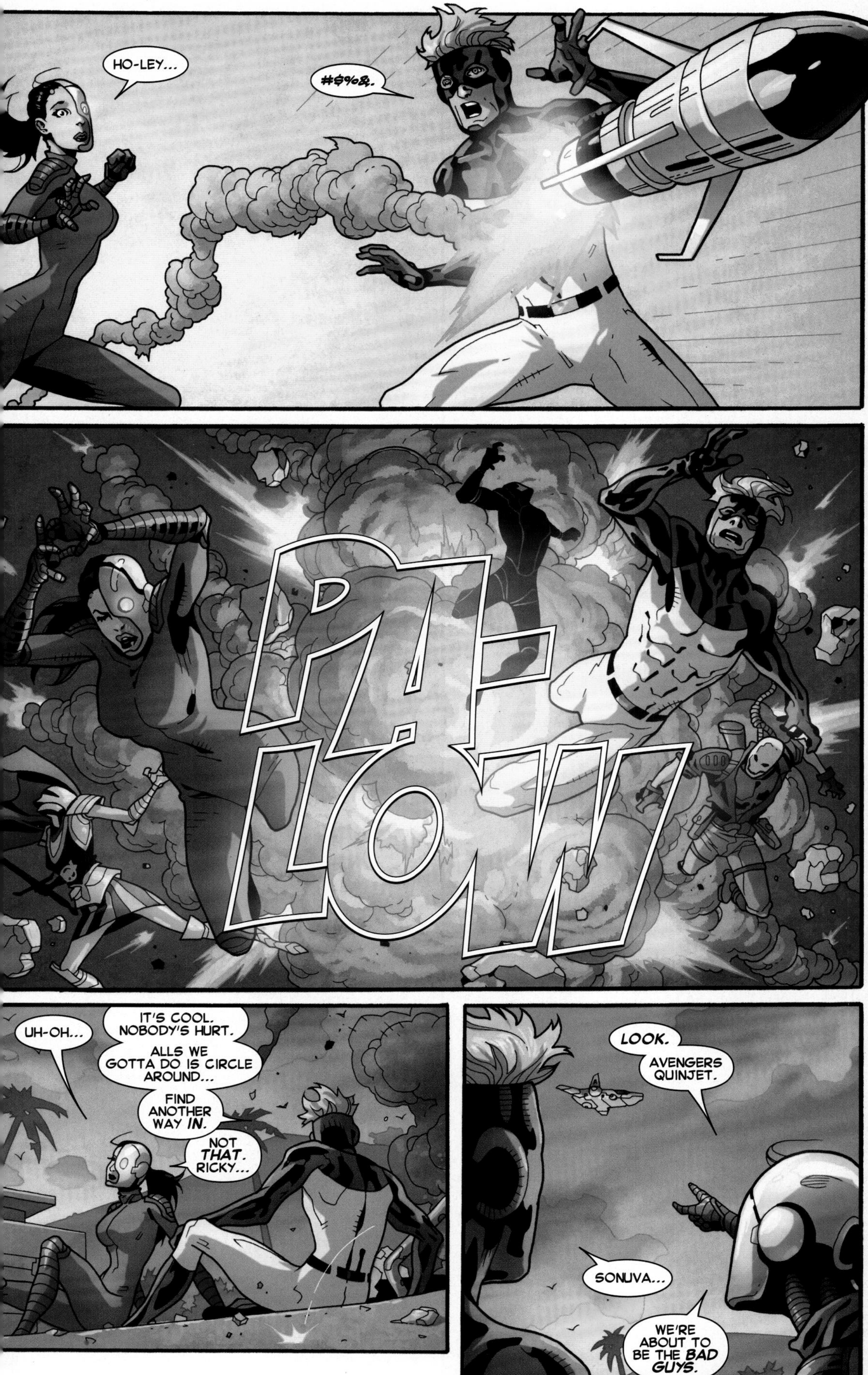
HO-LEY...
#$%&.
PA-LOW
UH-OH...
IT'S COOL. NOBODY'S HURT.
ALLS WE GOTTA DO IS CIRCLE AROUND...
FIND ANOTHER WAY IN.
NOT THAT. RICKY...
LOOK.
AVENGERS QUINJET.
SONUVA...
WE'RE ABOUT TO BE THE BAD GUYS.

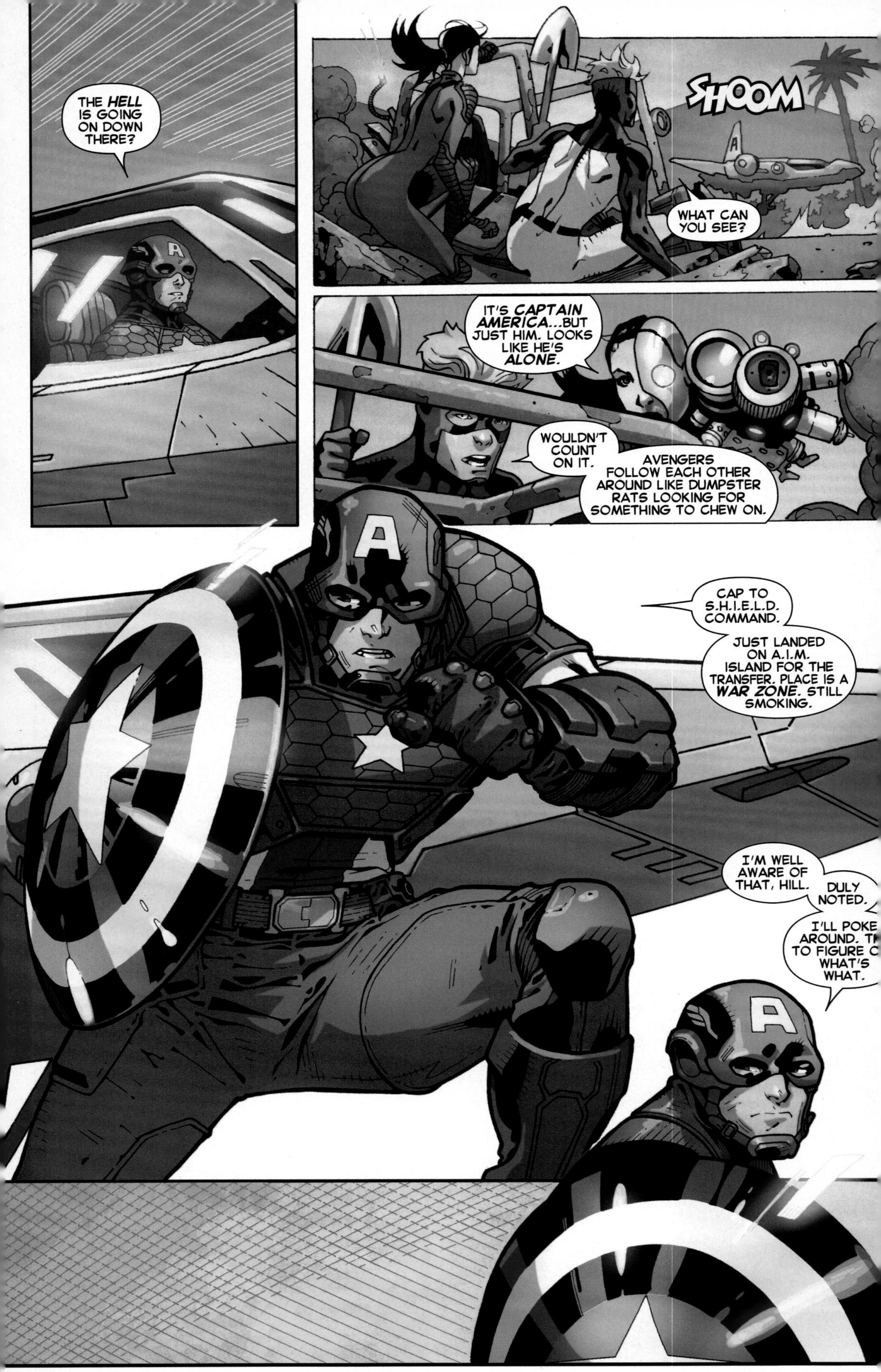

THE HELL IS GOING ON DOWN THERE?
SHOOM
WHAT CAN YOU SEE?
IT'S CAPTAIN AMERICA...BUT JUST HIM. LOOKS LIKE HE'S ALONE.
WOULDN'T COUNT ON IT.
AVENGERS FOLLOW EACH OTHER AROUND LIKE DUMPSTER RATS LOOKING FOR SOMETHING TO CHEW ON.
CAP TO S.H.I.E.L.D. COMMAND.
JUST LANDED ON A.I.M. ISLAND FOR THE TRANSFER. PLACE IS A WAR ZONE. STILL SMOKING.
I'M WELL AWARE OF THAT, HILL.
DULY NOTED.

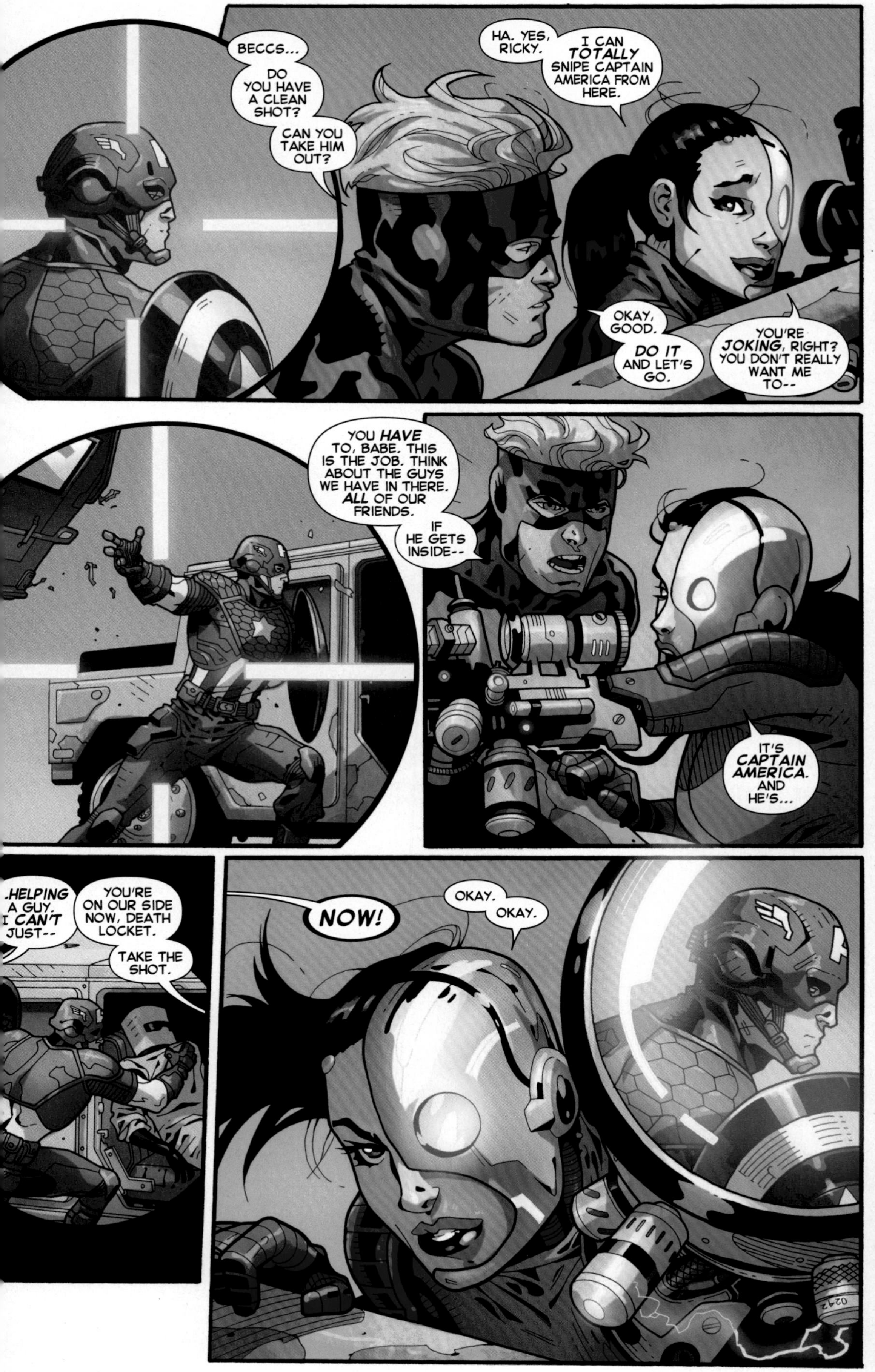
BECCS...
DO YOU HAVE A CLEAN SHOT?
CAN YOU TAKE HIM OUT?
HA. YES, RICKY.
I CAN TOTALLY SNIPE CAPTAIN AMERICA FROM HERE.
OKAY, GOOD.
DO IT AND LET'S GO.
YOU'RE JOKING, RIGHT? YOU DON'T REALLY WANT ME TO--
YOU HAVE TO, BABE. THIS IS THE JOB. THINK ABOUT THE GUYS WE HAVE IN THERE. ALL OF OUR FRIENDS.
IF HE GETS INSIDE--
IT'S CAPTAIN AMERICA. AND HE'S...
...HELPING A GUY. I CAN'T JUST--
YOU'RE ON OUR SIDE NOW, DEATH LOCKET.
TAKE THE SHOT.
NOW!
OKAY.
OKAY.

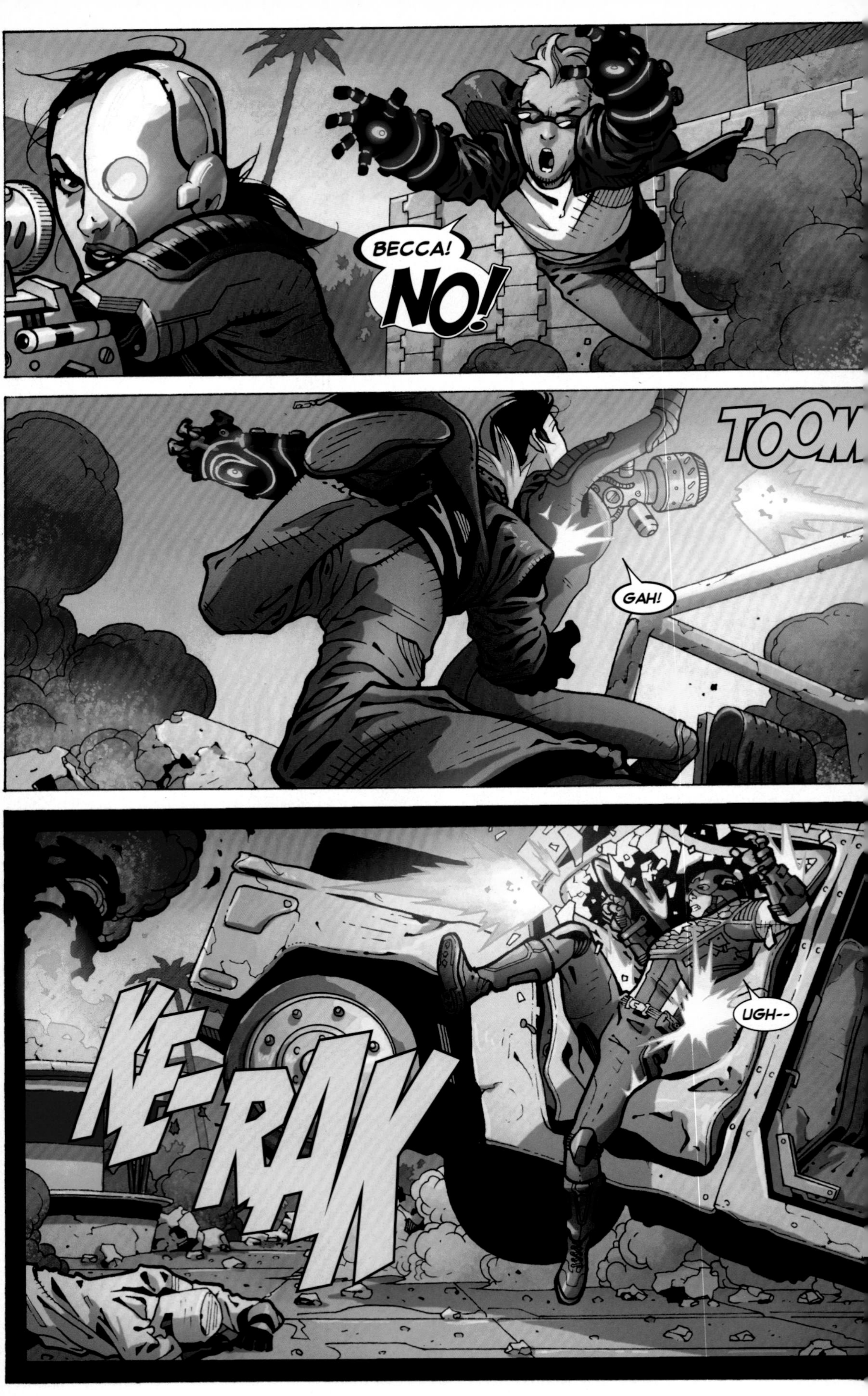
BECCA! NO!
TOOM
GAH!
KE-RAK
UGH--

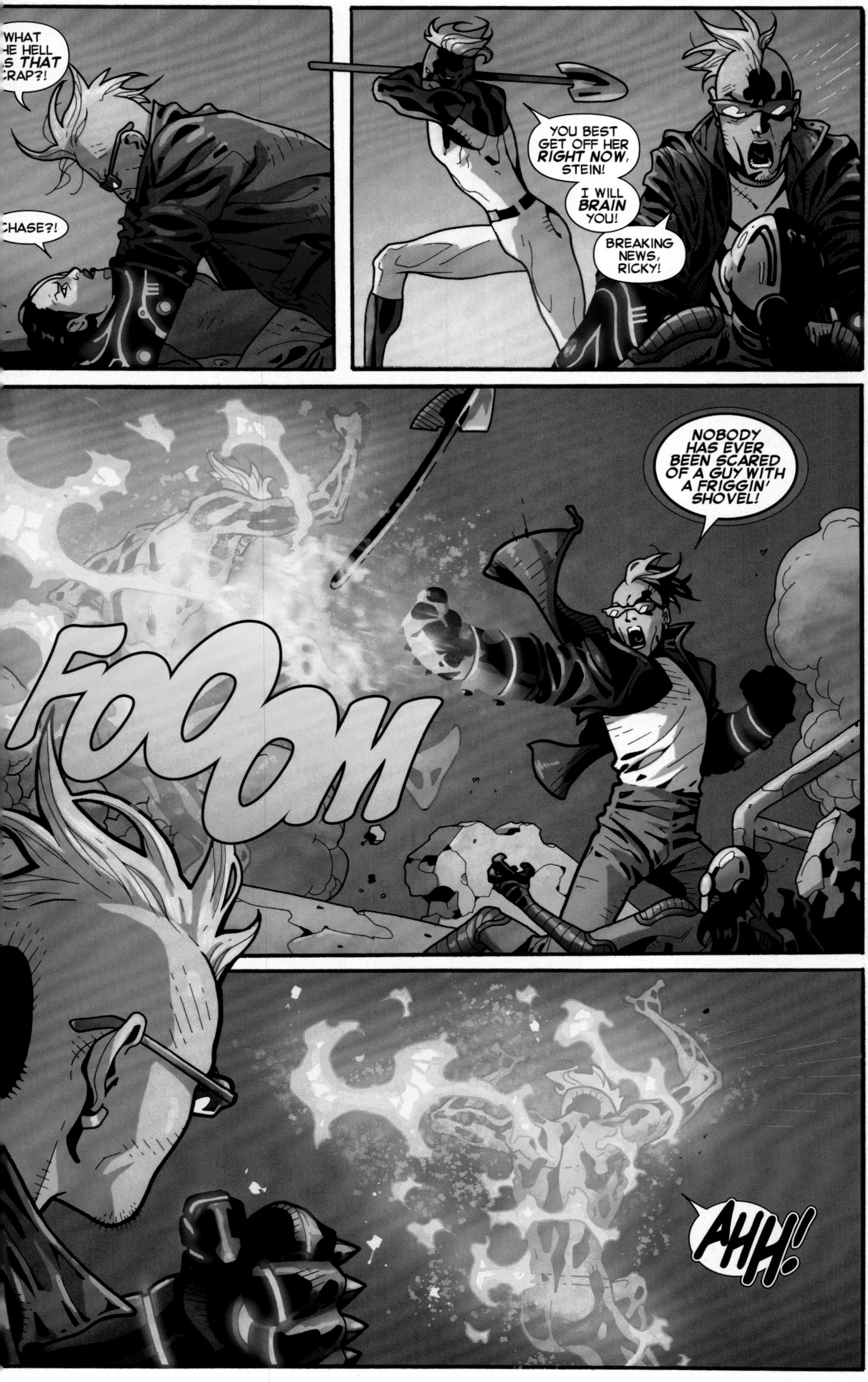
WHAT HE HELL S THAT CRAP?!
CHASE?!
YOU BEST GET OFF HER RIGHT NOW, STEIN!
I WILL BRAIN YOU!
BREAKING NEWS, RICKY!
NOBODY HAS EVER BEEN SCARED OF A GUY WITH A FRIGGIN' SHOVEL!
FOOOM
AHH!

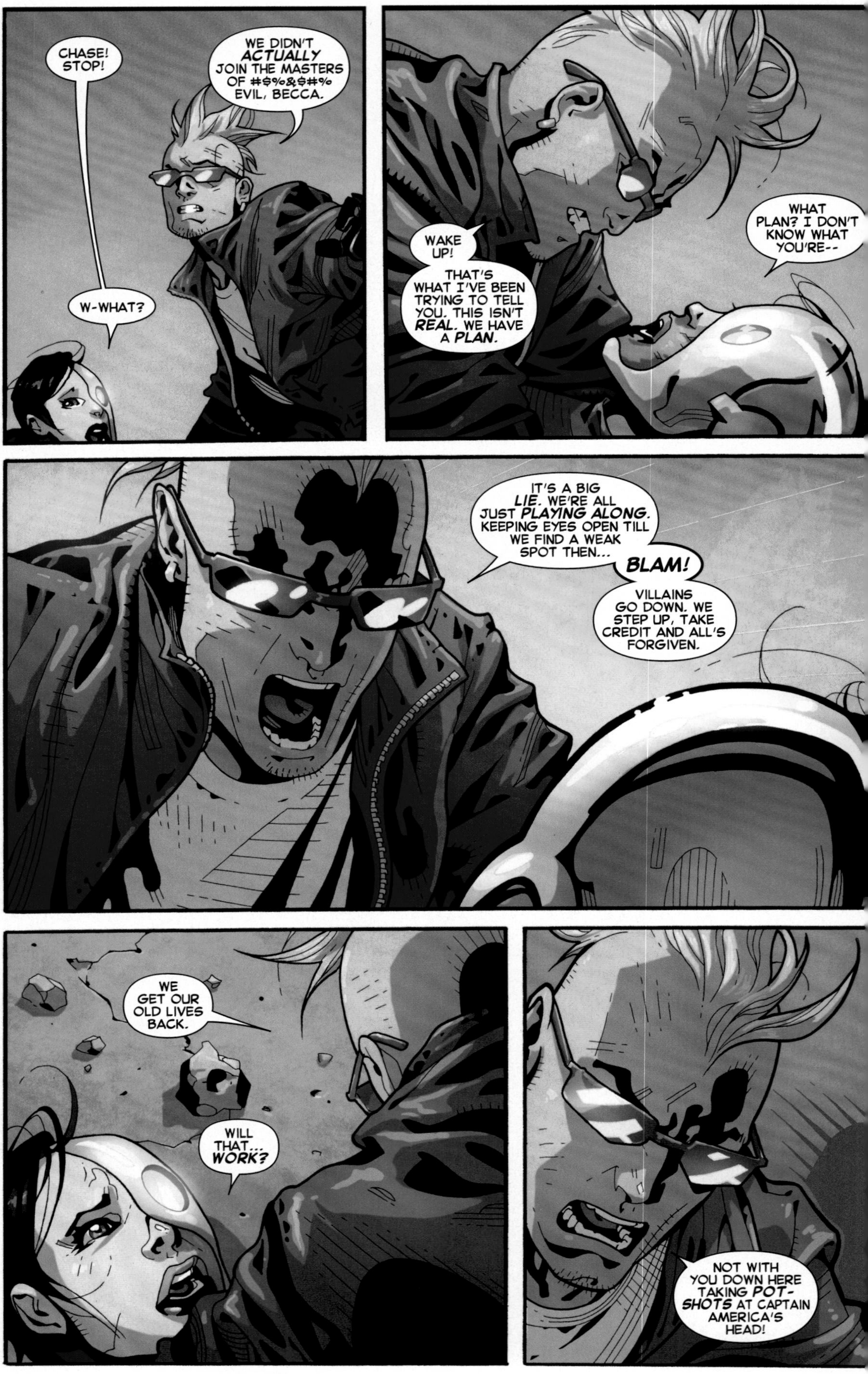
CHASE! STOP!
WE DIDN'T ACTUALLY JOIN THE MASTERS OF #$%&$#% EVIL, BECCA.
W-WHAT?
WAKE UP!
THAT'S WHAT I'VE BEEN TRYING TO TELL YOU. THIS ISN'T REAL. WE HAVE A PLAN.
WHAT PLAN? I DON'T KNOW WHAT YOU'RE--
IT'S A BIG LIE. WE'RE ALL JUST PLAYING ALONG. KEEPING EYES OPEN TILL WE FIND A WEAK SPOT THEN...
BLAM!
VILLAINS GO DOWN. WE STEP UP, TAKE CREDIT AND ALL'S FORGIVEN.
WE GET OUR OLD LIVES BACK.
WILL THAT... WORK?
NOT WITH YOU DOWN HERE TAKING POT-SHOTS AT CAPTAIN AMERICA'S HEAD!

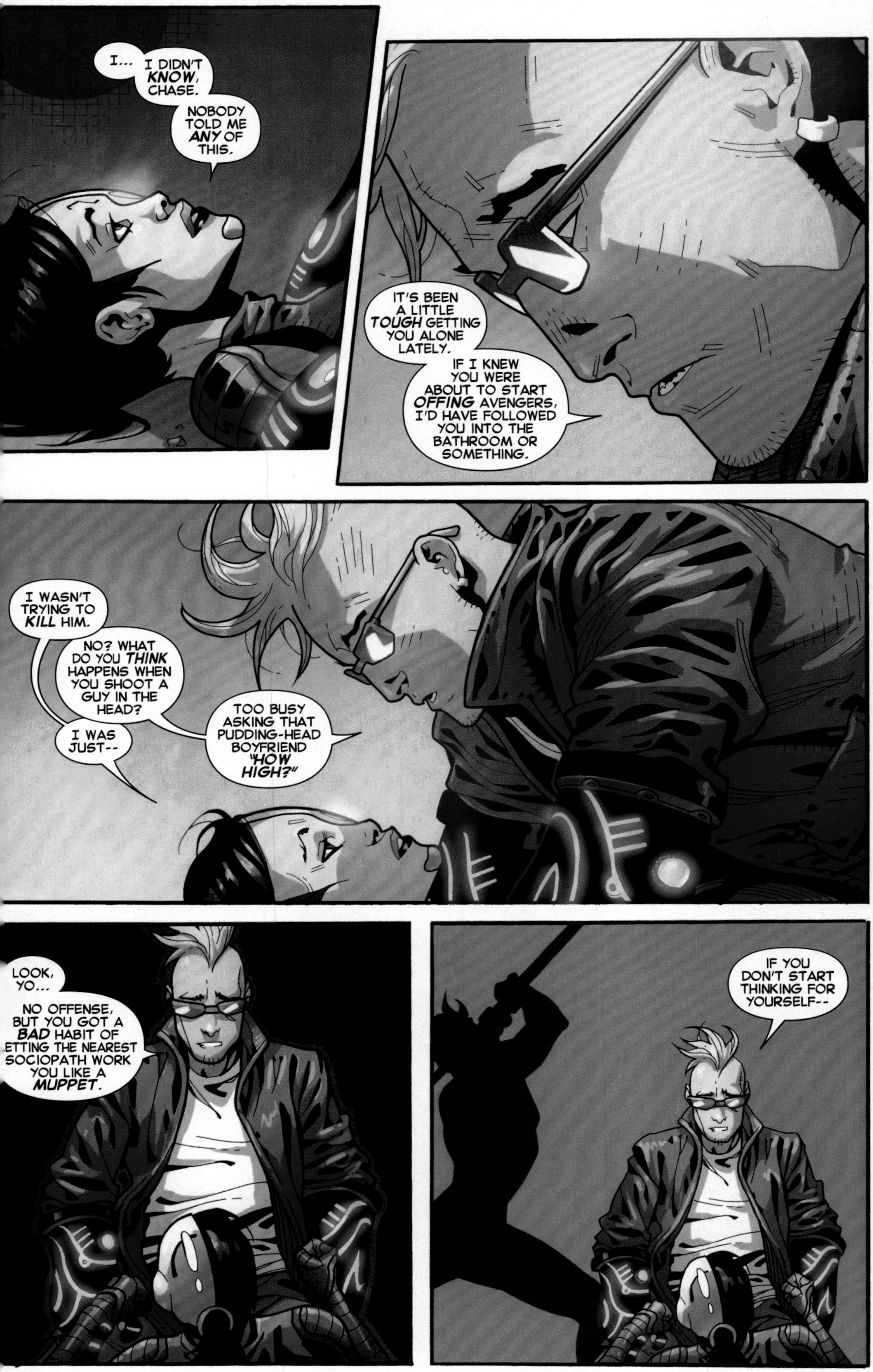

I...
I DIDN'T KNOW, CHASE.
NOBODY TOLD ME ANY OF THIS.
IT'S BEEN A LITTLE TOUGH GETTING YOU ALONE LATELY.
IF I KNEW YOU WERE ABOUT TO START OFFING AVENGERS, I'D HAVE FOLLOWED YOU INTO THE BATHROOM OR SOMETHING.
I WASN'T TRYING TO KILL HIM.
NO? WHAT DO YOU THINK HAPPENS WHEN YOU SHOOT A GUY IN THE HEAD?
I WAS JUST--
TOO BUSY ASKING THAT PUDDING-HEAD BOYFRIEND "HOW HIGH?"
LOOK, YO...
NO OFFENSE, BUT YOU GOT A BAD HABIT OF ETTING THE NEAREST SOCIOPATH WORK YOU LIKE A MUPPET.
IF YOU DON'T START THINKING FOR YOURSELF--

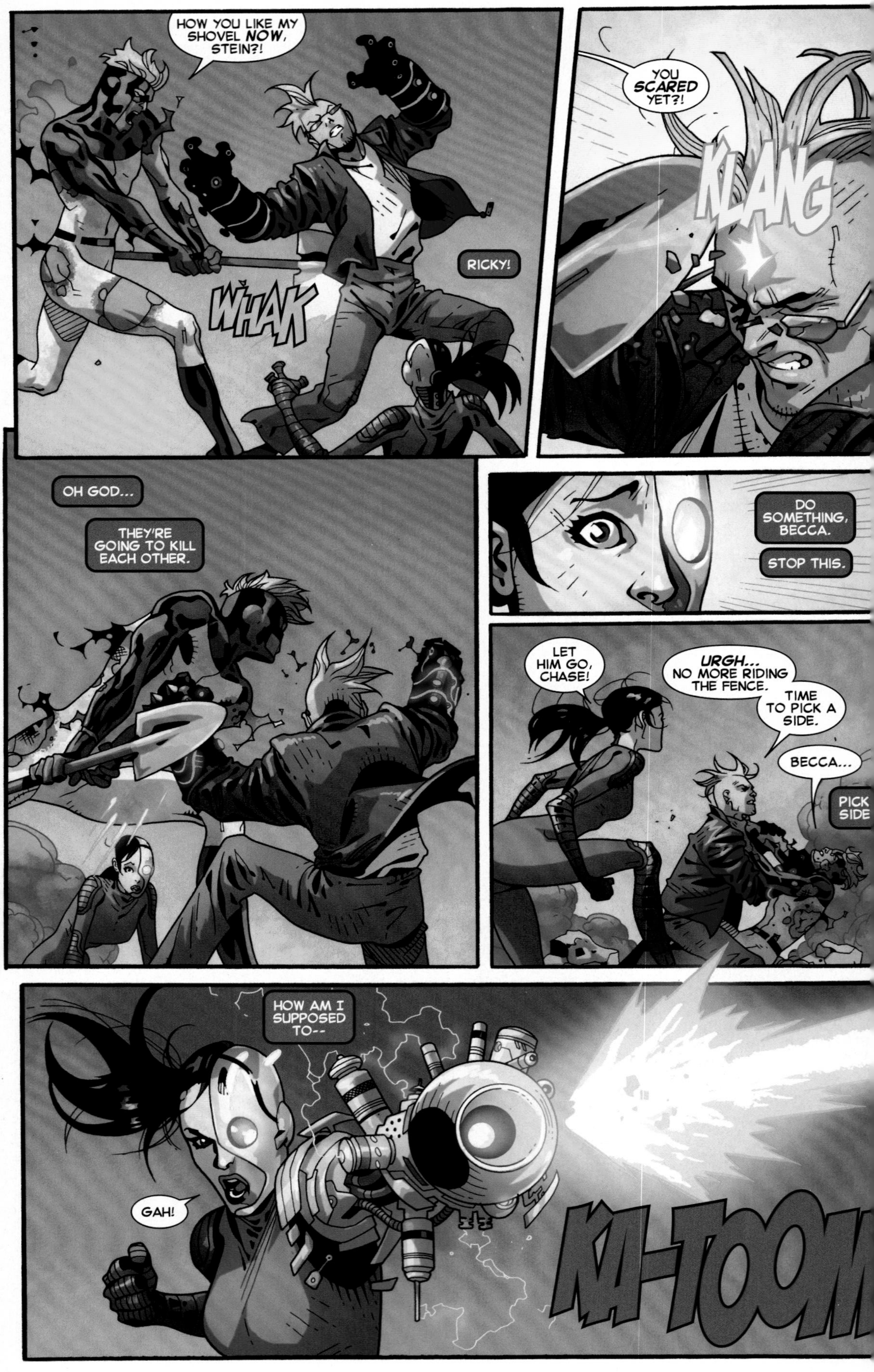

HOW YOU LIKE MY SHOVEL NOW, STEIN?!
RICKY!
WHAK
YOU SCARED YET?!
KLANG
OH GOD...
THEY'RE GOING TO KILL EACH OTHER.
DO SOMETHING, BECCA.
STOP THIS.
LET HIM GO, CHASE!
URGH... NO MORE RIDING THE FENCE.
TIME TO PICK A SIDE.
BECCA...
PICK SIDE
HOW AM I SUPPOSED TO--
GAH!
KA-TOOM

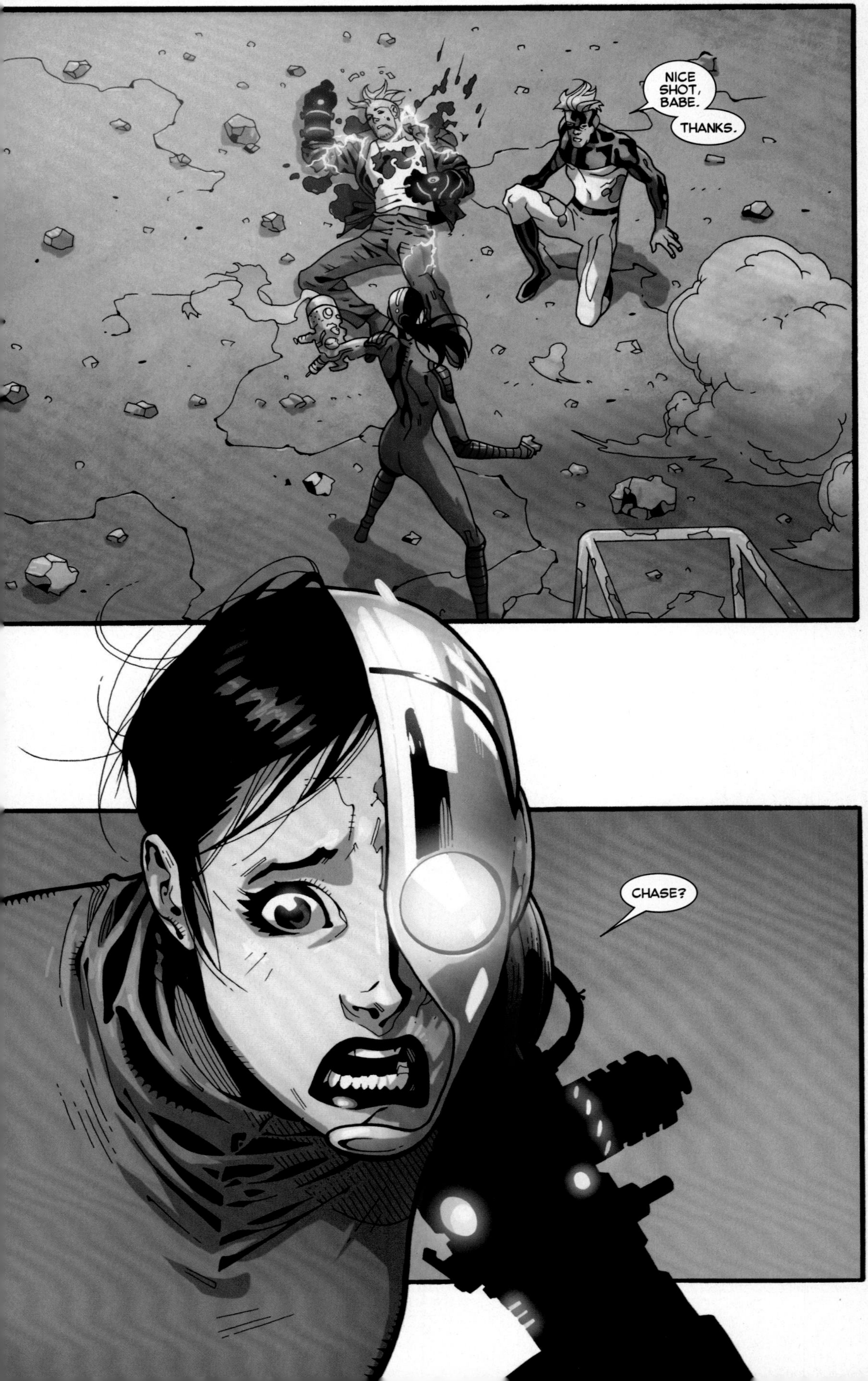
NICE SHOT, BABE.
THANKS.
CHASE?

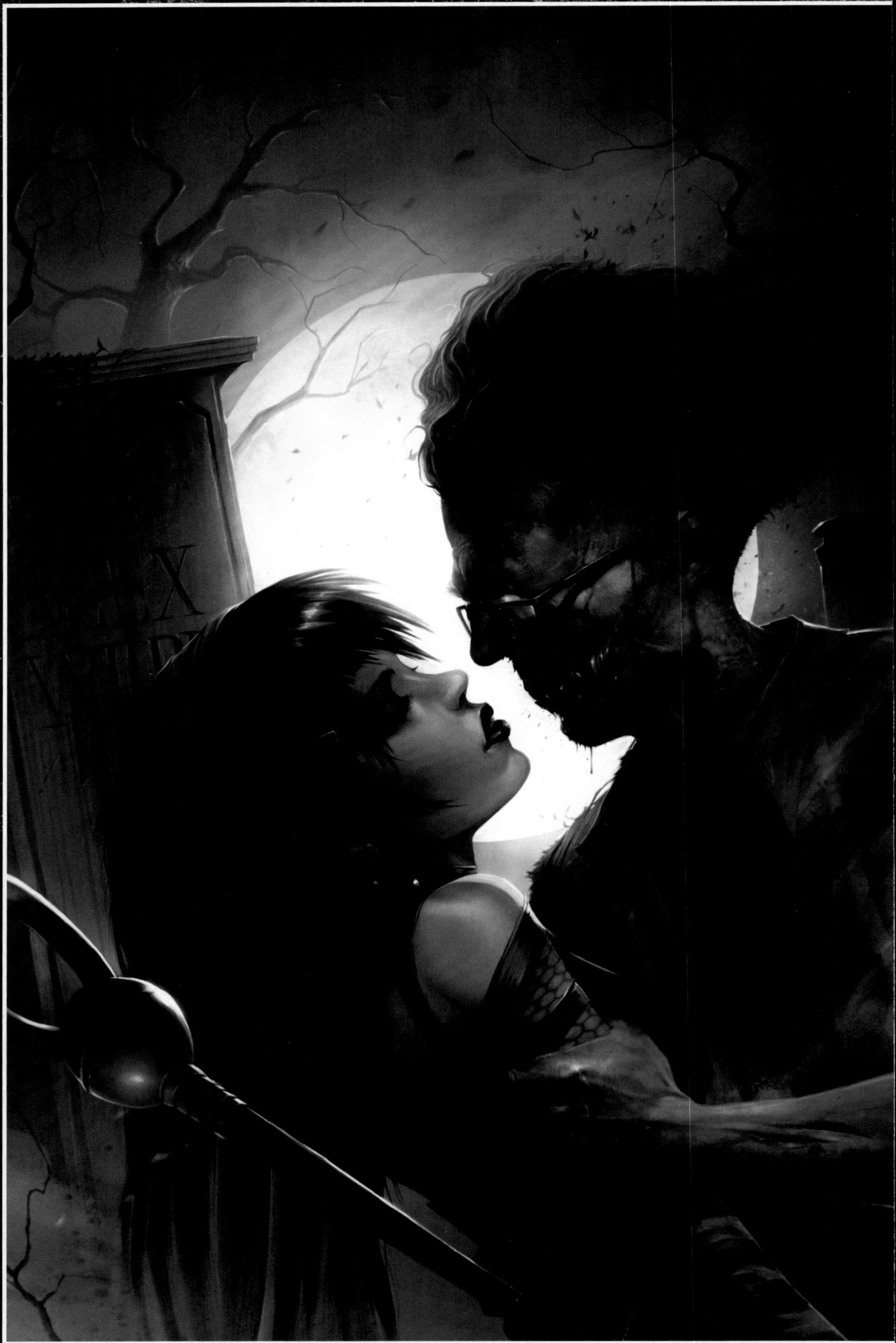

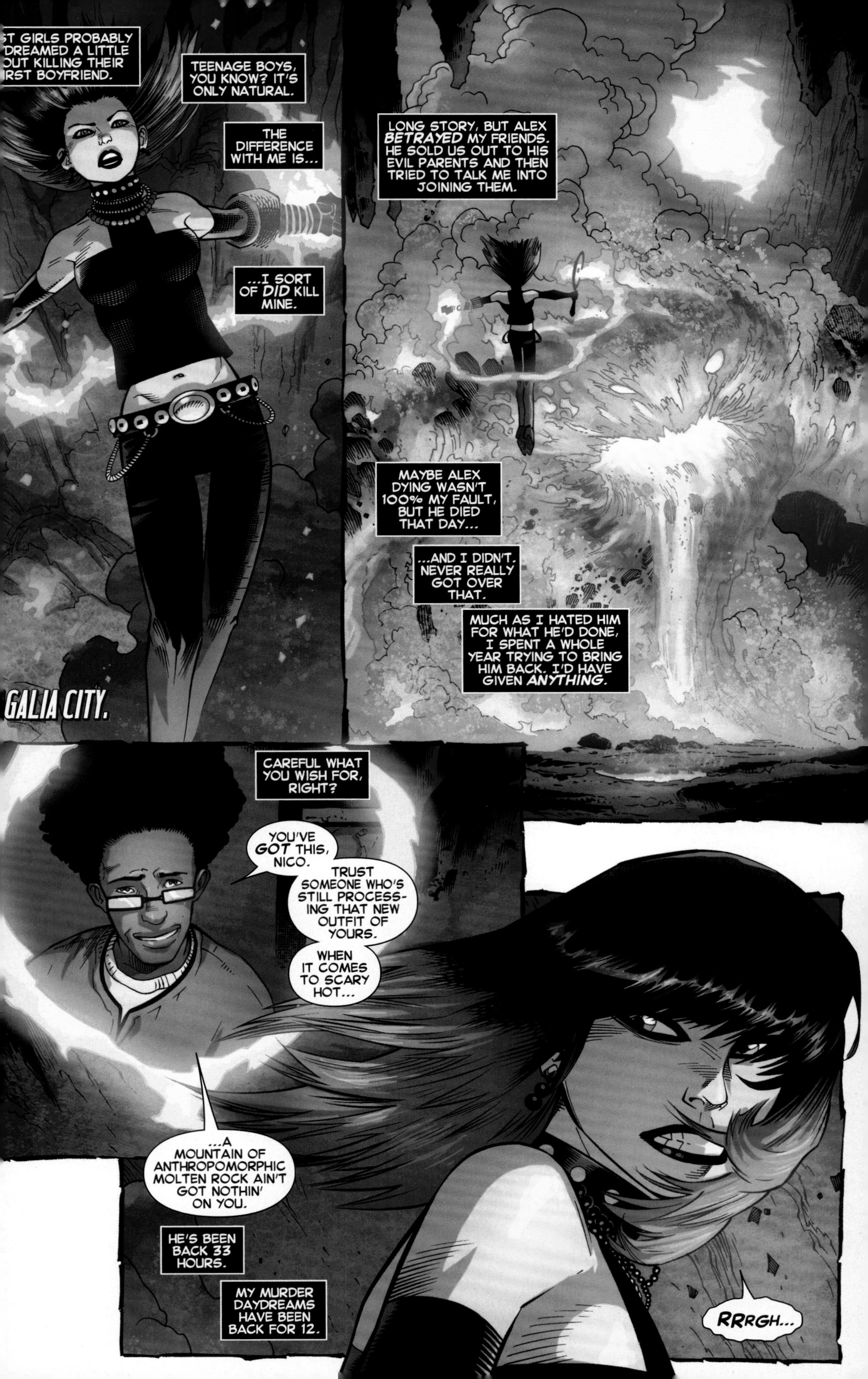
ST GIRLS PROBABLY DREAMED A LITTLE OUT KILLING THEIR IRST BOYFRIEND.
TEENAGE BOYS, YOU KNOW? IT'S ONLY NATURAL.
THE DIFFERENCE WITH ME IS...
...I SORT OF DID KILL MINE.
GALIA CITY.
LONG STORY, BUT ALEX BETRAYED MY FRIENDS. HE SOLD US OUT TO HIS EVIL PARENTS AND THEN TRIED TO TALK ME INTO JOINING THEM.
MAYBE ALEX DYING WASN'T 100% MY FAULT, BUT HE DIED THAT DAY...
...AND I DIDN'T. NEVER REALLY GOT OVER THAT.
MUCH AS I HATED HIM FOR WHAT HE'D DONE, I SPENT A WHOLE YEAR TRYING TO BRING HIM BACK. I'D HAVE GIVEN ANYTHING.
CAREFUL WHAT YOU WISH FOR, RIGHT?
YOU'VE GOT THIS, NICO.
TRUST SOMEONE WHO'S STILL PROCESSING THAT NEW OUTFIT OF YOURS.
WHEN IT COMES TO SCARY HOT...
...A MOUNTAIN OF ANTHROPOMORPHIC MOLTEN ROCK AIN'T GOT NOTHIN' ON YOU.
HE'S BEEN BACK 33 HOURS.
MY MURDER DAYDREAMS HAVE BEEN BACK FOR 12.
RRRGH...

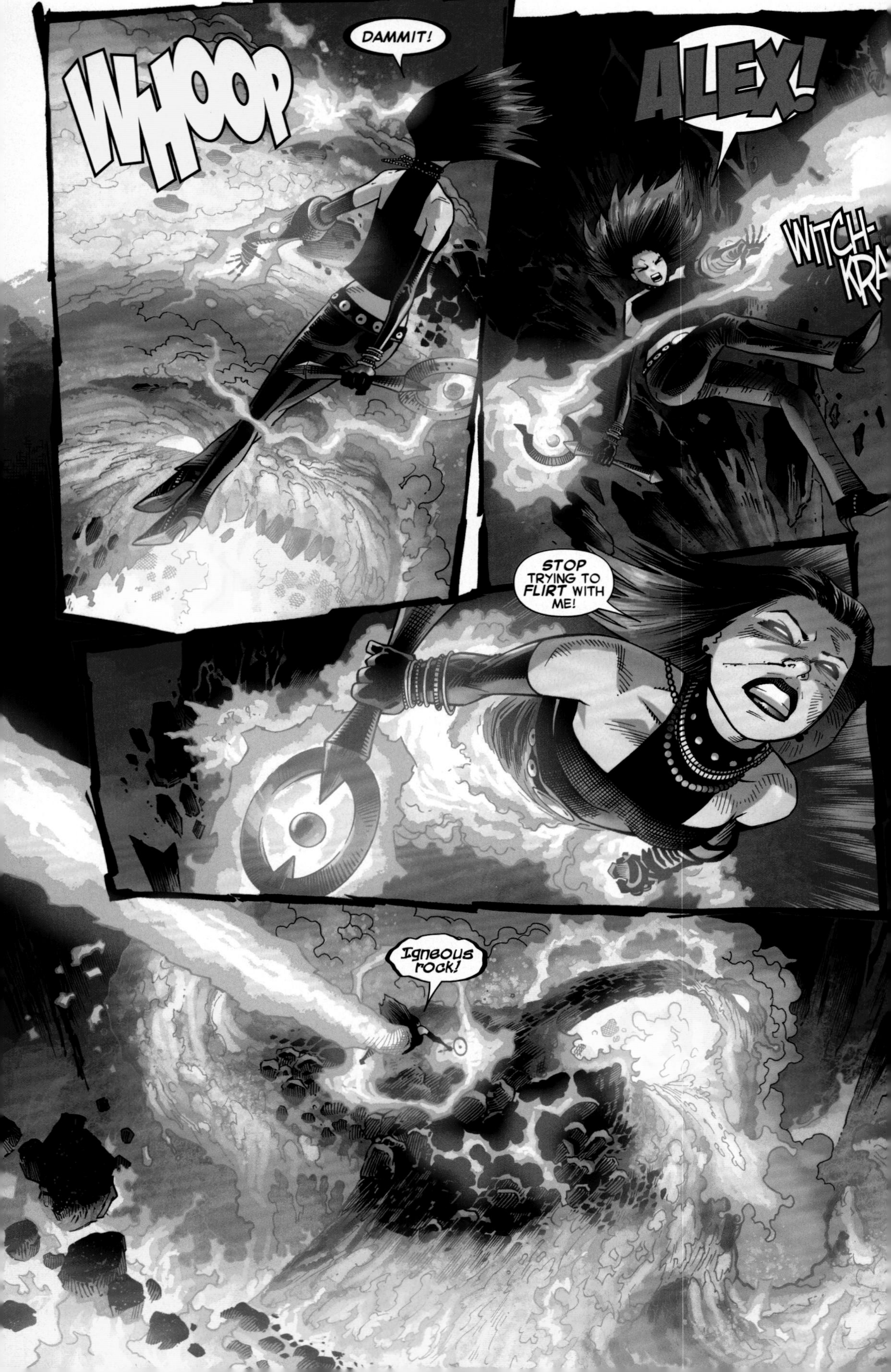
WHOOP
DAMMIT!
ALEX!
WITCH-KRA
STOP TRYING TO FLIRT WITH ME!
Igneous rock!

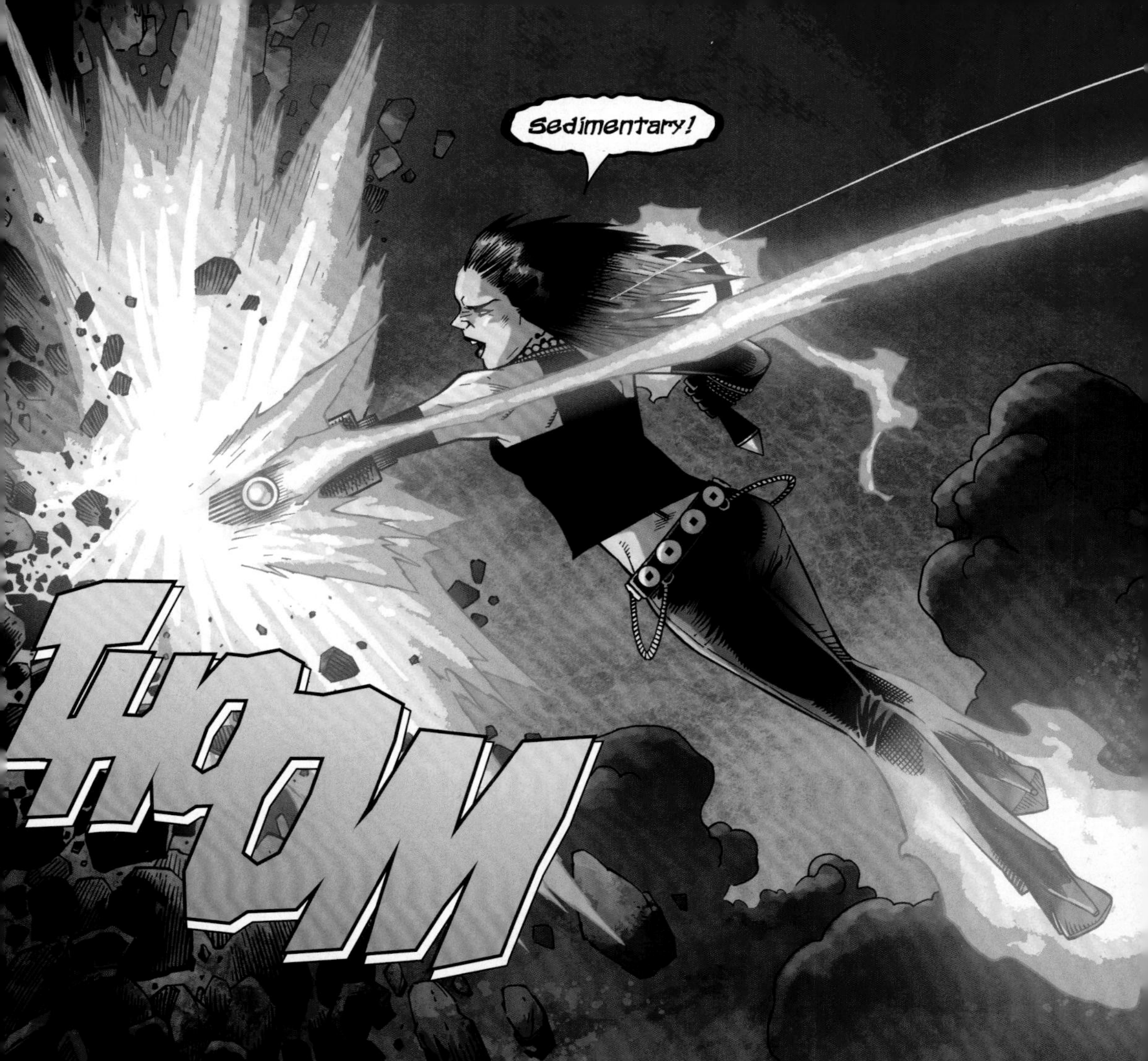
Sedimentary!
THOOM

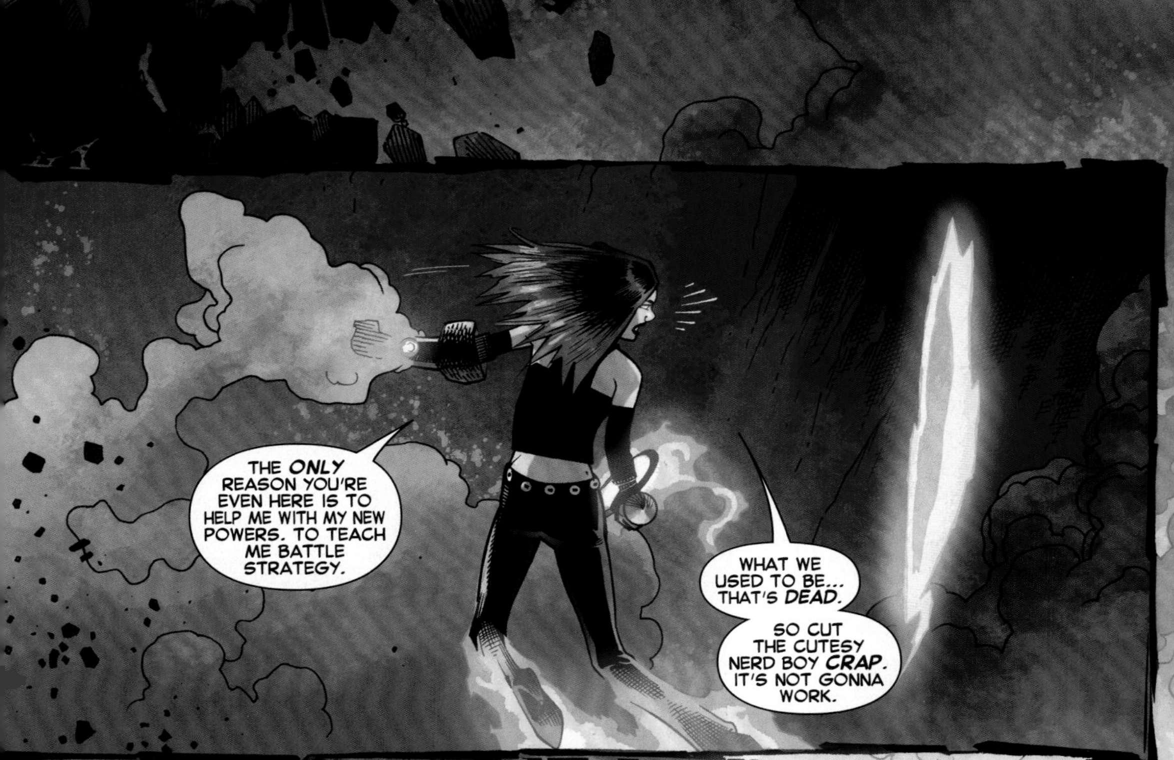
THE ONLY REASON YOU'RE EVEN HERE IS TO HELP ME WITH MY NEW POWERS. TO TEACH ME BATTLE STRATEGY.
WHAT WE USED TO BE... THAT'S DEAD.
SO CUT THE CUTESY NERD BOY CRAP. IT'S NOT GONNA WORK.

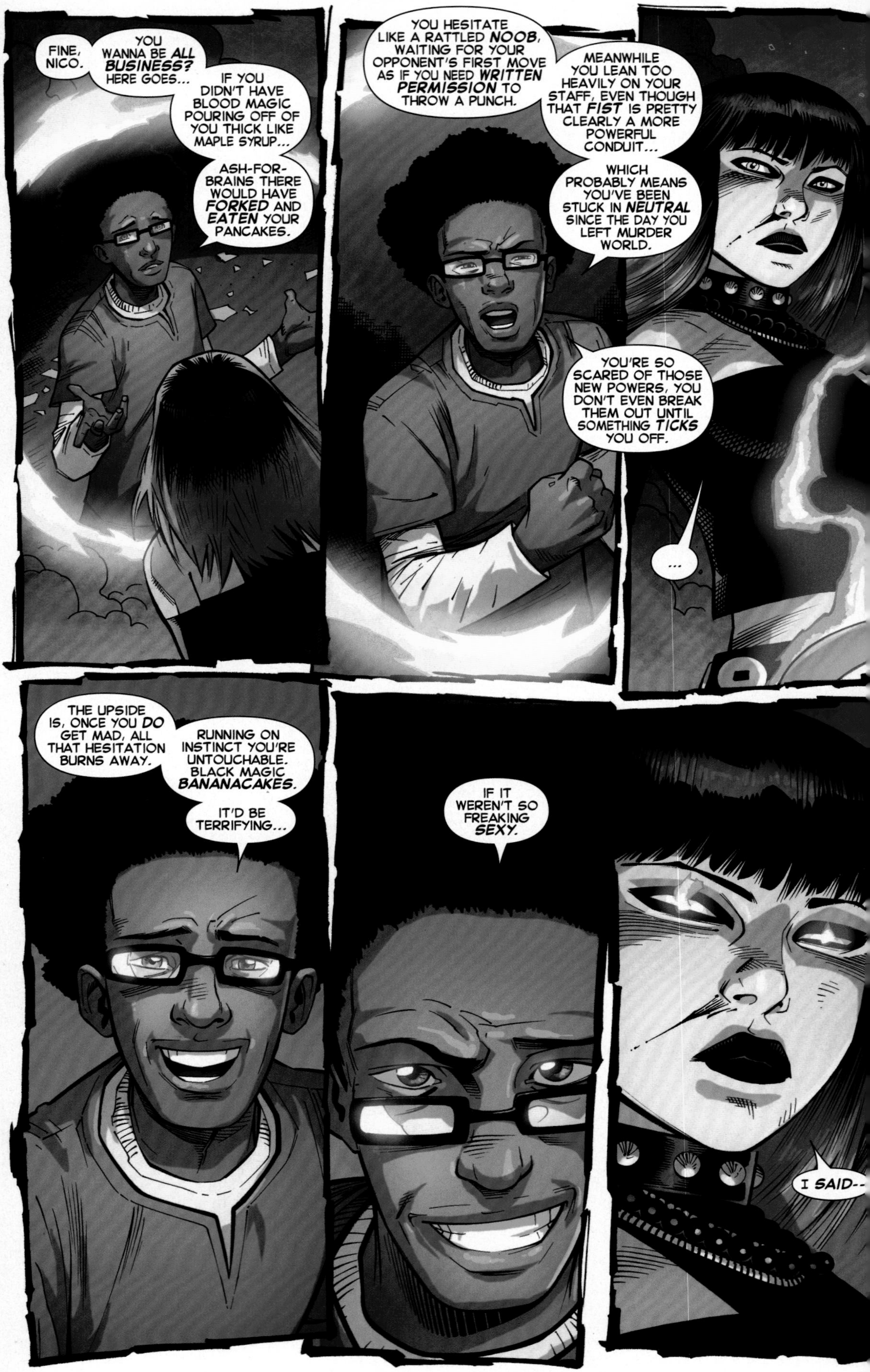
FINE, NICO.
YOU WANNA BE ALL BUSINESS? HERE GOES...
IF YOU DIDN'T HAVE BLOOD MAGIC POURING OFF OF YOU THICK LIKE MAPLE SYRUP...
ASH-FOR-BRAINS THERE WOULD HAVE FORKED AND EATEN YOUR PANCAKES.
YOU HESITATE LIKE A RATTLED NOOB, WAITING FOR YOUR OPPONENT'S FIRST MOVE AS IF YOU NEED WRITTEN PERMISSION TO THROW A PUNCH.
MEANWHILE YOU LEAN TOO HEAVILY ON YOUR STAFF, EVEN THOUGH THAT FIST IS PRETTY CLEARLY A MORE POWERFUL CONDUIT...
WHICH PROBABLY MEANS YOU'VE BEEN STUCK IN NEUTRAL SINCE THE DAY YOU LEFT MURDER WORLD.
YOU'RE SO SCARED OF THOSE NEW POWERS, YOU DON'T EVEN BREAK THEM OUT UNTIL SOMETHING TICKS YOU OFF.
...
THE UPSIDE IS, ONCE YOU DO GET MAD, ALL THAT HESITATION BURNS AWAY.
RUNNING ON INSTINCT YOU'RE UNTOUCHABLE. BLACK MAGIC BANANACAKES.
IT'D BE TERRIFYING...
IF IT WEREN'T SO FREAKING SEXY.
I SAID--

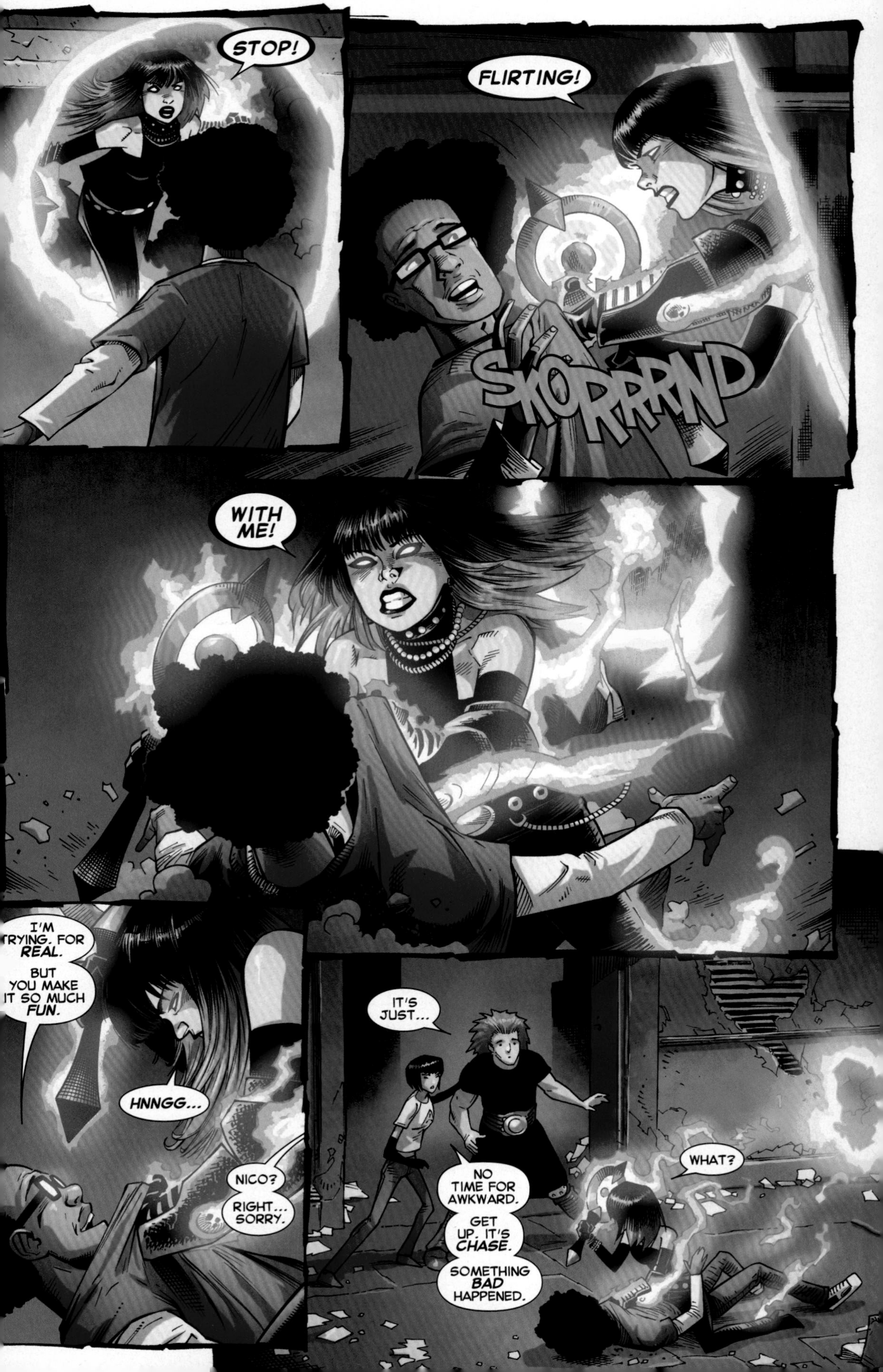
STOP!
FLIRTING!
SKORRRND
WITH ME!
I'M TRYING. FOR REAL.
BUT YOU MAKE IT SO MUCH FUN.
HNNGG...
NICO?
RIGHT... SORRY.
IT'S JUST...
NO TIME FOR AWKWARD.
GET UP. IT'S CHASE.
SOMETHING BAD HAPPENED.
WHAT?

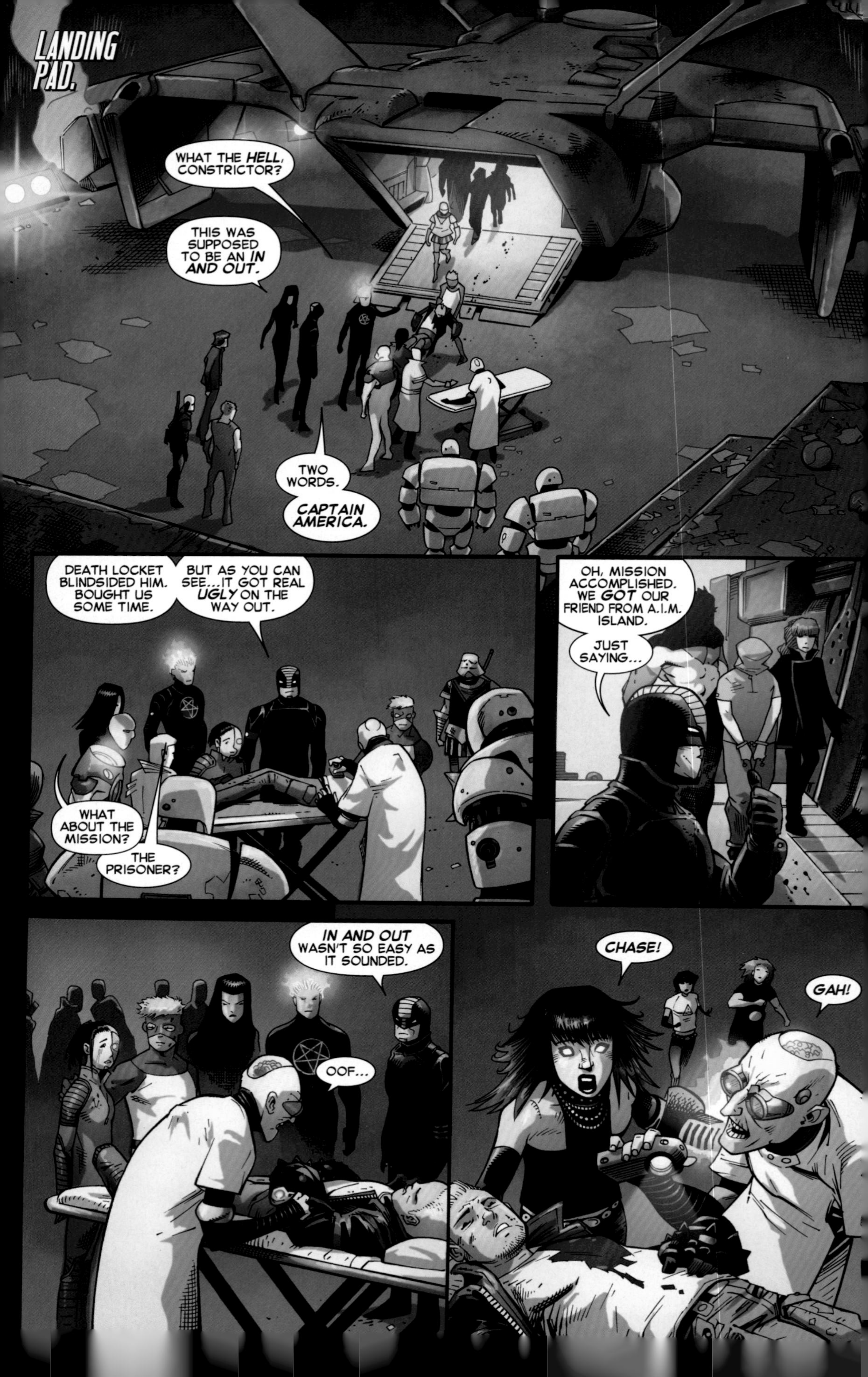
LANDING PAD.
WHAT THE HELL, CONSTRICTOR?
THIS WAS SUPPOSED TO BE AN IN AND OUT.
TWO WORDS.
CAPTAIN AMERICA.
DEATH LOCKET BLINDSIDED HIM. BOUGHT US SOME TIME.
BUT AS YOU CAN SEE...IT GOT REAL UGLY ON THE WAY OUT.
WHAT ABOUT THE MISSION?
THE PRISONER?
OH, MISSION ACCOMPLISHED. WE GOT OUR FRIEND FROM A.I.M. ISLAND.
JUST SAYING...
IN AND OUT WASN'T SO EASY AS IT SOUNDED.
OOF...
CHASE!
GAH!

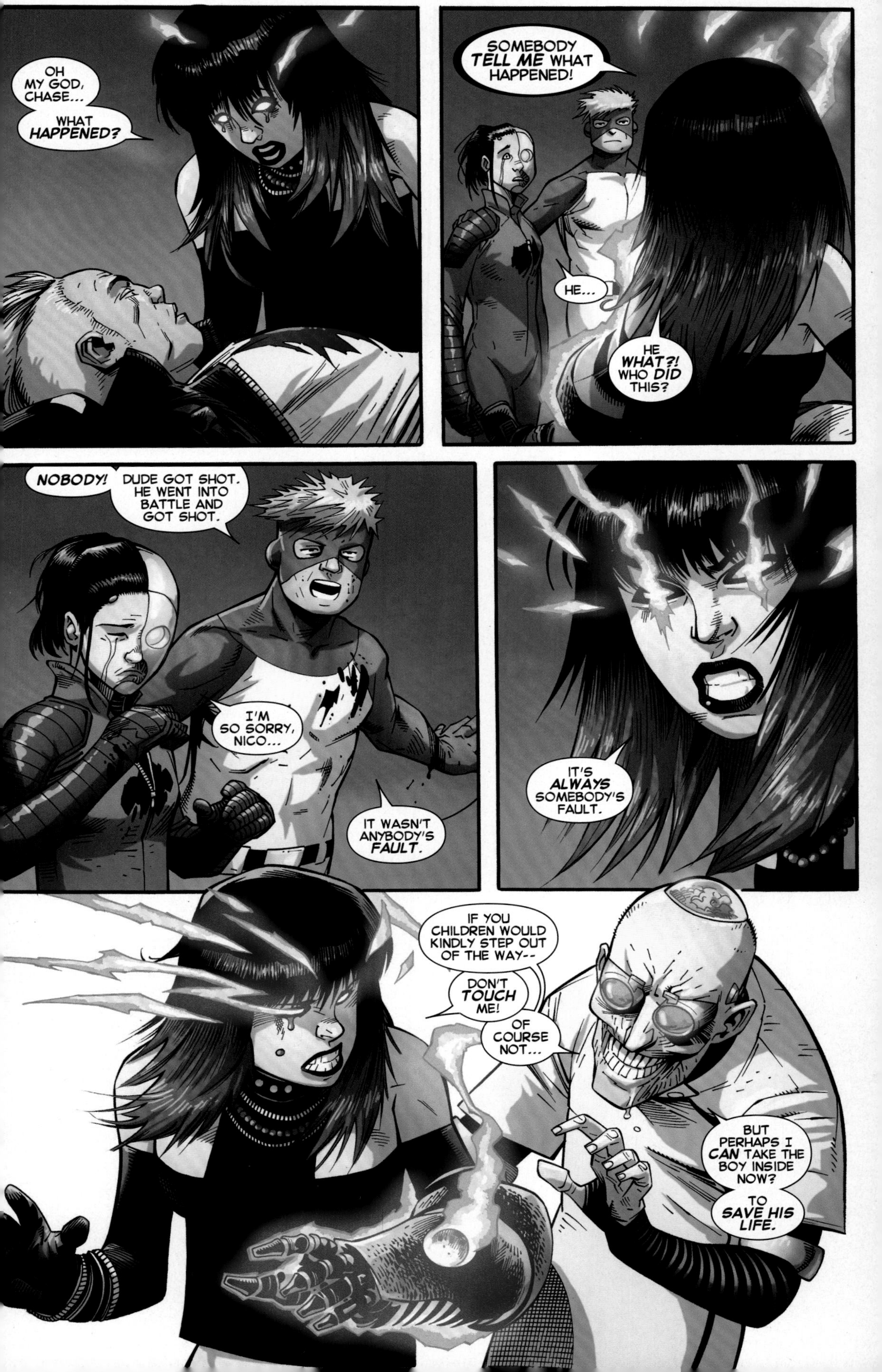
OH MY GOD, CHASE...
WHAT HAPPENED?
SOMEBODY TELL ME WHAT HAPPENED!
HE...
HE WHAT?! WHO DID THIS?
NOBODY!
DUDE GOT SHOT. HE WENT INTO BATTLE AND GOT SHOT.
I'M SO SORRY, NICO...
IT WASN'T ANYBODY'S FAULT.
IT'S ALWAYS SOMEBODY'S FAULT.
IF YOU CHILDREN WOULD KINDLY STEP OUT OF THE WAY--
DON'T TOUCH ME!
OF COURSE NOT...
BUT PERHAPS I CAN TAKE THE BOY INSIDE NOW?
TO SAVE HIS LIFE.

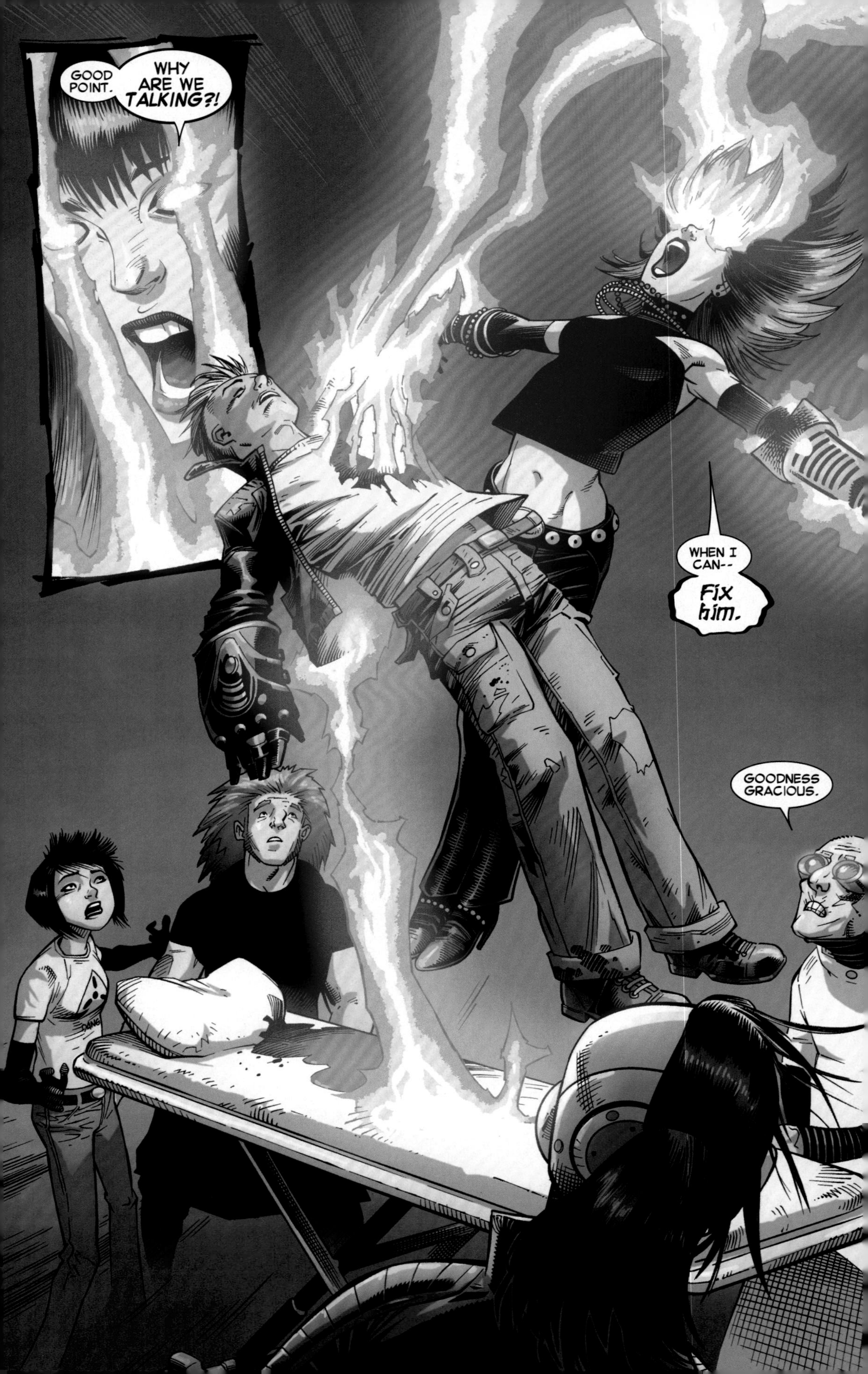
GOOD POINT.
WHY ARE WE TALKING?!
WHEN I CAN--
Fix him.
GOODNESS GRACIOUS.

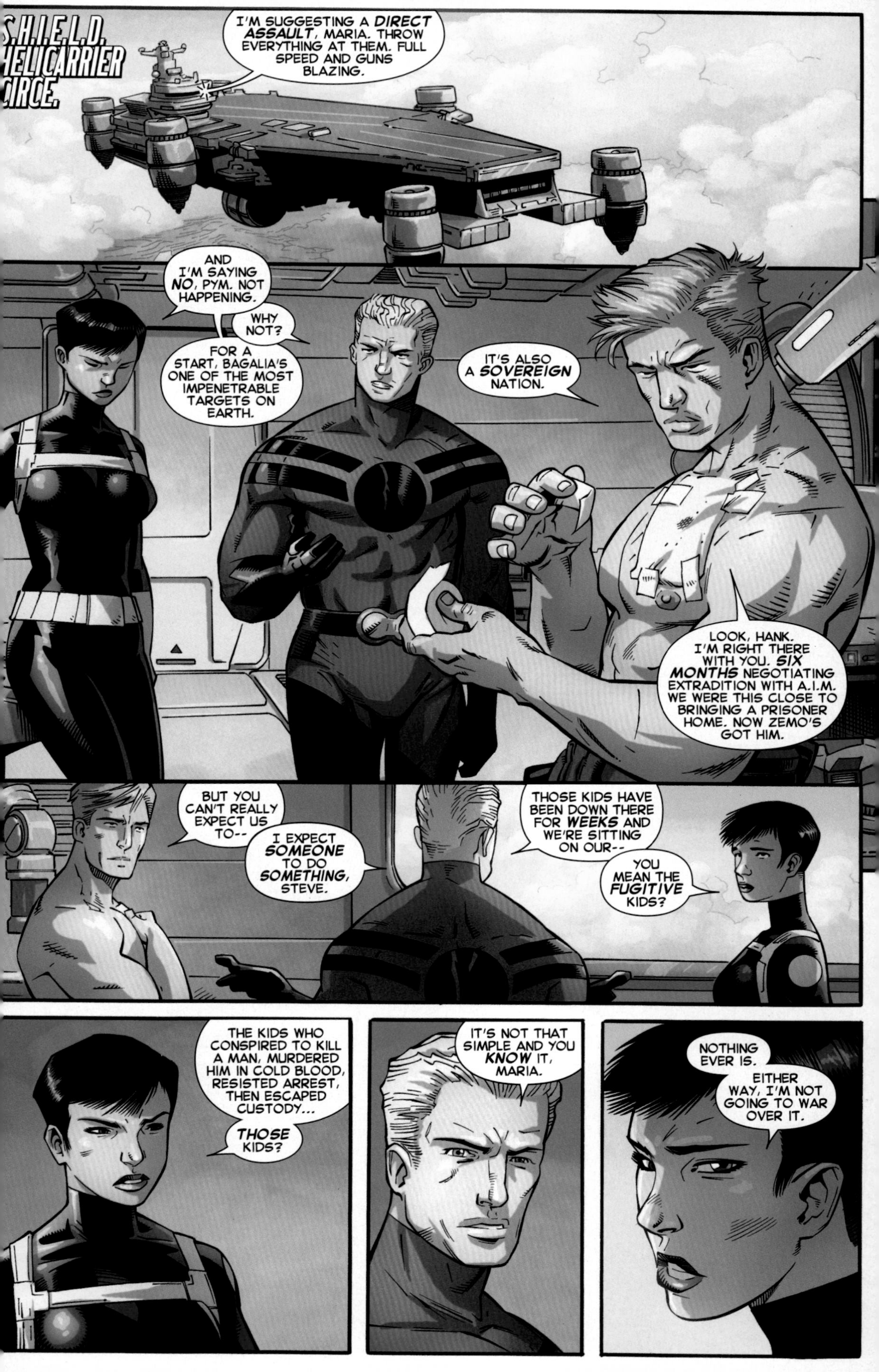
S.H.I.E.L.D. HELICARRIER CIRCE.
I'M SUGGESTING A DIRECT ASSAULT, MARIA. THROW EVERYTHING AT THEM. FULL SPEED AND GUNS BLAZING.
AND I'M SAYING NO, PYM. NOT HAPPENING.
WHY NOT?
FOR A START, BAGALIA'S ONE OF THE MOST IMPENETRABLE TARGETS ON EARTH.
IT'S ALSO A SOVEREIGN NATION.
LOOK, HANK. I'M RIGHT THERE WITH YOU. SIX MONTHS NEGOTIATING EXTRADITION WITH A.I.M. WE WERE THIS CLOSE TO BRINGING A PRISONER HOME. NOW ZEMO'S GOT HIM.
BUT YOU CAN'T REALLY EXPECT US TO--
I EXPECT SOMEONE TO DO SOMETHING, STEVE.
THOSE KIDS HAVE BEEN DOWN THERE FOR WEEKS AND WE'RE SITTING ON OUR--
YOU MEAN THE FUGITIVE KIDS?
THE KIDS WHO CONSPIRED TO KILL A MAN, MURDERED HIM IN COLD BLOOD, RESISTED ARREST, THEN ESCAPED CUSTODY...
THOSE KIDS?
IT'S NOT THAT SIMPLE AND YOU KNOW IT, MARIA.
NOTHING EVER IS.
EITHER WAY, I'M NOT GOING TO WAR OVER IT.

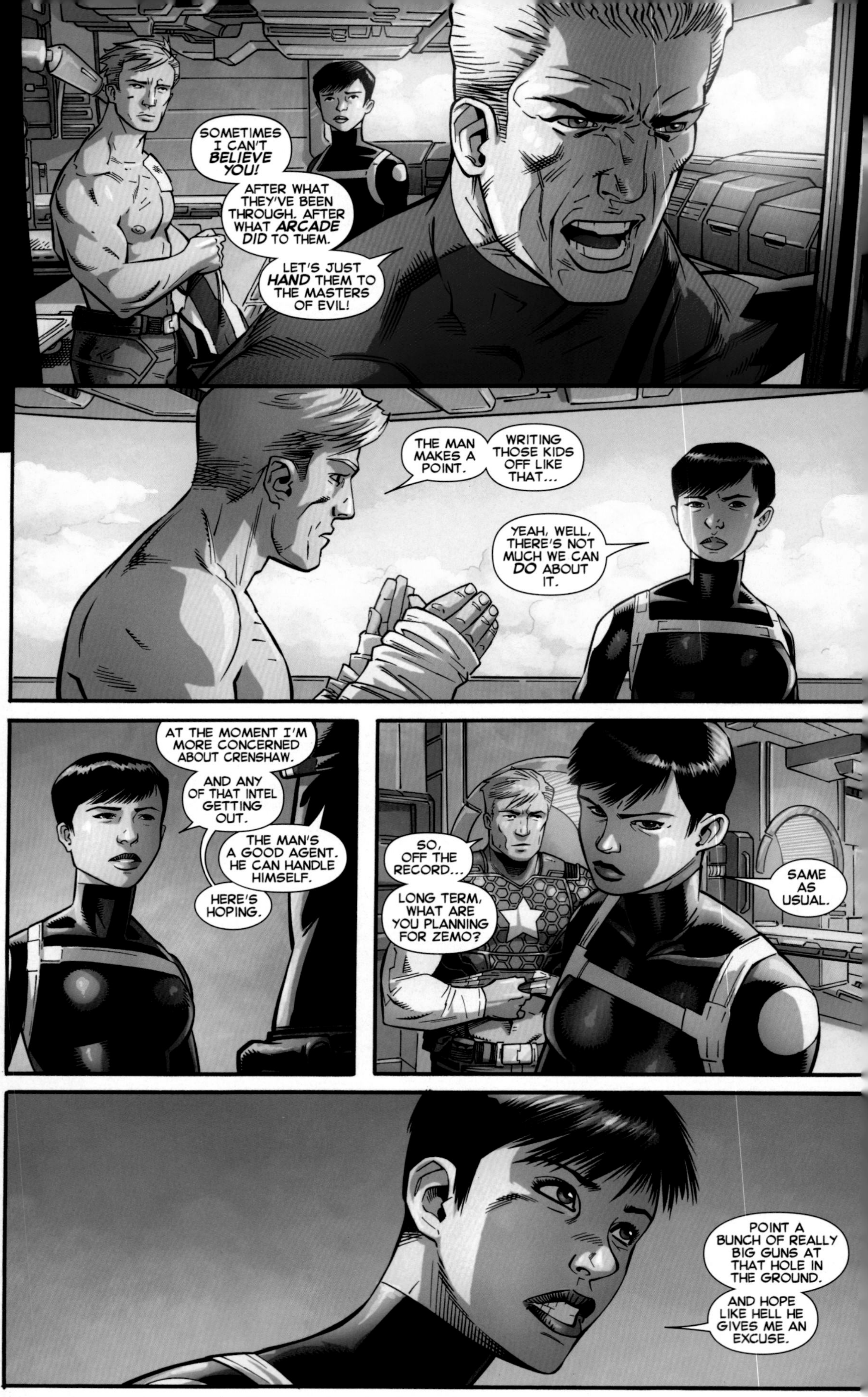
SOMETIMES I CAN'T BELIEVE YOU!
AFTER WHAT THEY'VE BEEN THROUGH. AFTER WHAT ARCADE DID TO THEM.
LET'S JUST HAND THEM TO THE MASTERS OF EVIL!
THE MAN MAKES A POINT.
WRITING THOSE KIDS OFF LIKE THAT...
YEAH, WELL, THERE'S NOT MUCH WE CAN DO ABOUT IT.
AT THE MOMENT I'M MORE CONCERNED ABOUT CRENSHAW.
AND ANY OF THAT INTEL GETTING OUT.
THE MAN'S A GOOD AGENT. HE CAN HANDLE HIMSELF.
HERE'S HOPING.
SO, OFF THE RECORD...
LONG TERM, WHAT ARE YOU PLANNING FOR ZEMO?
SAME AS USUAL.
POINT A BUNCH OF REALLY BIG GUNS AT THAT HOLE IN THE GROUND.
AND HOPE LIKE HELL HE GIVES ME AN EXCUSE.

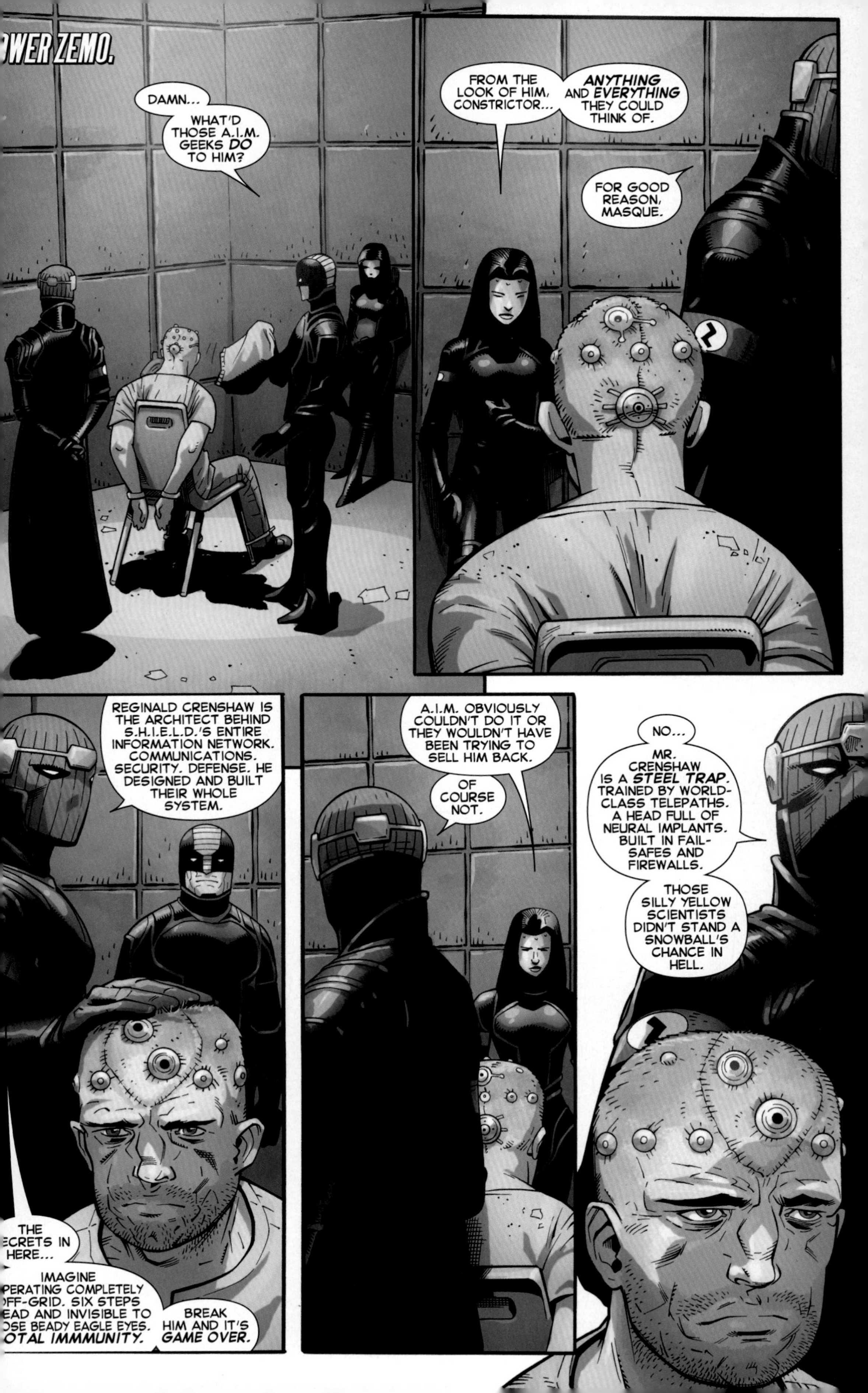

WER ZEMO.
DAMN...
WHAT'D THOSE A.I.M. GEEKS DO TO HIM?
FROM THE LOOK OF HIM, CONSTRICTOR...
ANYTHING AND EVERYTHING THEY COULD THINK OF.
FOR GOOD REASON, MASQUE.
REGINALD CRENSHAW IS THE ARCHITECT BEHIND S.H.I.E.L.D.'S ENTIRE INFORMATION NETWORK. COMMUNICATIONS. SECURITY. DEFENSE. HE DESIGNED AND BUILT THEIR WHOLE SYSTEM.
THE ECRETS IN HERE...
IMAGINE PERATING COMPLETELY FF-GRID. SIX STEPS EAD AND INVISIBLE TO OSE BEADY EAGLE EYES. OTAL IMMMUNITY.
BREAK HIM AND IT'S GAME OVER.
A.I.M. OBVIOUSLY COULDN'T DO IT OR THEY WOULDN'T HAVE BEEN TRYING TO SELL HIM BACK.
OF COURSE NOT.
NO...
MR. CRENSHAW IS A STEEL TRAP. TRAINED BY WORLD-CLASS TELEPATHS. A HEAD FULL OF NEURAL IMPLANTS. BUILT IN FAIL-SAFES AND FIREWALLS.
THOSE SILLY YELLOW SCIENTISTS DIDN'T STAND A SNOWBALL'S CHANCE IN HELL.

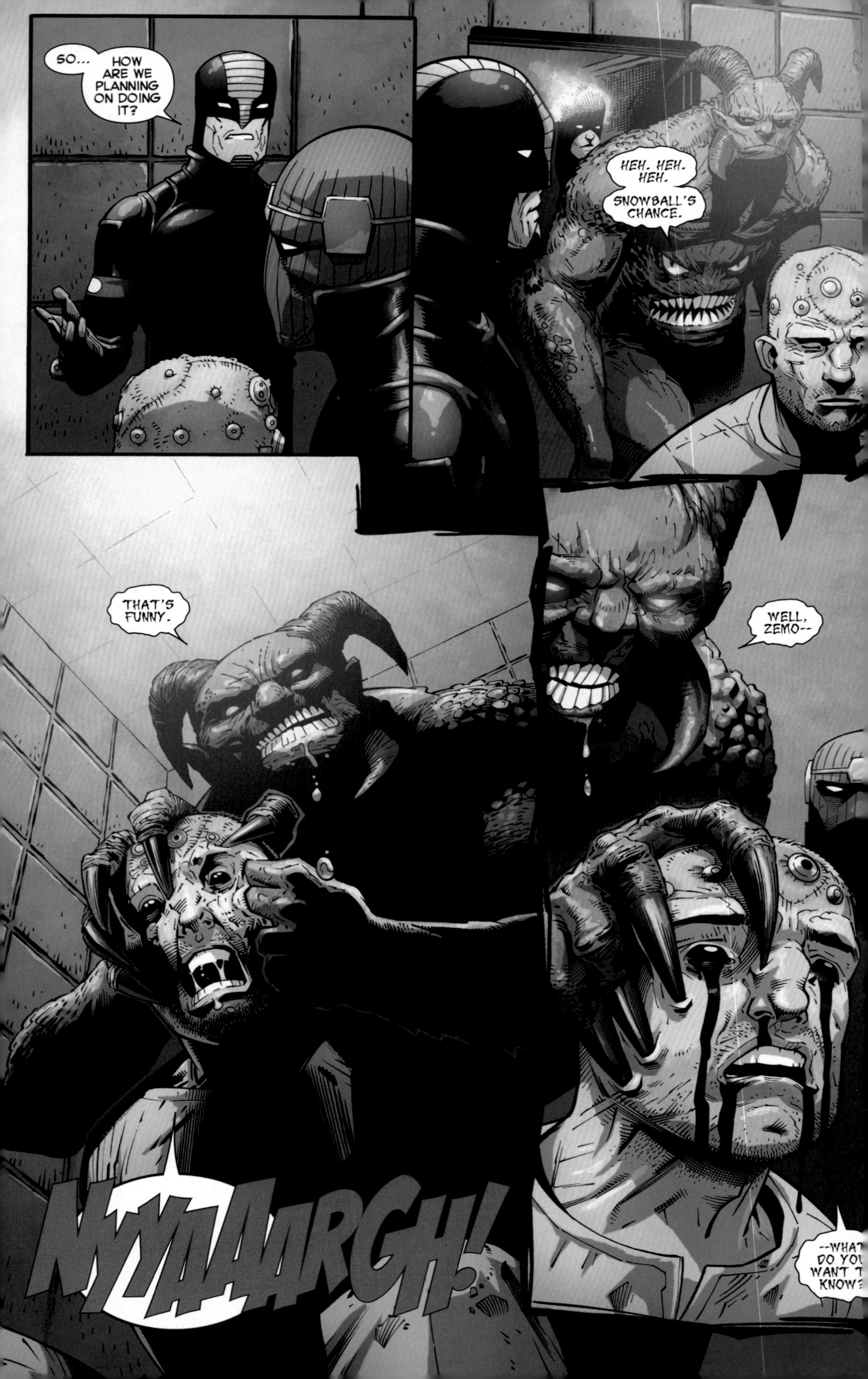
SO...
HOW ARE WE PLANNING ON DOING IT?
HEH. HEH. HEH.
SNOWBALL'S CHANCE.
THAT'S FUNNY.
WELL, ZEMO--
MYAAARGH!
--WHAT DO YOU WANT TO KNOW?

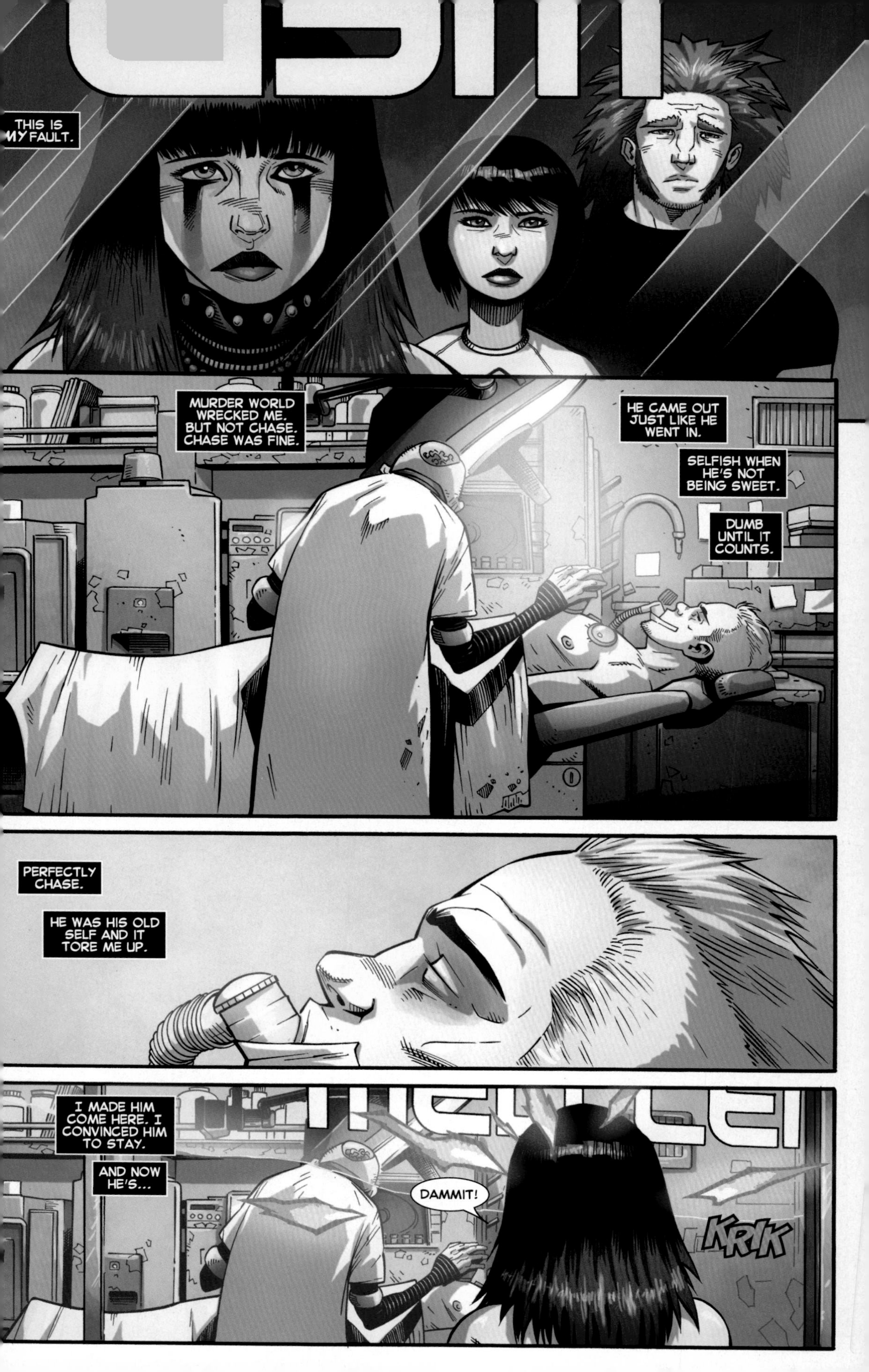
THIS IS MY FAULT.
MURDER WORLD WRECKED ME. BUT NOT CHASE. CHASE WAS FINE.
HE CAME OUT JUST LIKE HE WENT IN.
SELFISH WHEN HE'S NOT BEING SWEET.
DUMB UNTIL IT COUNTS.
PERFECTLY CHASE.
HE WAS HIS OLD SELF AND IT TORE ME UP.
I MADE HIM COME HERE. I CONVINCED HIM TO STAY.
AND NOW HE'S...
DAMMIT!
KRIK

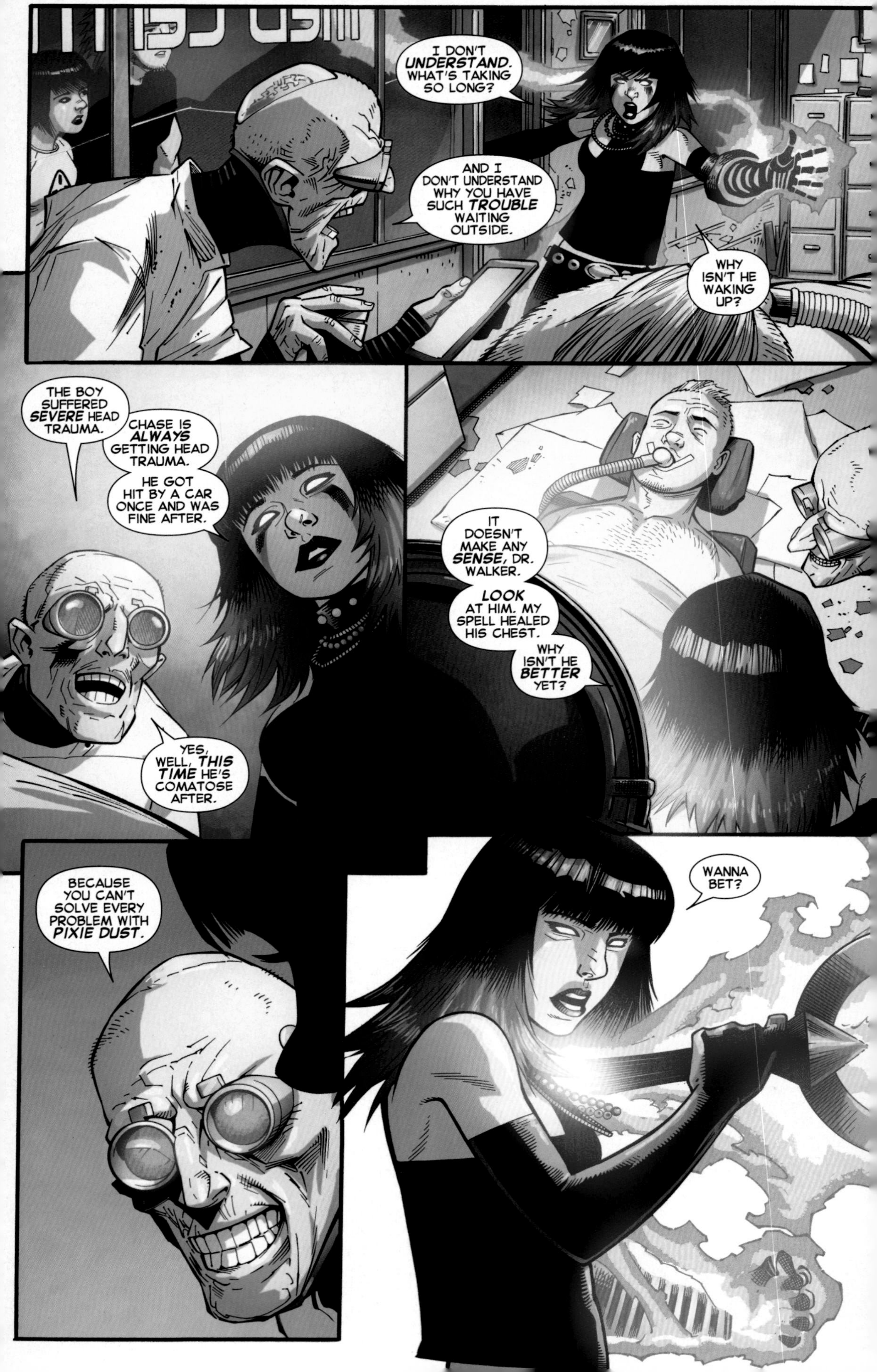
I DON'T UNDERSTAND. WHAT'S TAKING SO LONG?
AND I DON'T UNDERSTAND WHY YOU HAVE SUCH TROUBLE WAITING OUTSIDE.
WHY ISN'T HE WAKING UP?
THE BOY SUFFERED SEVERE HEAD TRAUMA.
CHASE IS ALWAYS GETTING HEAD TRAUMA.
HE GOT HIT BY A CAR ONCE AND WAS FINE AFTER.
YES, WELL, THIS TIME HE'S COMATOSE AFTER.
IT DOESN'T MAKE ANY SENSE, DR. WALKER.
LOOK AT HIM. MY SPELL HEALED HIS CHEST.
WHY ISN'T HE BETTER YET?
BECAUSE YOU CAN'T SOLVE EVERY PROBLEM WITH PIXIE DUST.
WANNA BET?

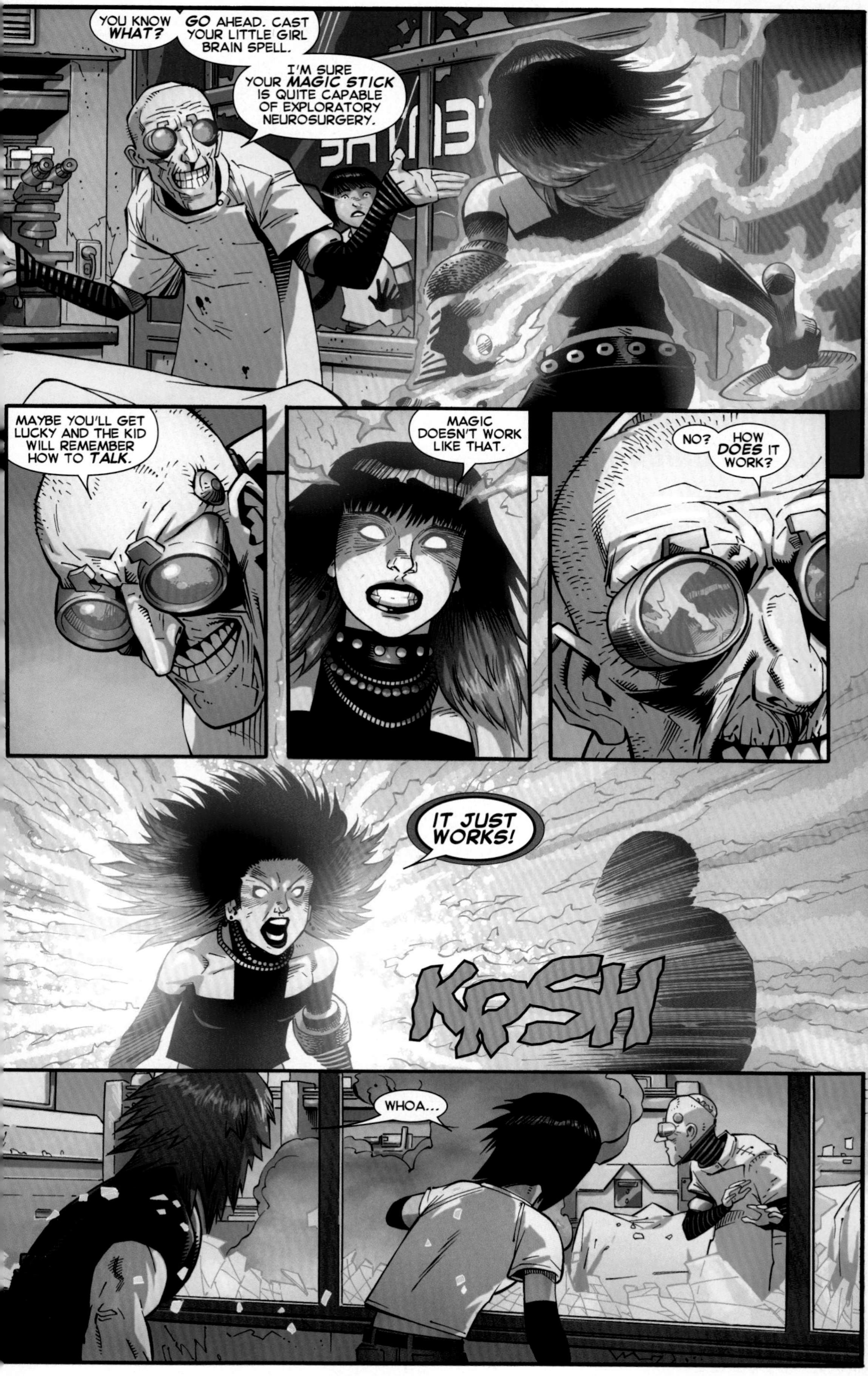
YOU KNOW WHAT?
GO AHEAD. CAST YOUR LITTLE GIRL BRAIN SPELL.
I'M SURE YOUR MAGIC STICK IS QUITE CAPABLE OF EXPLORATORY NEUROSURGERY.
MAYBE YOU'LL GET LUCKY AND THE KID WILL REMEMBER HOW TO TALK.
MAGIC DOESN'T WORK LIKE THAT.
NO?
HOW DOES IT WORK?
IT JUST WORKS!
KRSH
WHOA...

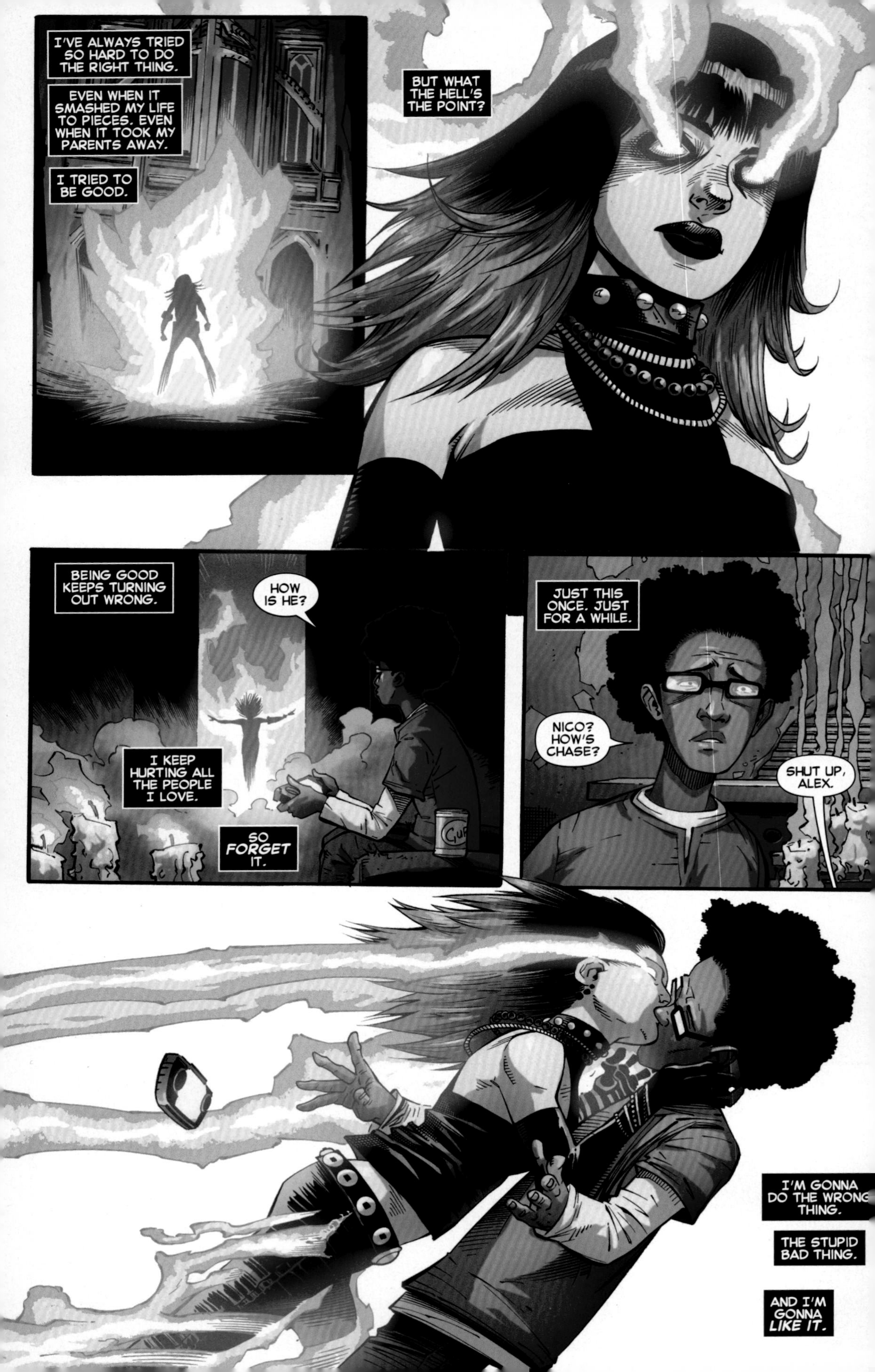
I'VE ALWAYS TRIED SO HARD TO DO THE RIGHT THING.
EVEN WHEN IT SMASHED MY LIFE TO PIECES. EVEN WHEN IT TOOK MY PARENTS AWAY.
I TRIED TO BE GOOD.
BUT WHAT THE HELL'S THE POINT?
BEING GOOD KEEPS TURNING OUT WRONG.
HOW IS HE?
I KEEP HURTING ALL THE PEOPLE I LOVE.
SO FORGET IT.
JUST THIS ONCE. JUST FOR A WHILE.
NICO? HOW'S CHASE?
SHUT UP, ALEX.
I'M GONNA DO THE WRONG THING.
THE STUPID BAD THING.
AND I'M GONNA LIKE IT.

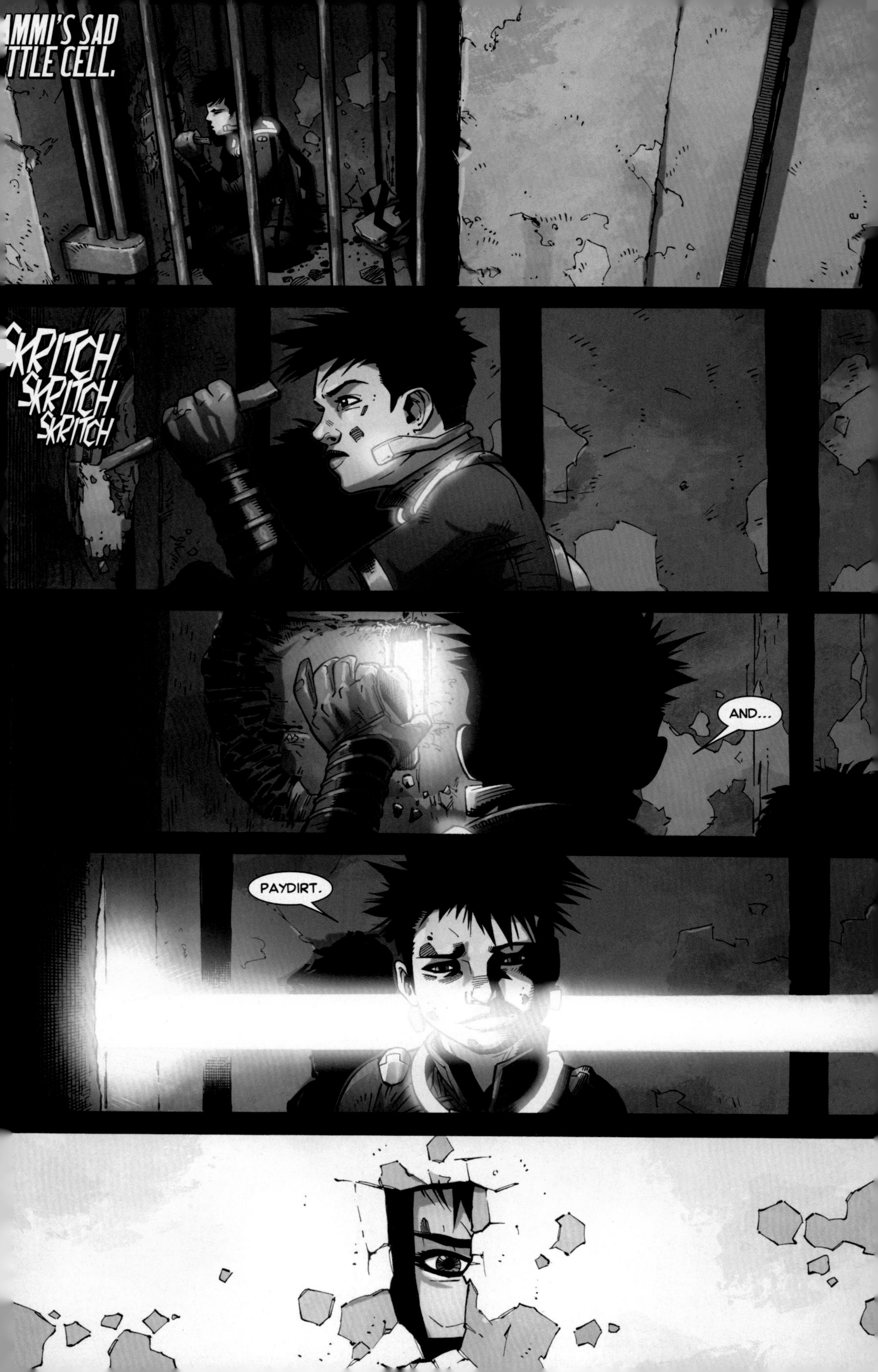

MMI'S SAD
TTLE CELL.
SKRITCH
SKRITCH
SKRITCH
AND...
PAYDIRT.

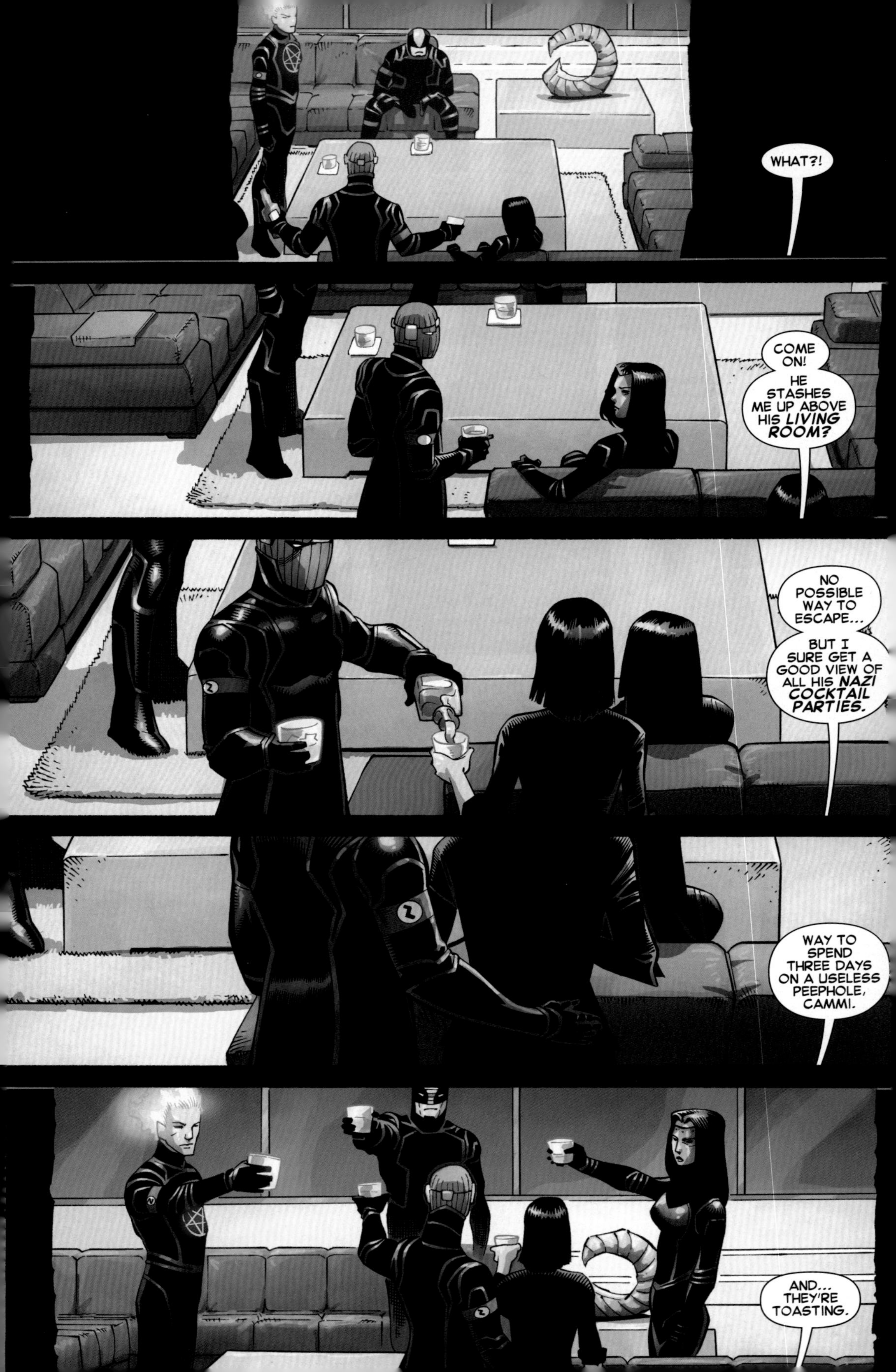
WHAT?!
COME ON!
HE STASHES ME UP ABOVE HIS LIVING ROOM?
NO POSSIBLE WAY TO ESCAPE...
BUT I SURE GET A GOOD VIEW OF ALL HIS NAZI COCKTAIL PARTIES.
WAY TO SPEND THREE DAYS ON A USELESS PEEPHOLE, CAMMI.
AND... THEY'RE TOASTING.

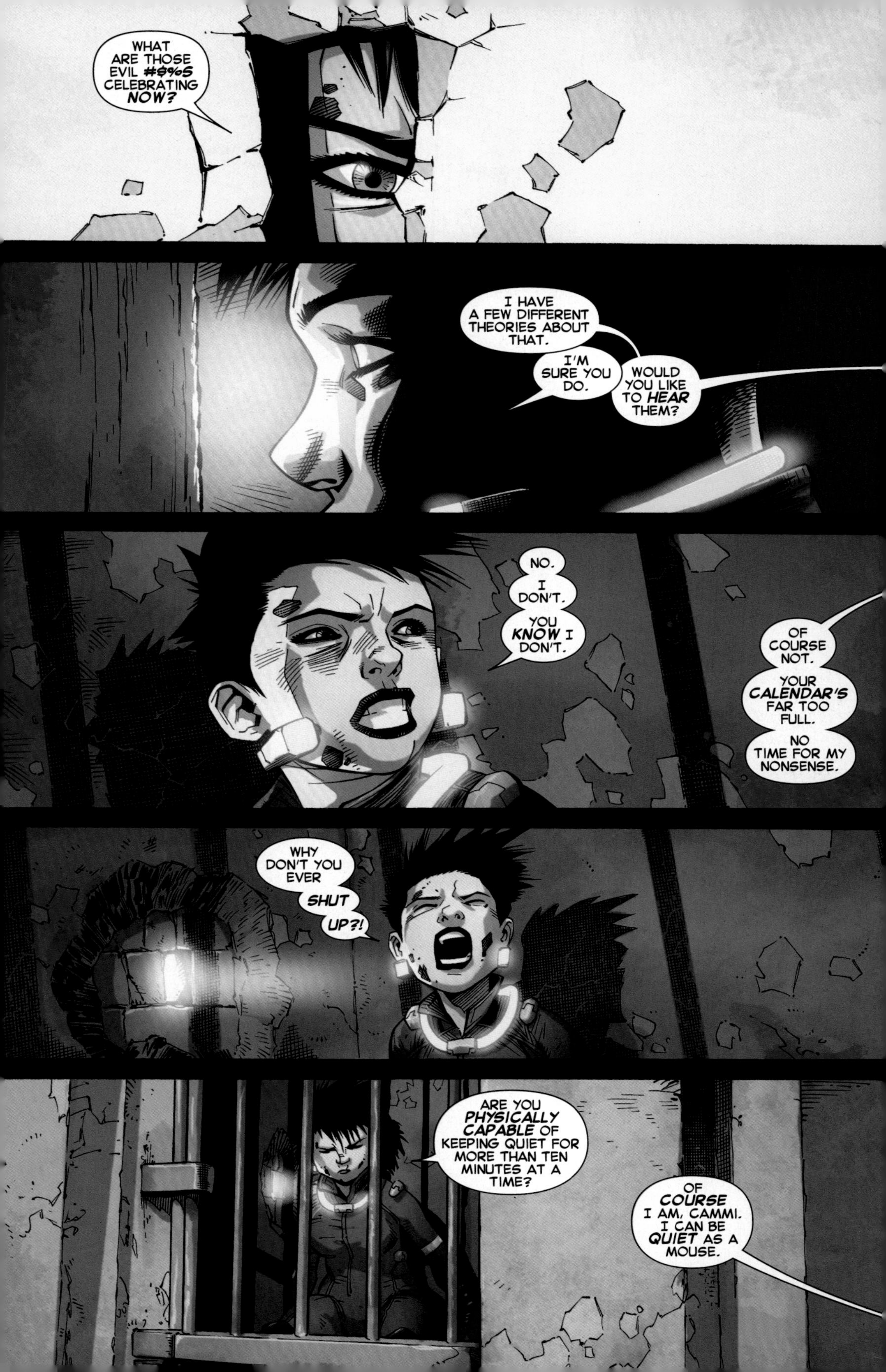
WHAT ARE THOSE EVIL #$%S CELEBRATING NOW?
I HAVE A FEW DIFFERENT THEORIES ABOUT THAT.
I'M SURE YOU DO.
WOULD YOU LIKE TO HEAR THEM?
NO.
I DON'T.
YOU KNOW I DON'T.
OF COURSE NOT.
YOUR CALENDAR'S FAR TOO FULL.
NO TIME FOR MY NONSENSE.
WHY DON'T YOU EVER SHUT UP?!
ARE YOU PHYSICALLY CAPABLE OF KEEPING QUIET FOR MORE THAN TEN MINUTES AT A TIME?
OF COURSE I AM, CAMMI. I CAN BE QUIET AS A MOUSE.

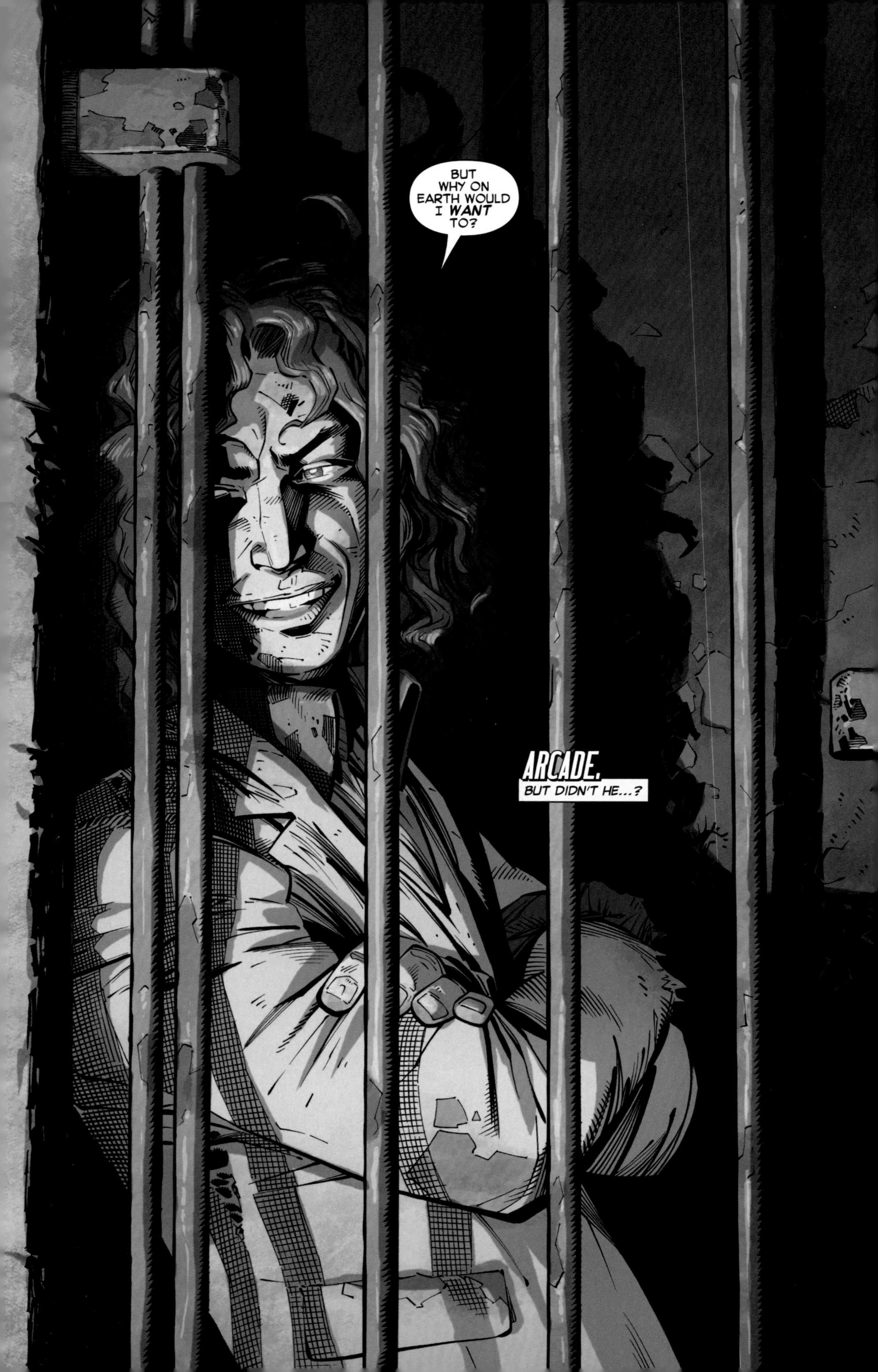
BUT WHY ON EARTH WOULD I *WANT* TO?
ARCADE.
BUT DIDN'T HE...?

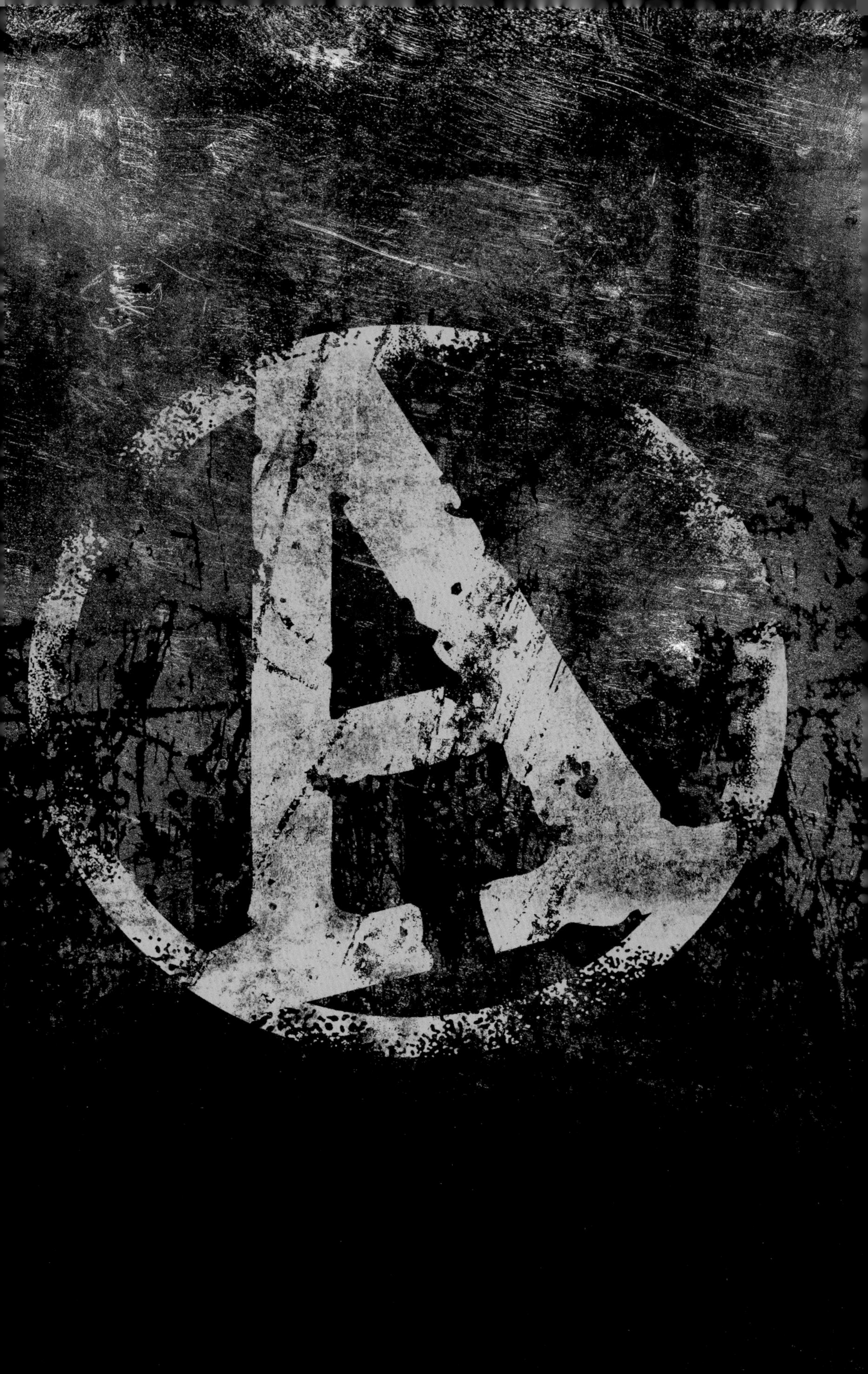

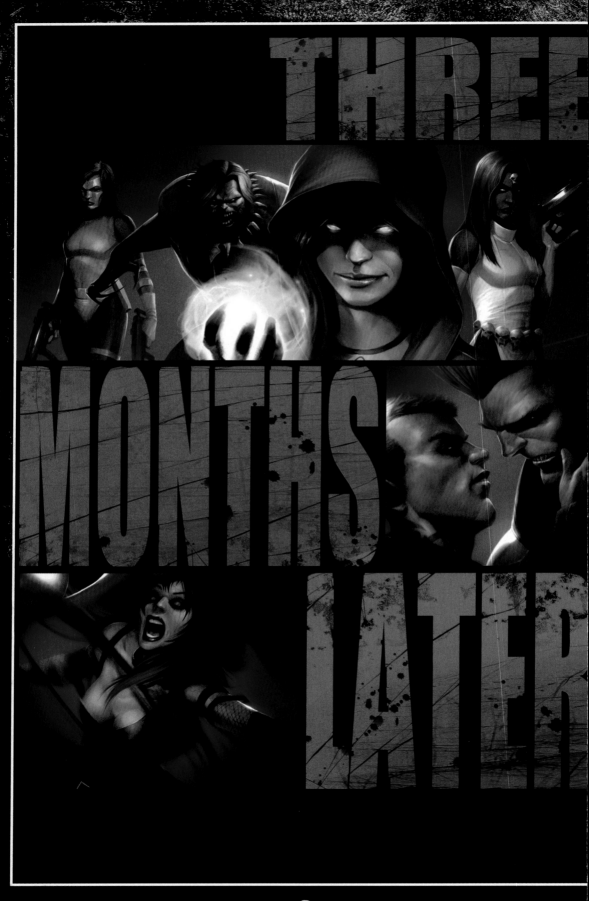

THREE

MONTHS

LATER

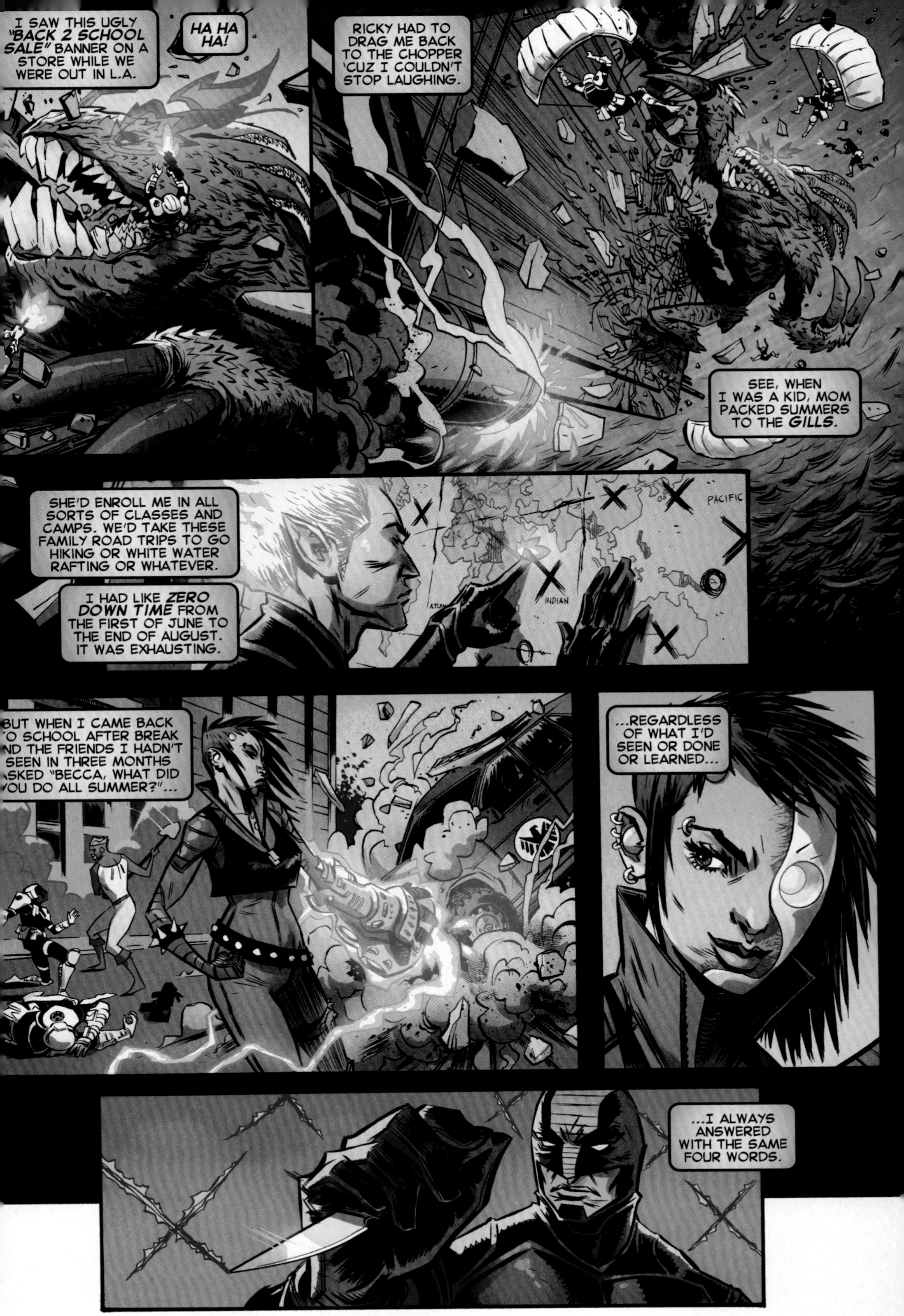
I SAW THIS UGLY "BACK 2 SCHOOL SALE" BANNER ON A STORE WHILE WE WERE OUT IN L.A.
HA HA HA!
RICKY HAD TO DRAG ME BACK TO THE CHOPPER 'CUZ I COULDN'T STOP LAUGHING.
SEE, WHEN I WAS A KID, MOM PACKED SUMMERS TO THE GILLS.
SHE'D ENROLL ME IN ALL SORTS OF CLASSES AND CAMPS. WE'D TAKE THESE FAMILY ROAD TRIPS TO GO HIKING OR WHITE WATER RAFTING OR WHATEVER.
I HAD LIKE ZERO DOWN TIME FROM THE FIRST OF JUNE TO THE END OF AUGUST. IT WAS EXHAUSTING.
PACIFIC
INDIAN
BUT WHEN I CAME BACK TO SCHOOL AFTER BREAK AND THE FRIENDS I HADN'T SEEN IN THREE MONTHS ASKED "BECCA, WHAT DID YOU DO ALL SUMMER?"...
...REGARDLESS OF WHAT I'D SEEN OR DONE OR LEARNED...
...I ALWAYS ANSWERED WITH THE SAME FOUR WORDS.

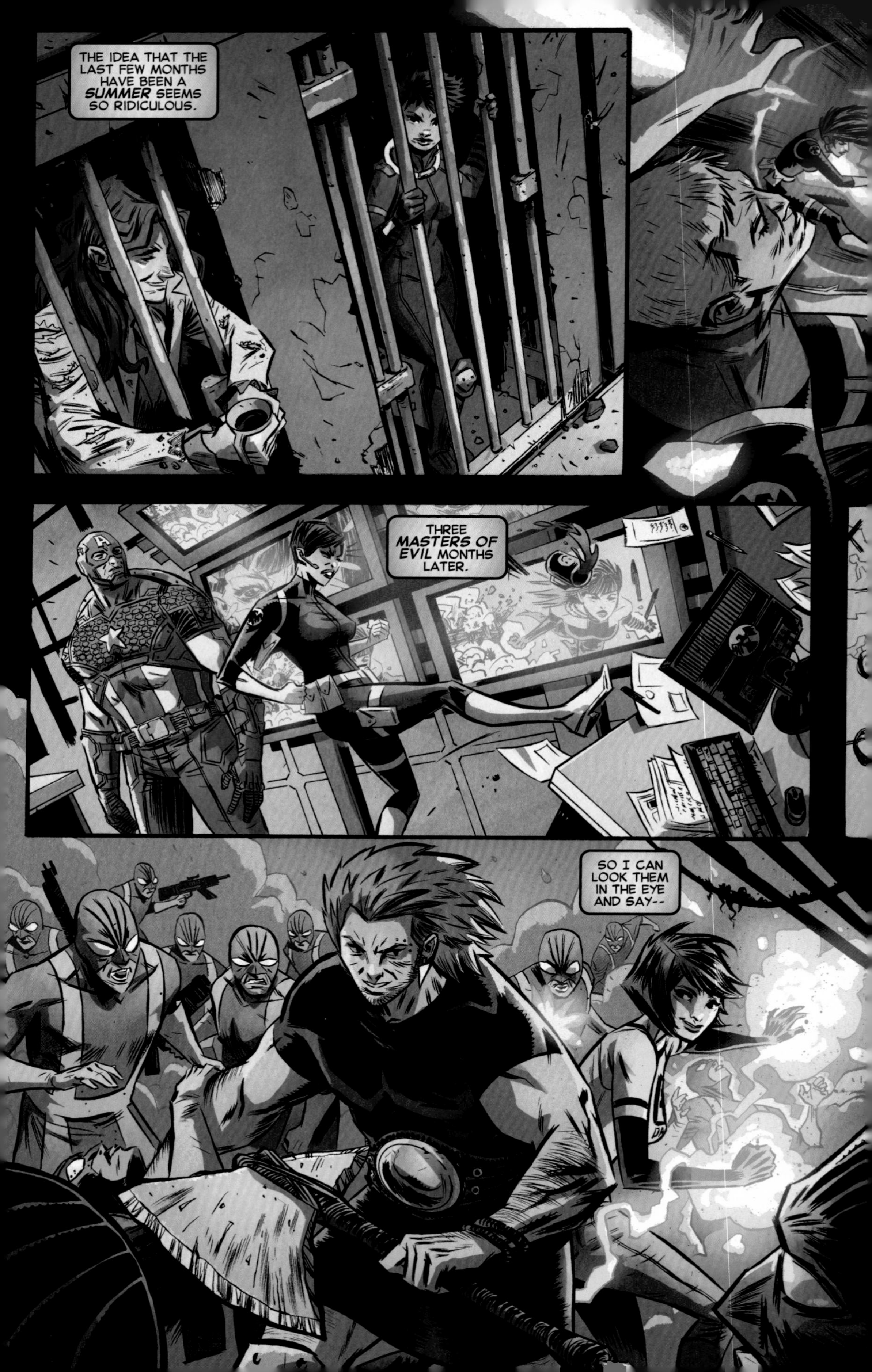
THE IDEA THAT THE LAST FEW MONTHS HAVE BEEN A SUMMER SEEMS SO RIDICULOUS.
THREE MASTERS OF EVIL MONTHS LATER.
SO I CAN LOOK THEM IN THE EYE AND SAY--

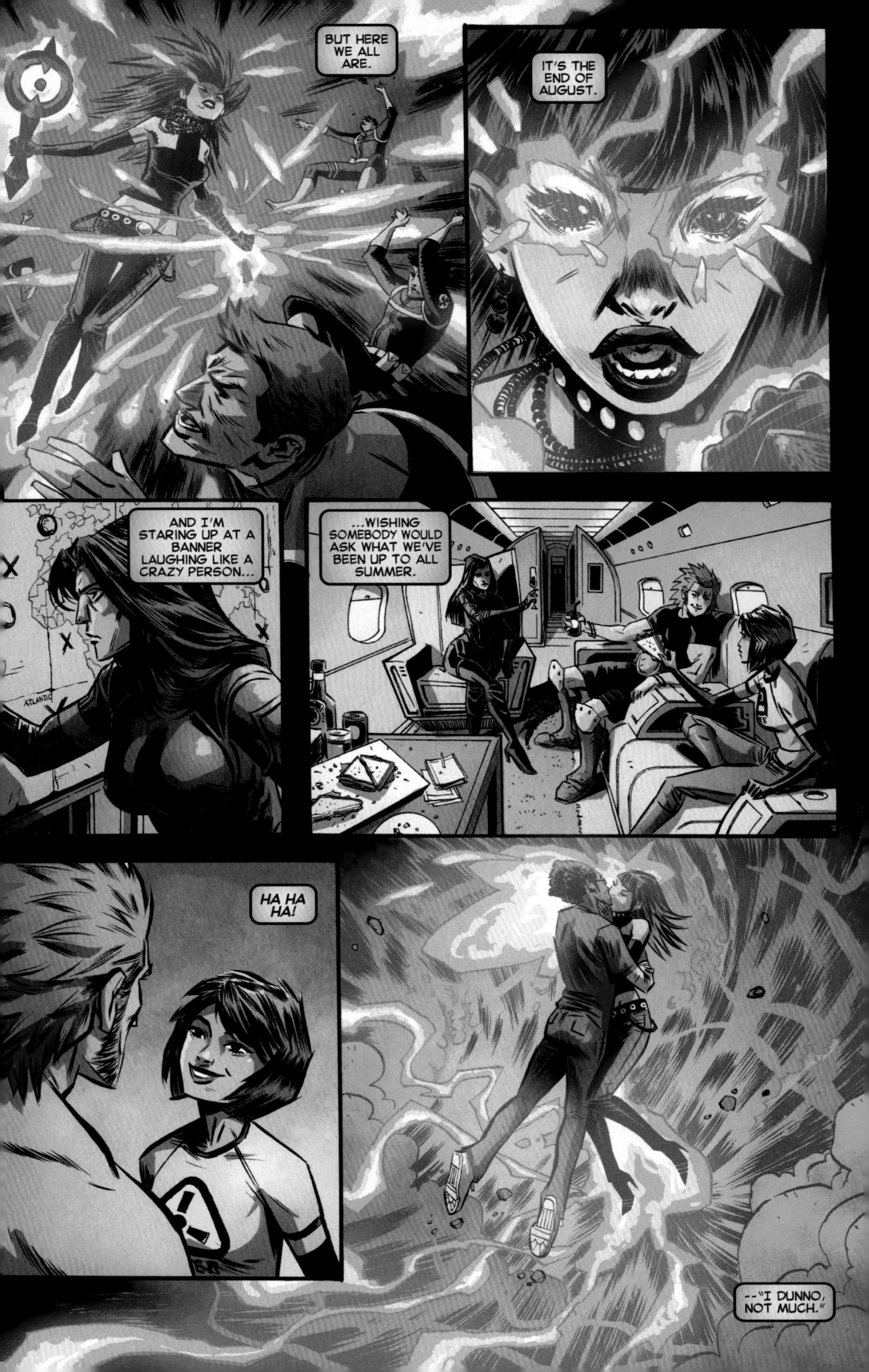
BUT HERE WE ALL ARE.
IT'S THE END OF AUGUST.
AND I'M STARING UP AT A BANNER LAUGHING LIKE A CRAZY PERSON...
...WISHING SOMEBODY WOULD ASK WHAT WE'VE BEEN UP TO ALL SUMMER.
HA HA HA!
--"I DUNNO, NOT MUCH."

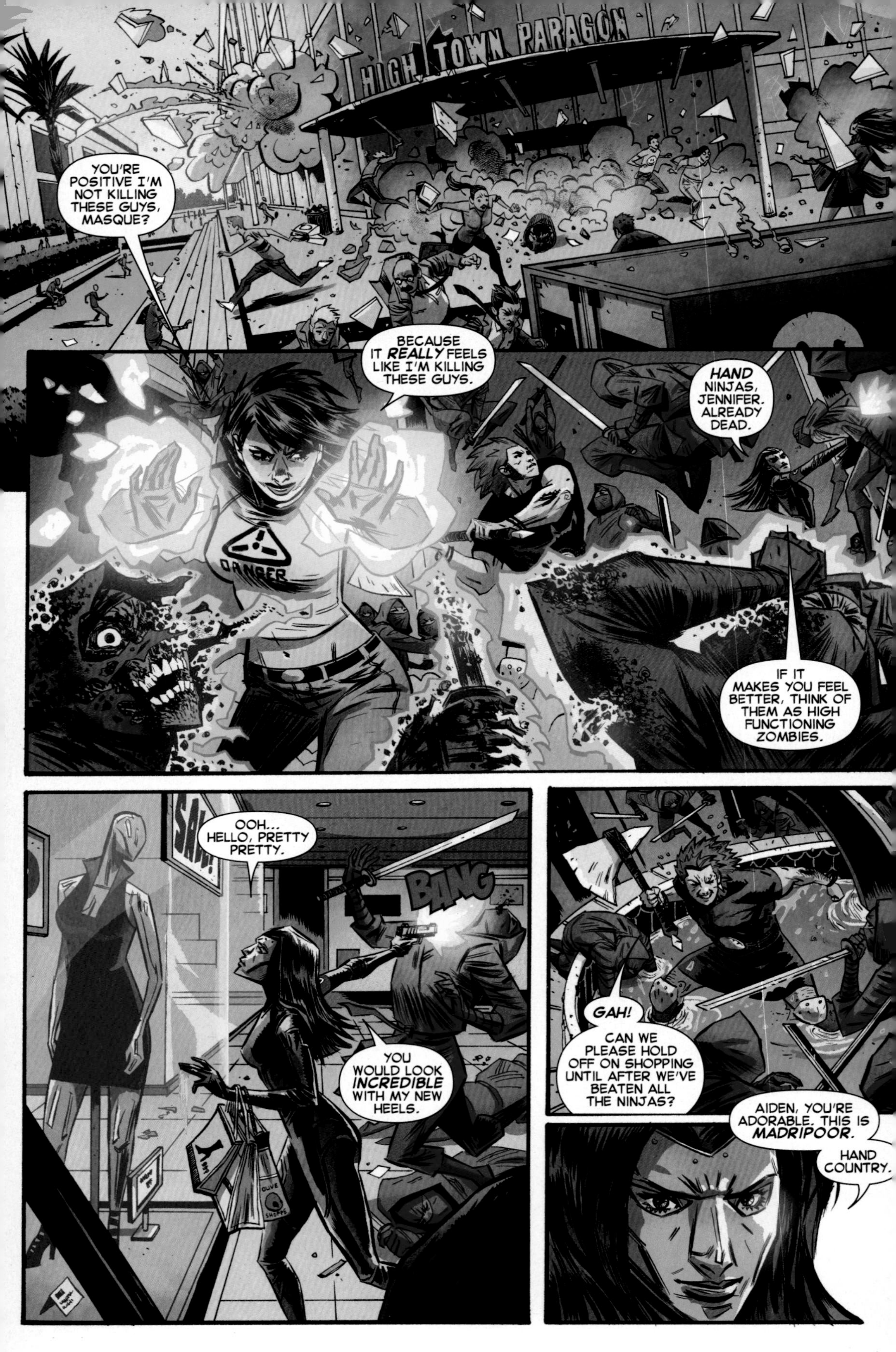

HIGH TOWN PARAGON
YOU'RE POSITIVE I'M NOT KILLING THESE GUYS, MASQUE?
BECAUSE IT REALLY FEELS LIKE I'M KILLING THESE GUYS.
HAND NINJAS, JENNIFER. ALREADY DEAD.
DANGER
IF IT MAKES YOU FEEL BETTER, THINK OF THEM AS HIGH FUNCTIONING ZOMBIES.
OOH... HELLO, PRETTY PRETTY.
BANG
YOU WOULD LOOK INCREDIBLE WITH MY NEW HEELS.
GAH!
CAN WE PLEASE HOLD OFF ON SHOPPING UNTIL AFTER WE'VE BEATEN ALL THE NINJAS?
AIDEN, YOU'RE ADORABLE. THIS IS MADRIPOOR.
HAND COUNTRY.

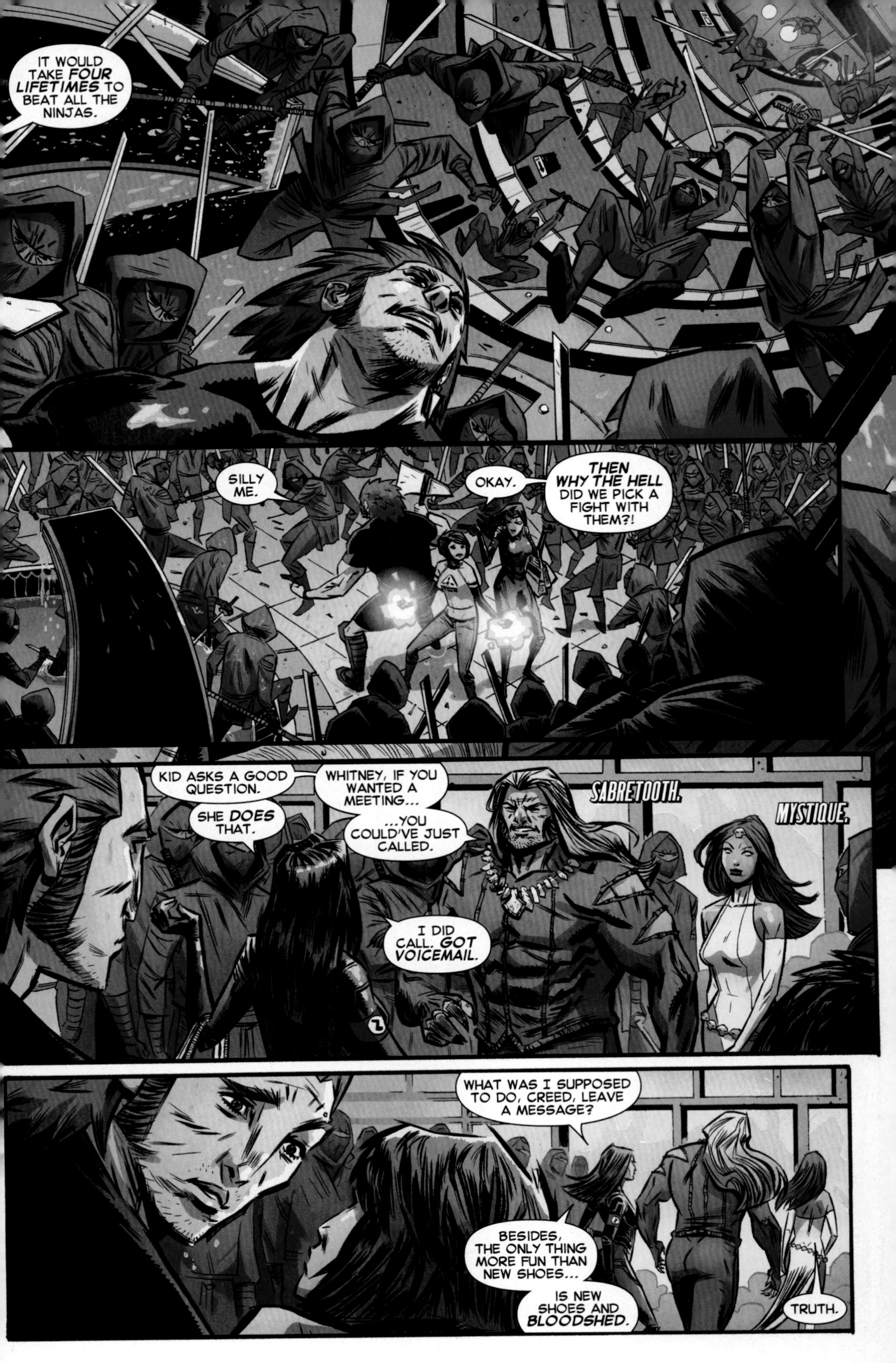
IT WOULD TAKE FOUR LIFETIMES TO BEAT ALL THE NINJAS.
SILLY ME.
OKAY.
THEN WHY THE HELL DID WE PICK A FIGHT WITH THEM?!
KID ASKS A GOOD QUESTION.
SHE DOES THAT.
WHITNEY, IF YOU WANTED A MEETING...
...YOU COULD'VE JUST CALLED.
SABRETOOTH.
MYSTIQUE.
I DID CALL. GOT VOICEMAIL.
WHAT WAS I SUPPOSED TO DO, CREED, LEAVE A MESSAGE?
BESIDES, THE ONLY THING MORE FUN THAN NEW SHOES...
IS NEW SHOES AND BLOODSHED.
TRUTH.

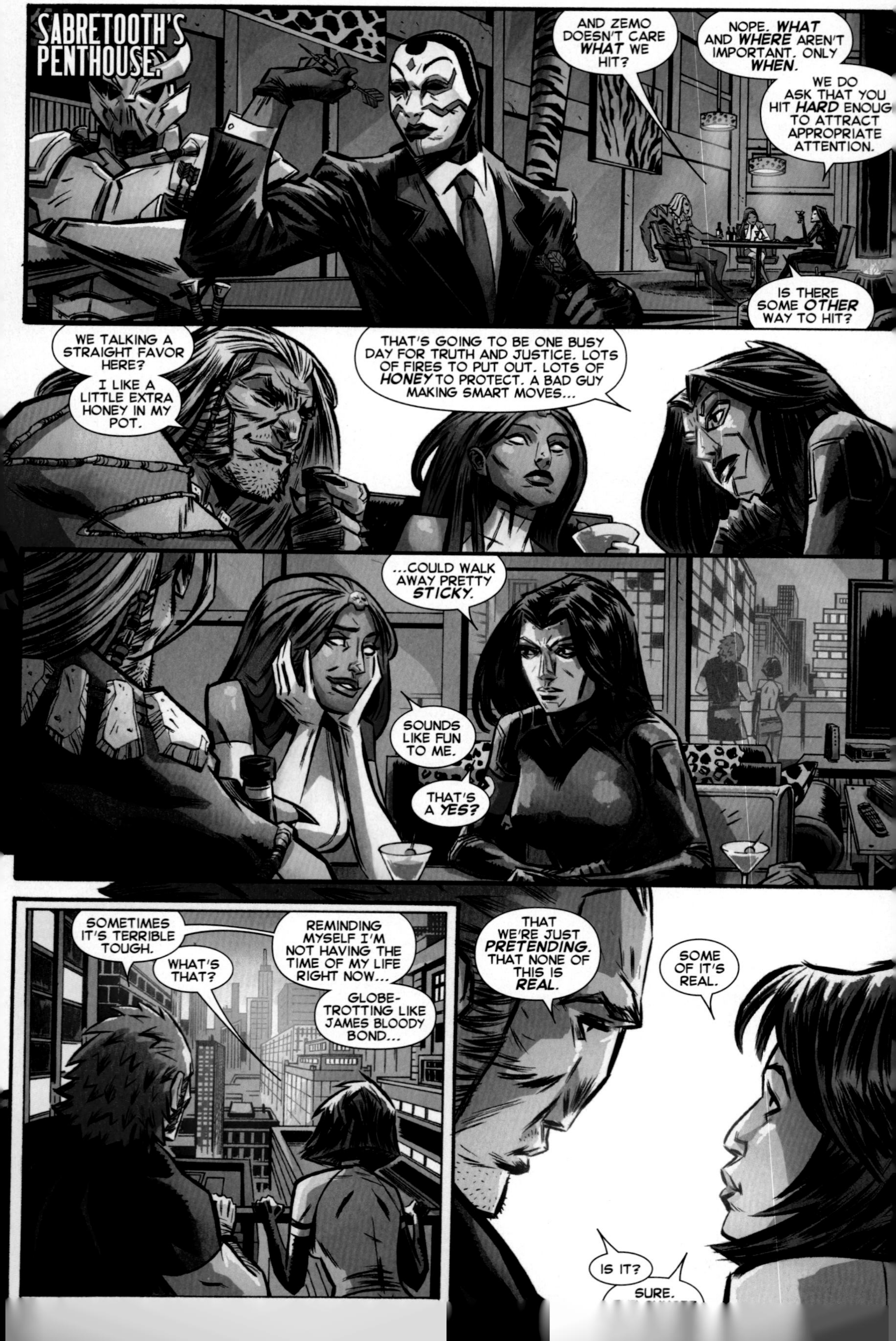
SABRETOOTH'S PENTHOUSE.
AND ZEMO DOESN'T CARE WHAT WE HIT?
NOPE. WHAT AND WHERE AREN'T IMPORTANT. ONLY WHEN.
WE DO ASK THAT YOU HIT HARD ENOUG TO ATTRACT APPROPRIATE ATTENTION.
IS THERE SOME OTHER WAY TO HIT?
WE TALKING A STRAIGHT FAVOR HERE?
I LIKE A LITTLE EXTRA HONEY IN MY POT.
THAT'S GOING TO BE ONE BUSY DAY FOR TRUTH AND JUSTICE. LOTS OF FIRES TO PUT OUT. LOTS OF HONEY TO PROTECT. A BAD GUY MAKING SMART MOVES...
...COULD WALK AWAY PRETTY STICKY.
SOUNDS LIKE FUN TO ME.
THAT'S A YES?
SOMETIMES IT'S TERRIBLE TOUGH.
WHAT'S THAT?
REMINDING MYSELF I'M NOT HAVING THE TIME OF MY LIFE RIGHT NOW...
GLOBE-TROTTING LIKE JAMES BLOODY BOND...
THAT WE'RE JUST PRETENDING. THAT NONE OF THIS IS REAL.
SOME OF IT'S REAL.
IS IT?
SURE.

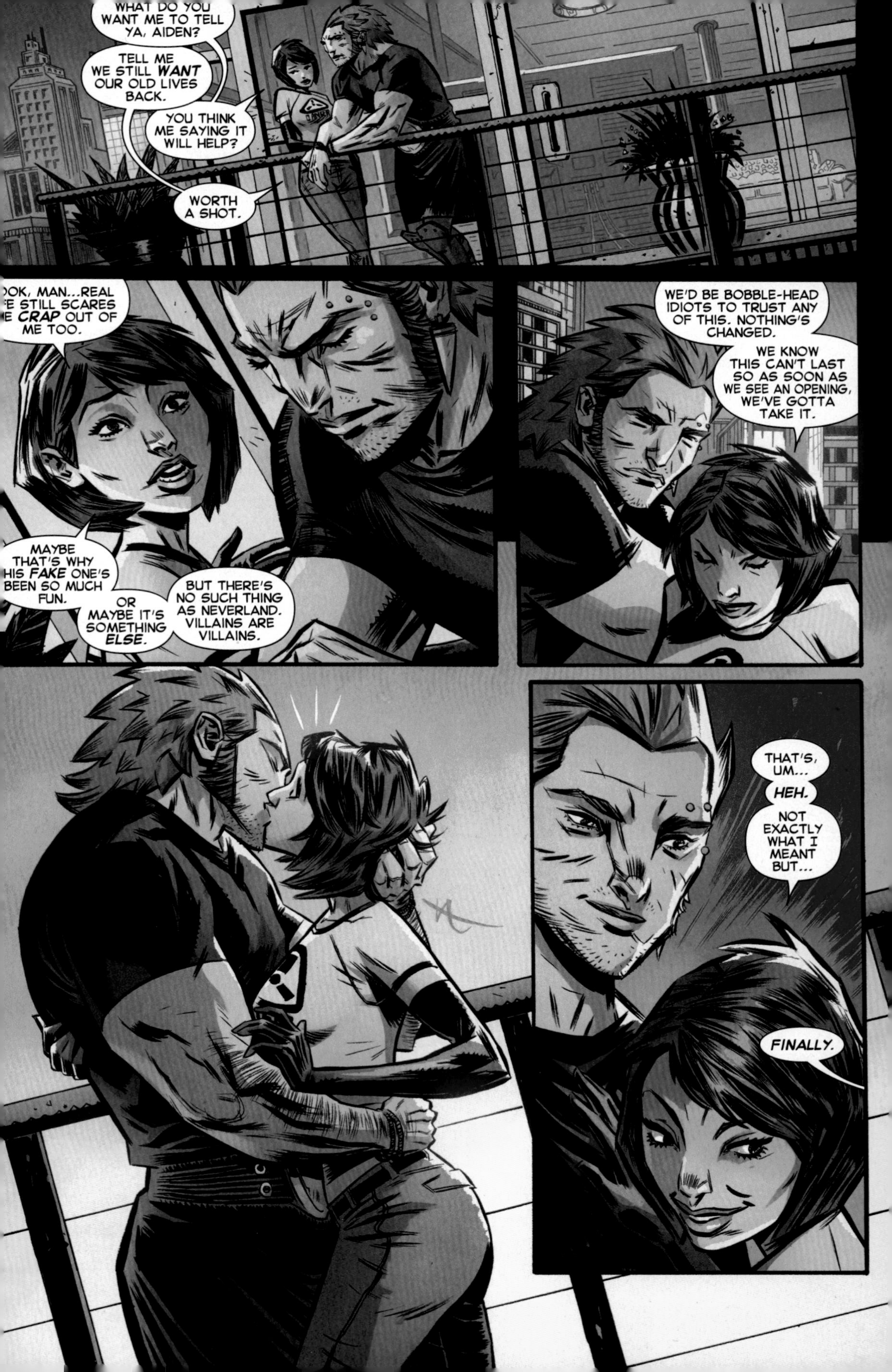
WHAT DO YOU WANT ME TO TELL YA, AIDEN?
TELL ME WE STILL WANT OUR OLD LIVES BACK.
YOU THINK ME SAYING IT WILL HELP?
WORTH A SHOT.
OOK, MAN...REAL FE STILL SCARES E CRAP OUT OF ME TOO.
MAYBE THAT'S WHY HIS FAKE ONE'S BEEN SO MUCH FUN.
OR MAYBE IT'S SOMETHING ELSE.
BUT THERE'S NO SUCH THING AS NEVERLAND. VILLAINS ARE VILLAINS.
WE'D BE BOBBLE-HEAD IDIOTS TO TRUST ANY OF THIS. NOTHING'S CHANGED.
WE KNOW THIS CAN'T LAST SO AS SOON AS WE SEE AN OPENING, WE'VE GOTTA TAKE IT.
THAT'S, UM...
HEH.
NOT EXACTLY WHAT I MEANT BUT...
FINALLY.

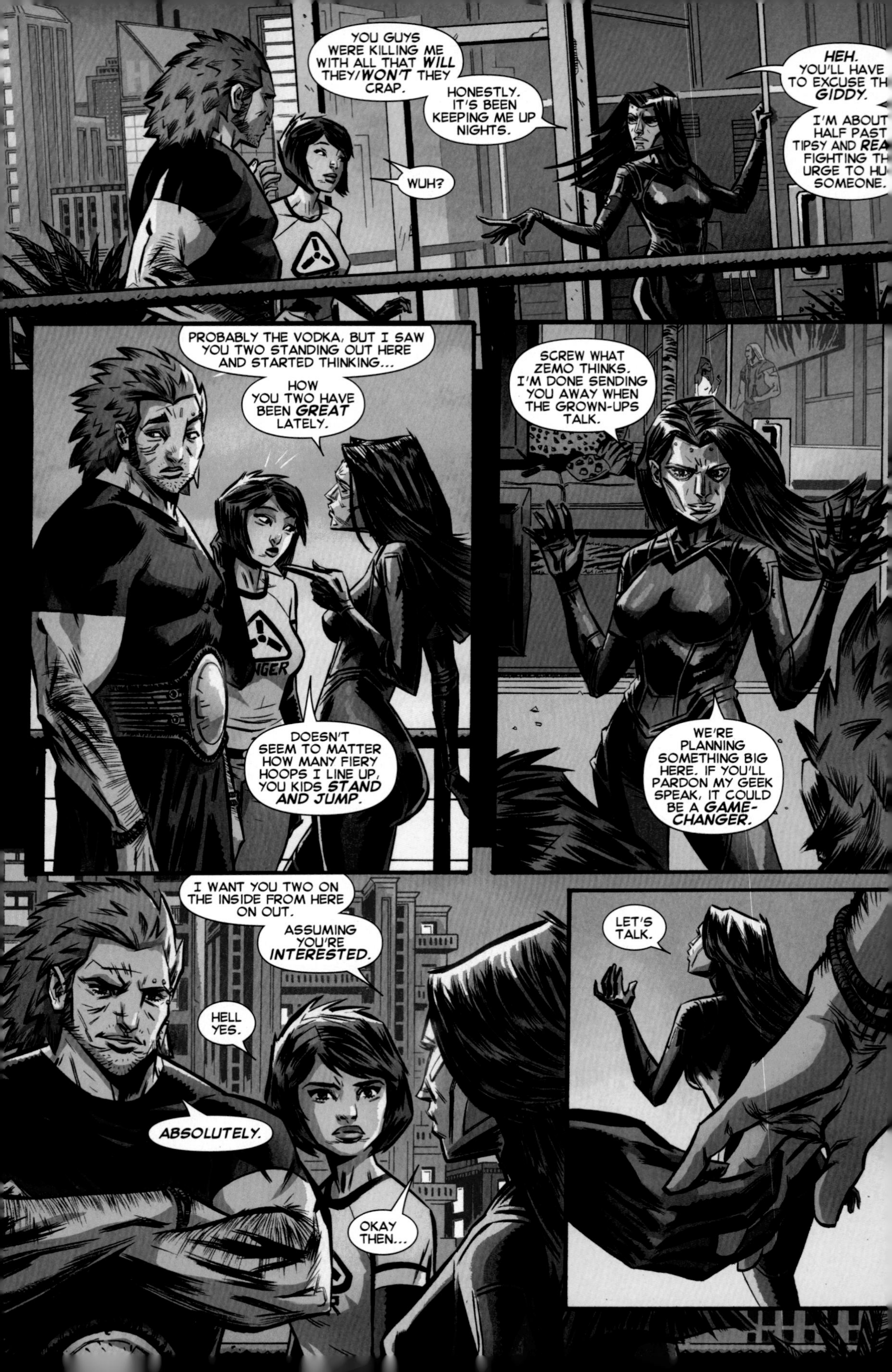
YOU GUYS WERE KILLING ME WITH ALL THAT *WILL* THEY/*WON'T* THEY CRAP.
HONESTLY. IT'S BEEN KEEPING ME UP NIGHTS.
WUH?
HEH. YOU'LL HAVE TO EXCUSE TH *GIDDY.*
I'M ABOUT HALF PAST TIPSY AND *REA* FIGHTING TH URGE TO HU SOMEONE.
PROBABLY THE VODKA, BUT I SAW YOU TWO STANDING OUT HERE AND STARTED THINKING...
HOW YOU TWO HAVE BEEN *GREAT* LATELY.
DOESN'T SEEM TO MATTER HOW MANY FIERY HOOPS I LINE UP, YOU KIDS *STAND AND JUMP.*
SCREW WHAT ZEMO THINKS. I'M DONE SENDING YOU AWAY WHEN THE GROWN-UPS TALK.
WE'RE PLANNING SOMETHING BIG HERE. IF YOU'LL PARDON MY GEEK SPEAK, IT COULD BE A *GAME-CHANGER.*
I WANT YOU TWO ON THE INSIDE FROM HERE ON OUT.
ASSUMING YOU'RE *INTERESTED.*
HELL YES.
ABSOLUTELY.
OKAY THEN...
LET'S TALK.

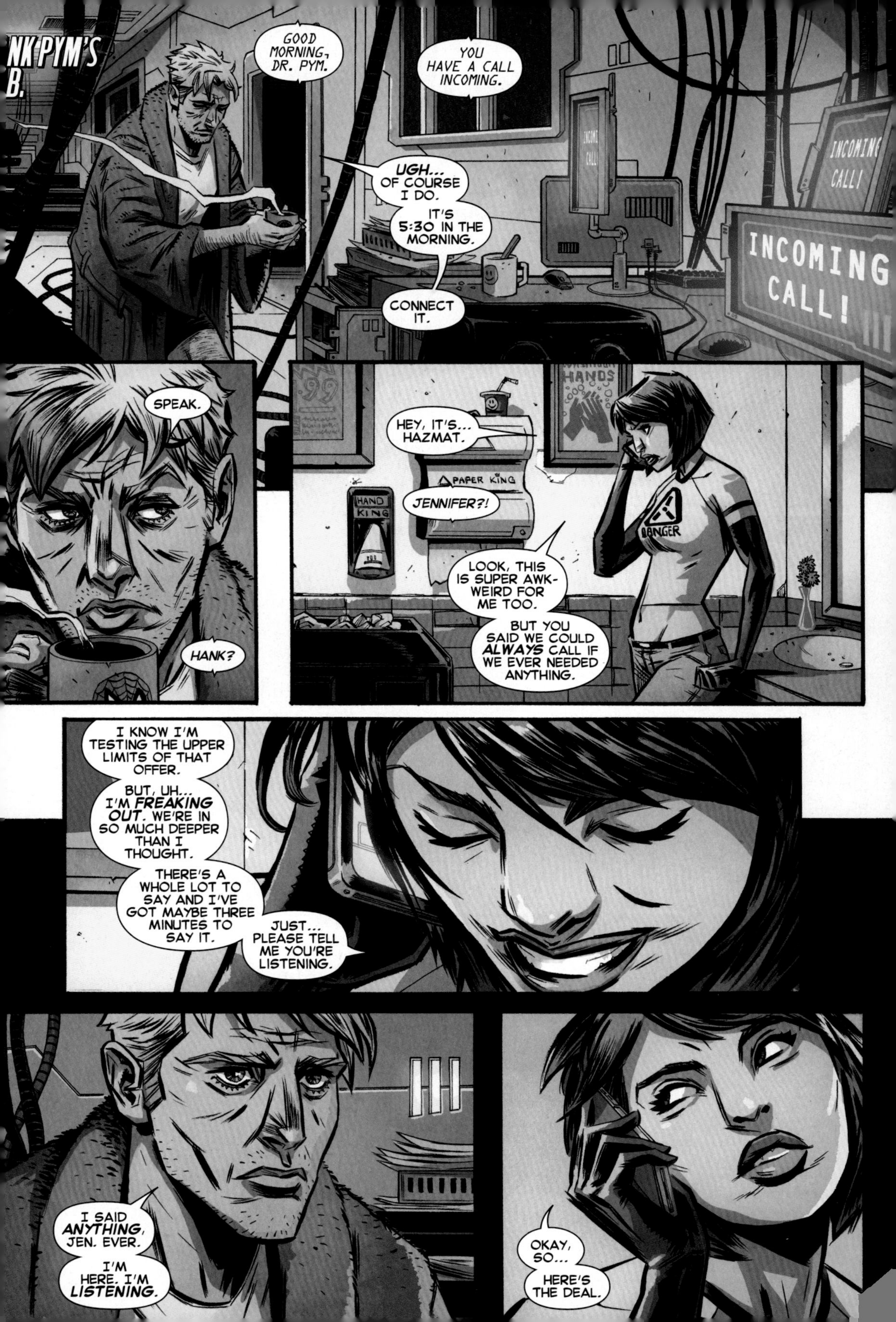
NK PYM'S
B.
GOOD MORNING, DR. PYM.
YOU HAVE A CALL INCOMING.
INCOMING CALL!
INCOMING CALL!
INCOMING CALL!
UGH... OF COURSE I DO.
IT'S 5:30 IN THE MORNING.
CONNECT IT.
SPEAK.
HEY, IT'S... HAZMAT.
PAPER KING
HAND KING
HANDS
JENNIFER?!
DANGER
LOOK, THIS IS SUPER AWK-WEIRD FOR ME TOO.
BUT YOU SAID WE COULD ALWAYS CALL IF WE EVER NEEDED ANYTHING.
HANK?
I KNOW I'M TESTING THE UPPER LIMITS OF THAT OFFER.
BUT, UH... I'M FREAKING OUT. WE'RE IN SO MUCH DEEPER THAN I THOUGHT.
THERE'S A WHOLE LOT TO SAY AND I'VE GOT MAYBE THREE MINUTES TO SAY IT.
JUST... PLEASE TELL ME YOU'RE LISTENING.
I SAID ANYTHING, JEN. EVER.
I'M HERE. I'M LISTENING.
OKAY, SO...
HERE'S THE DEAL.

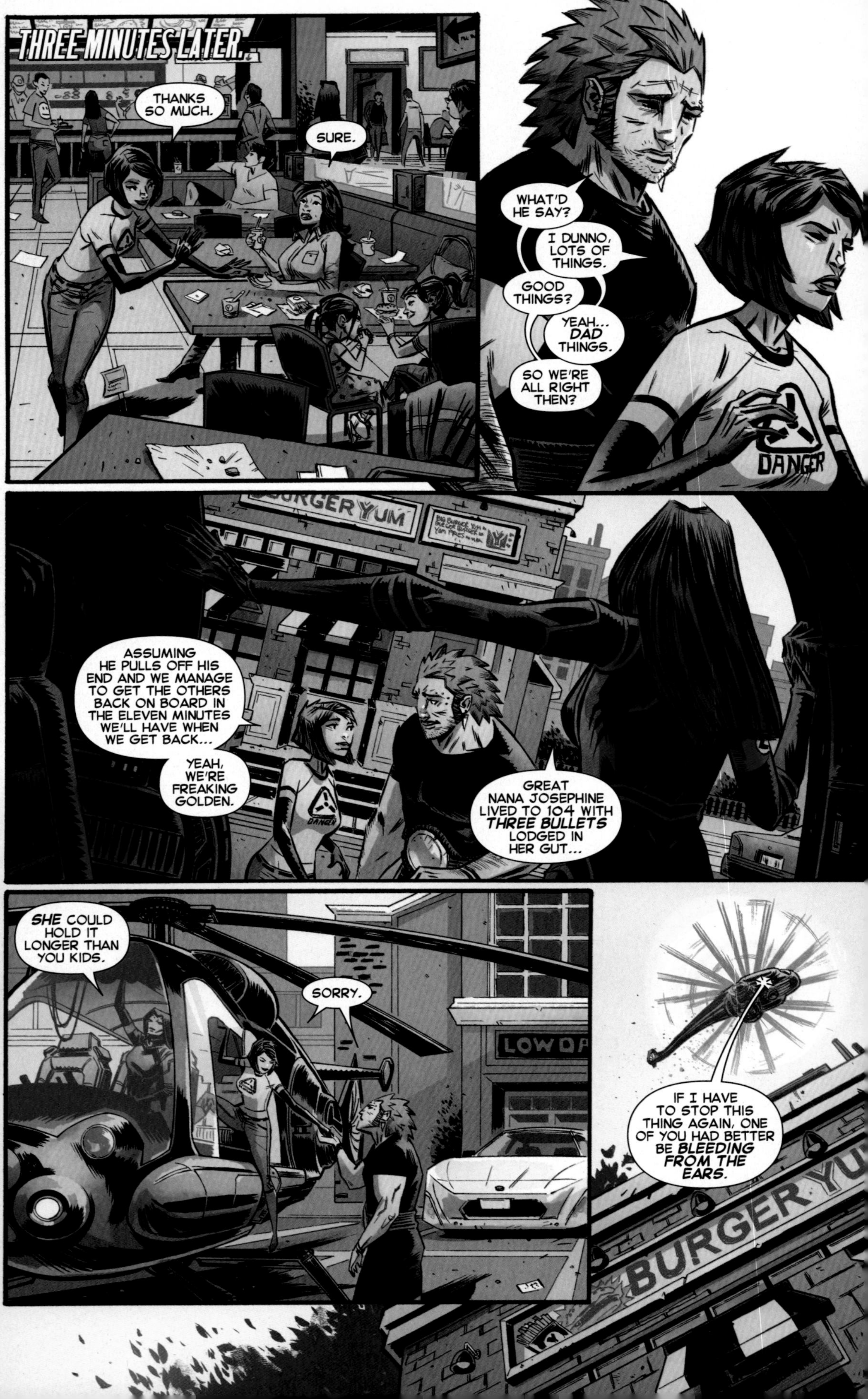
THREE MINUTES LATER.
THANKS SO MUCH.
SURE.
WHAT'D HE SAY?
I DUNNO, LOTS OF THINGS.
GOOD THINGS?
YEAH... DAD THINGS.
SO WE'RE ALL RIGHT THEN?
DANGER
BURGER YUM
ASSUMING HE PULLS OFF HIS END AND WE MANAGE TO GET THE OTHERS BACK ON BOARD IN THE ELEVEN MINUTES WE'LL HAVE WHEN WE GET BACK...
YEAH, WE'RE FREAKING GOLDEN.
DANGER
GREAT NANA JOSEPHINE LIVED TO 104 WITH THREE BULLETS LODGED IN HER GUT...
SHE COULD HOLD IT LONGER THAN YOU KIDS.
SORRY.
IF I HAVE TO STOP THIS THING AGAIN, ONE OF YOU HAD BETTER BE BLEEDING FROM THE EARS.
BURGER YU

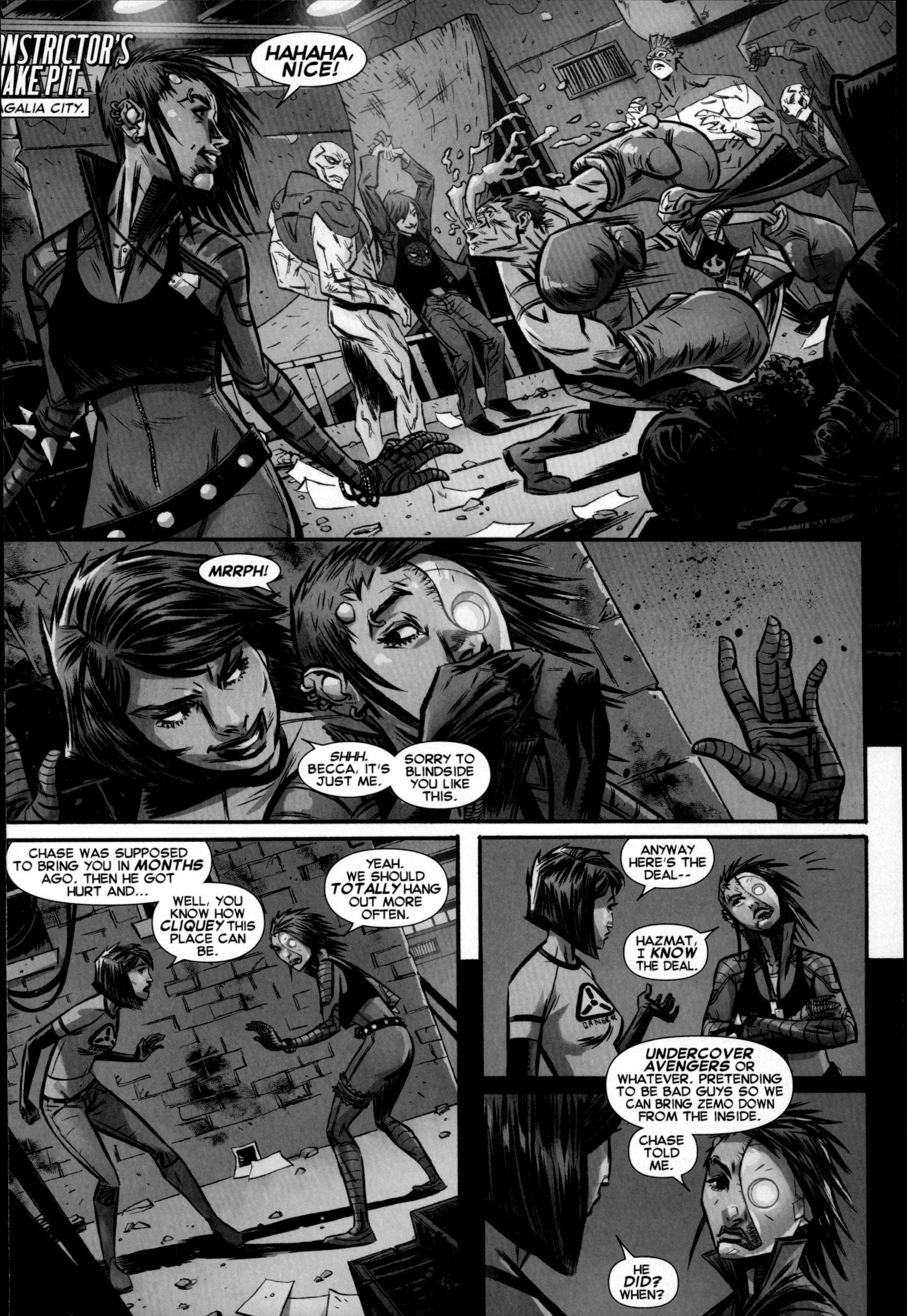

ONSTRICTOR'S
AKE PIT.
AGALIA CITY.
HAHAHA, NICE!
MRRPH!
SHHH. BECCA, IT'S JUST ME.
SORRY TO BLINDSIDE YOU LIKE THIS.
CHASE WAS SUPPOSED TO BRING YOU IN MONTHS AGO. THEN HE GOT HURT AND...
WELL, YOU KNOW HOW CLIQUEY THIS PLACE CAN BE.
YEAH. WE SHOULD TOTALLY HANG OUT MORE OFTEN.
ANYWAY HERE'S THE DEAL--
HAZMAT, I KNOW THE DEAL.
UNDERCOVER AVENGERS OR WHATEVER. PRETENDING TO BE BAD GUYS SO WE CAN BRING ZEMO DOWN FROM THE INSIDE.
CHASE TOLD ME.
HE DID? WHEN?

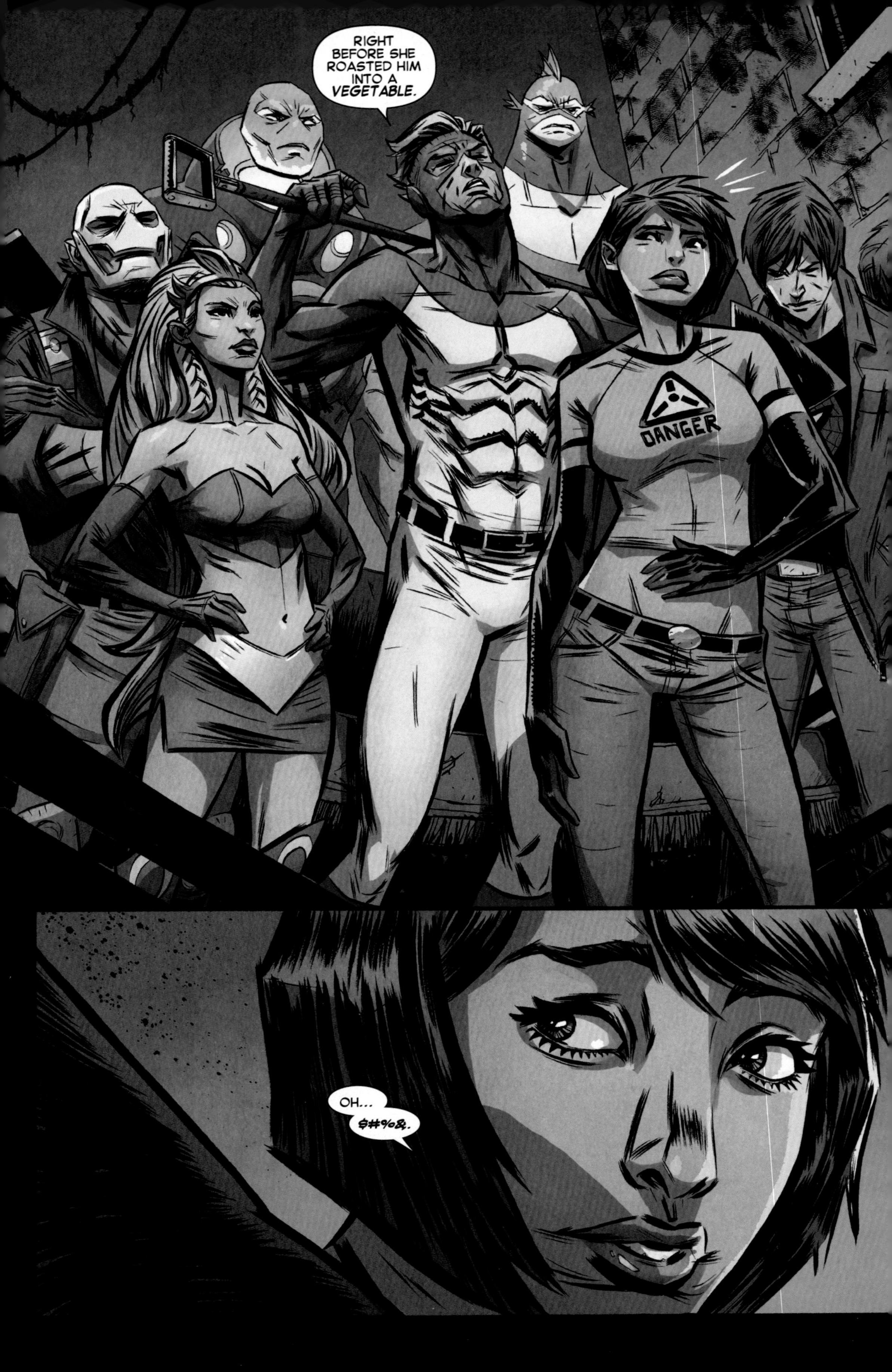
RIGHT BEFORE SHE ROASTED HIM INTO A VEGETABLE.
DANGER
OH... $#%&.

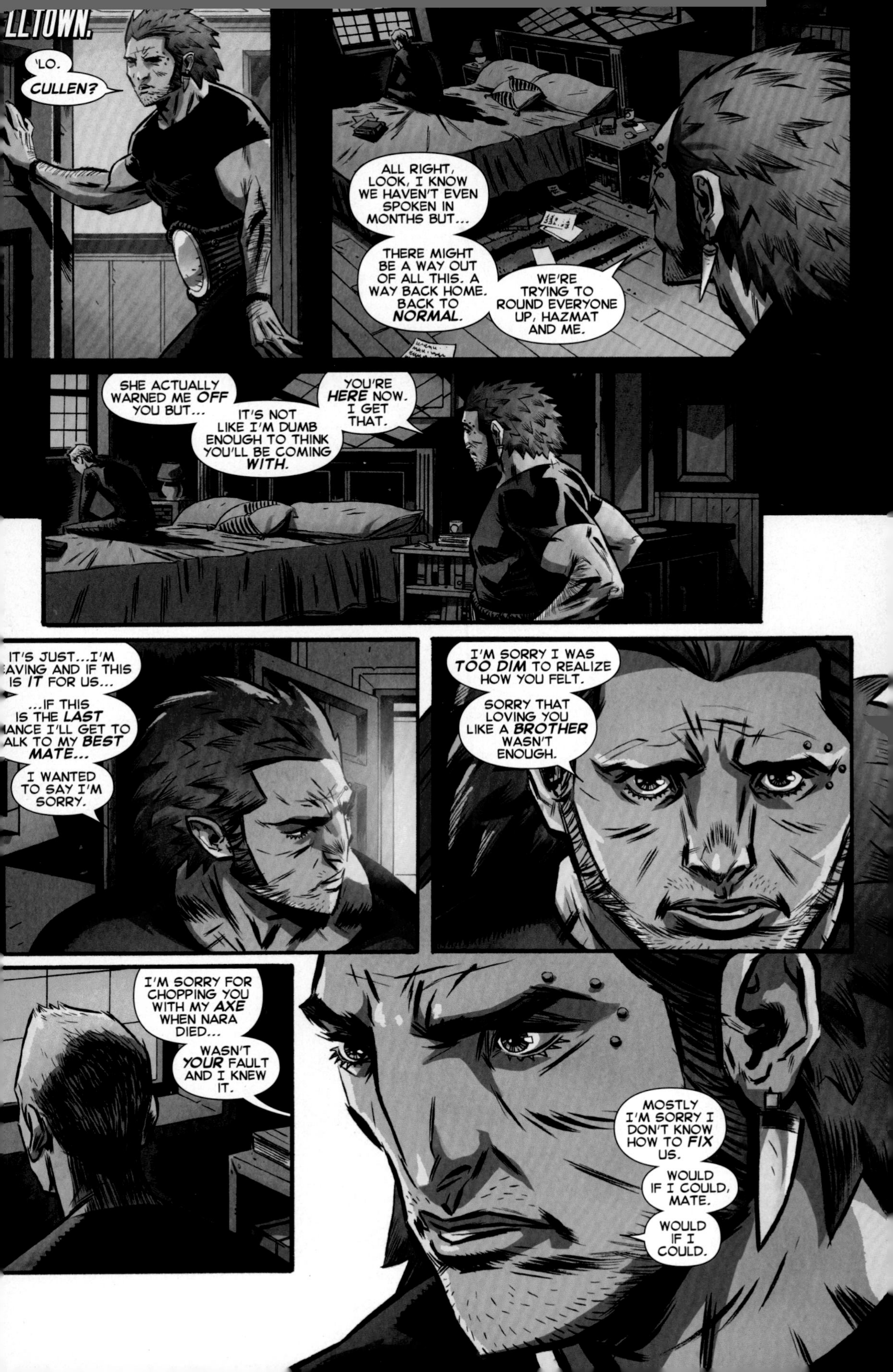

LLTOWN.
'LO.
CULLEN?
ALL RIGHT, LOOK, I KNOW WE HAVEN'T EVEN SPOKEN IN MONTHS BUT...
THERE MIGHT BE A WAY OUT OF ALL THIS. A WAY BACK HOME. BACK TO NORMAL.
WE'RE TRYING TO ROUND EVERYONE UP, HAZMAT AND ME.
SHE ACTUALLY WARNED ME OFF YOU BUT...
IT'S NOT LIKE I'M DUMB ENOUGH TO THINK YOU'LL BE COMING WITH.
YOU'RE HERE NOW. I GET THAT.
IT'S JUST...I'M EAVING AND IF THIS IS IT FOR US...
...IF THIS IS THE LAST HANCE I'LL GET TO ALK TO MY BEST MATE...
I WANTED TO SAY I'M SORRY.
I'M SORRY I WAS TOO DIM TO REALIZE HOW YOU FELT.
SORRY THAT LOVING YOU LIKE A BROTHER WASN'T ENOUGH.
I'M SORRY FOR CHOPPING YOU WITH MY AXE WHEN NARA DIED...
WASN'T YOUR FAULT AND I KNEW IT.
MOSTLY I'M SORRY I DON'T KNOW HOW TO FIX US.
WOULD IF I COULD, MATE.
WOULD IF I COULD.

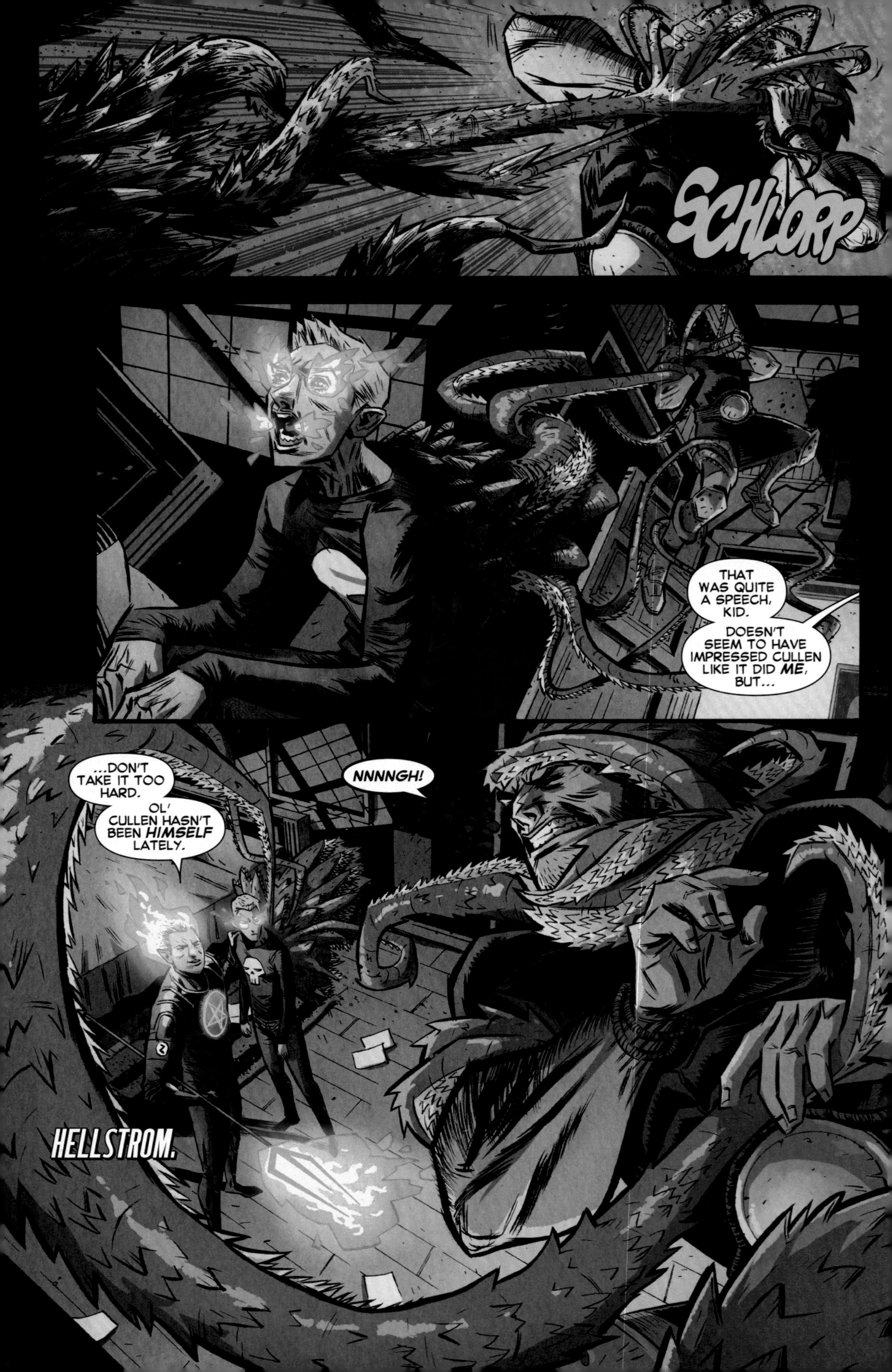
SCHLORP
THAT WAS QUITE A SPEECH, KID.
DOESN'T SEEM TO HAVE IMPRESSED CULLEN LIKE IT DID *ME*, BUT...
...DON'T TAKE IT TOO HARD.
OL' CULLEN HASN'T BEEN *HIMSELF* LATELY.
NNNNGH!
HELLSTROM.

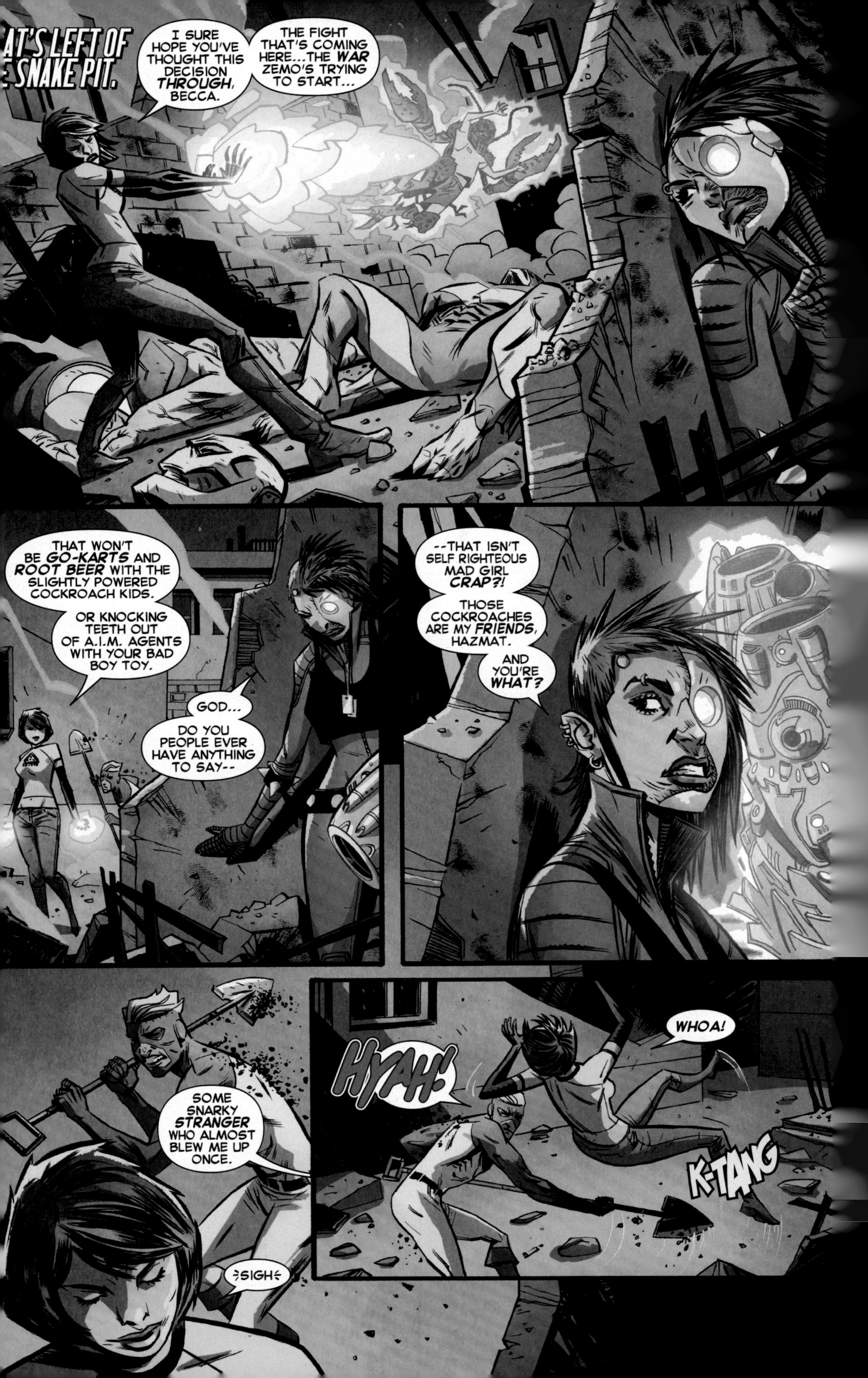

AT'S LEFT OF
E SNAKE PIT.
I SURE HOPE YOU'VE THOUGHT THIS DECISION THROUGH, BECCA.
THE FIGHT THAT'S COMING HERE...THE WAR ZEMO'S TRYING TO START...
THAT WON'T BE GO-KARTS AND ROOT BEER WITH THE SLIGHTLY POWERED COCKROACH KIDS.
OR KNOCKING TEETH OUT OF A.I.M. AGENTS WITH YOUR BAD BOY TOY.
GOD...
DO YOU PEOPLE EVER HAVE ANYTHING TO SAY--
--THAT ISN'T SELF RIGHTEOUS MAD GIRL CRAP?!
THOSE COCKROACHES ARE MY FRIENDS, HAZMAT.
AND YOU'RE WHAT?
SOME SNARKY STRANGER WHO ALMOST BLEW ME UP ONCE.
SIGH
HYAH!
WHOA!
K-TANG

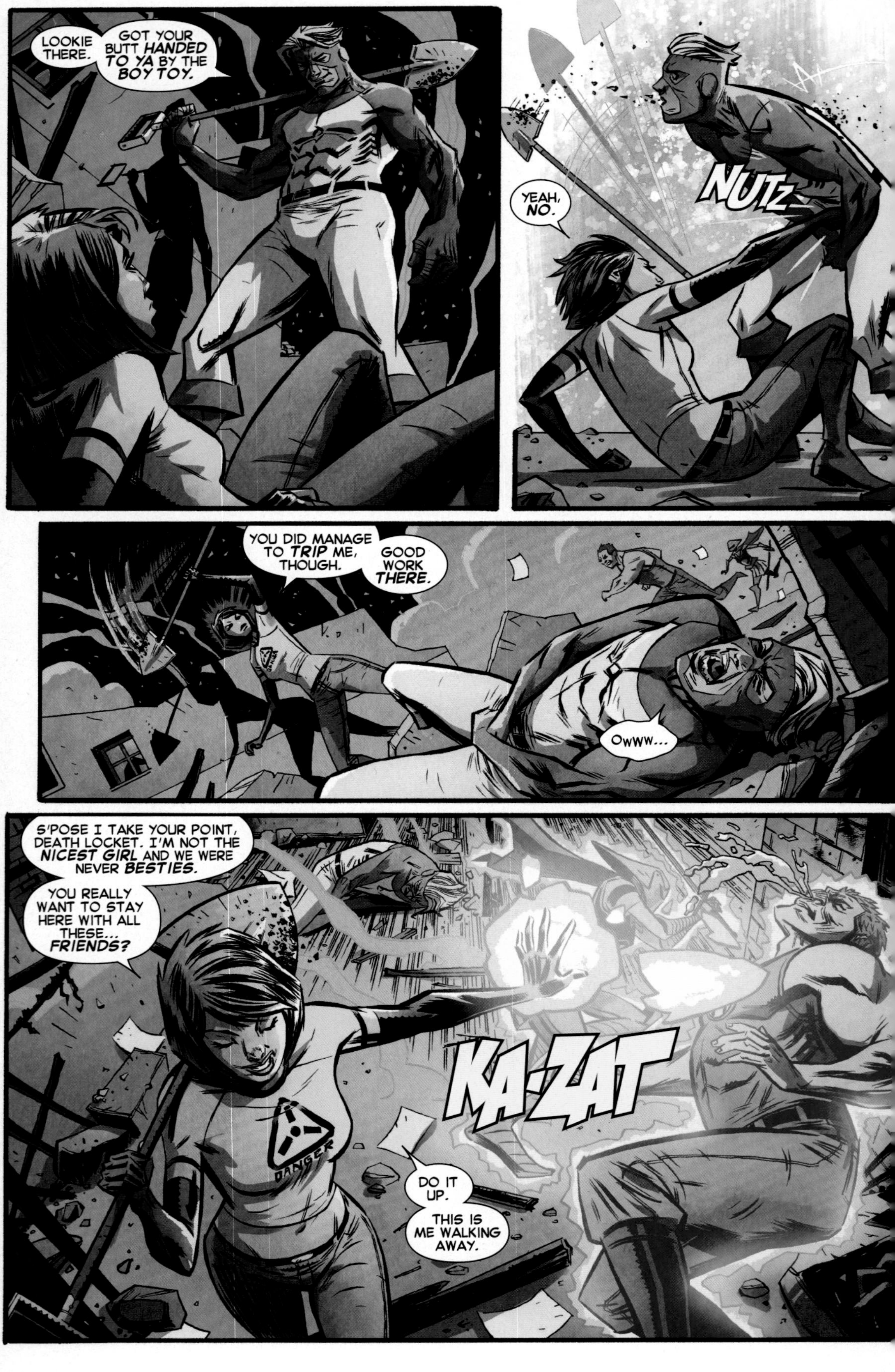
LOOKIE THERE.
GOT YOUR BUTT HANDED TO YA BY THE BOY TOY.
YEAH, NO.
NUTZ
YOU DID MANAGE TO TRIP ME, THOUGH.
GOOD WORK THERE.
OWWW...
S'POSE I TAKE YOUR POINT, DEATH LOCKET. I'M NOT THE NICEST GIRL AND WE WERE NEVER BESTIES.
YOU REALLY WANT TO STAY HERE WITH ALL THESE... FRIENDS?
KA-ZAT
DO IT UP.
THIS IS ME WALKING AWAY.
DANGER

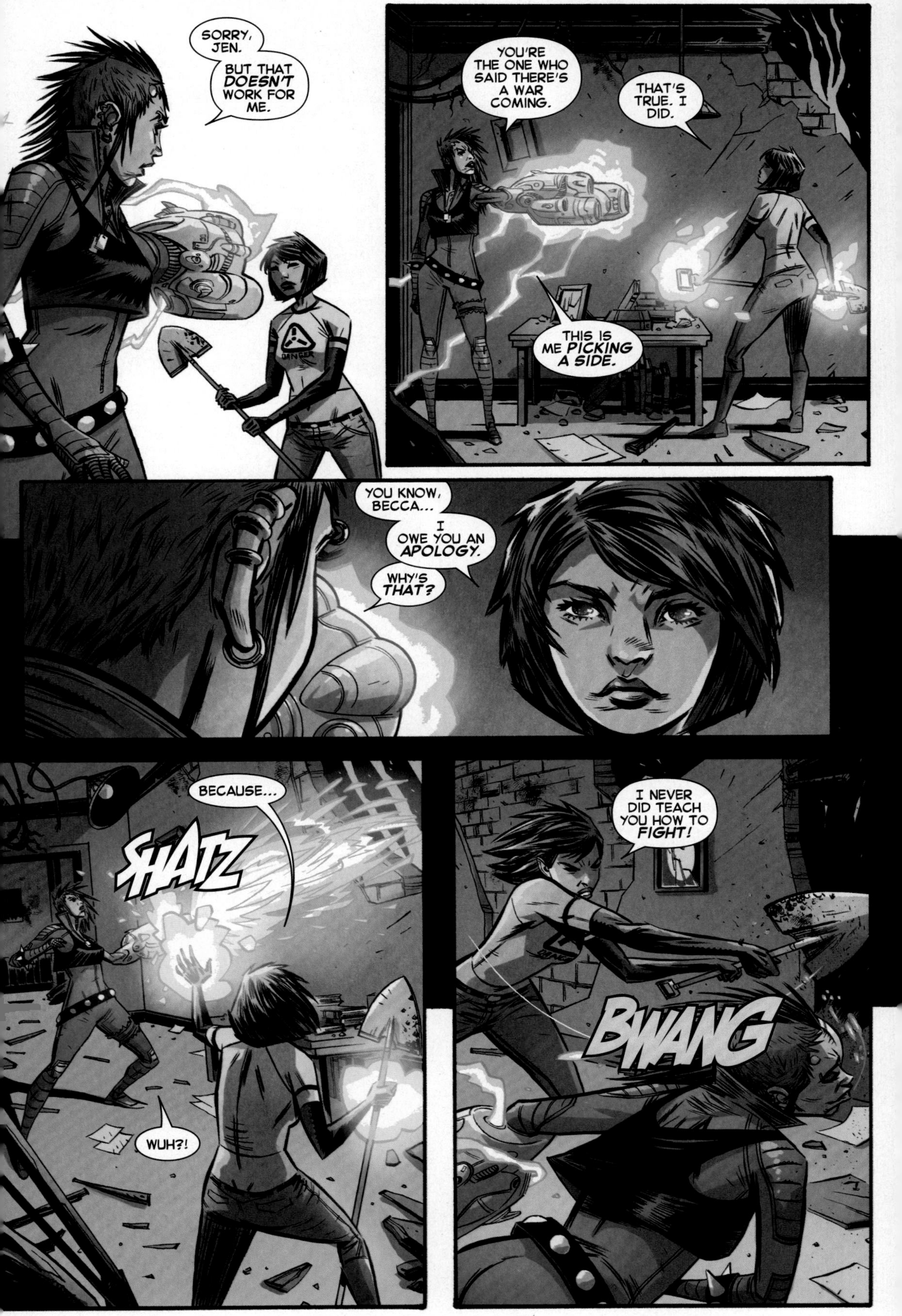
SORRY, JEN.
BUT THAT DOESN'T WORK FOR ME.
YOU'RE THE ONE WHO SAID THERE'S A WAR COMING.
THAT'S TRUE. I DID.
THIS IS ME PICKING A SIDE.
YOU KNOW, BECCA...
I OWE YOU AN APOLOGY.
WHY'S THAT?
BECAUSE...
SHATZ
WUH?!
I NEVER DID TEACH YOU HOW TO FIGHT!
BWANG

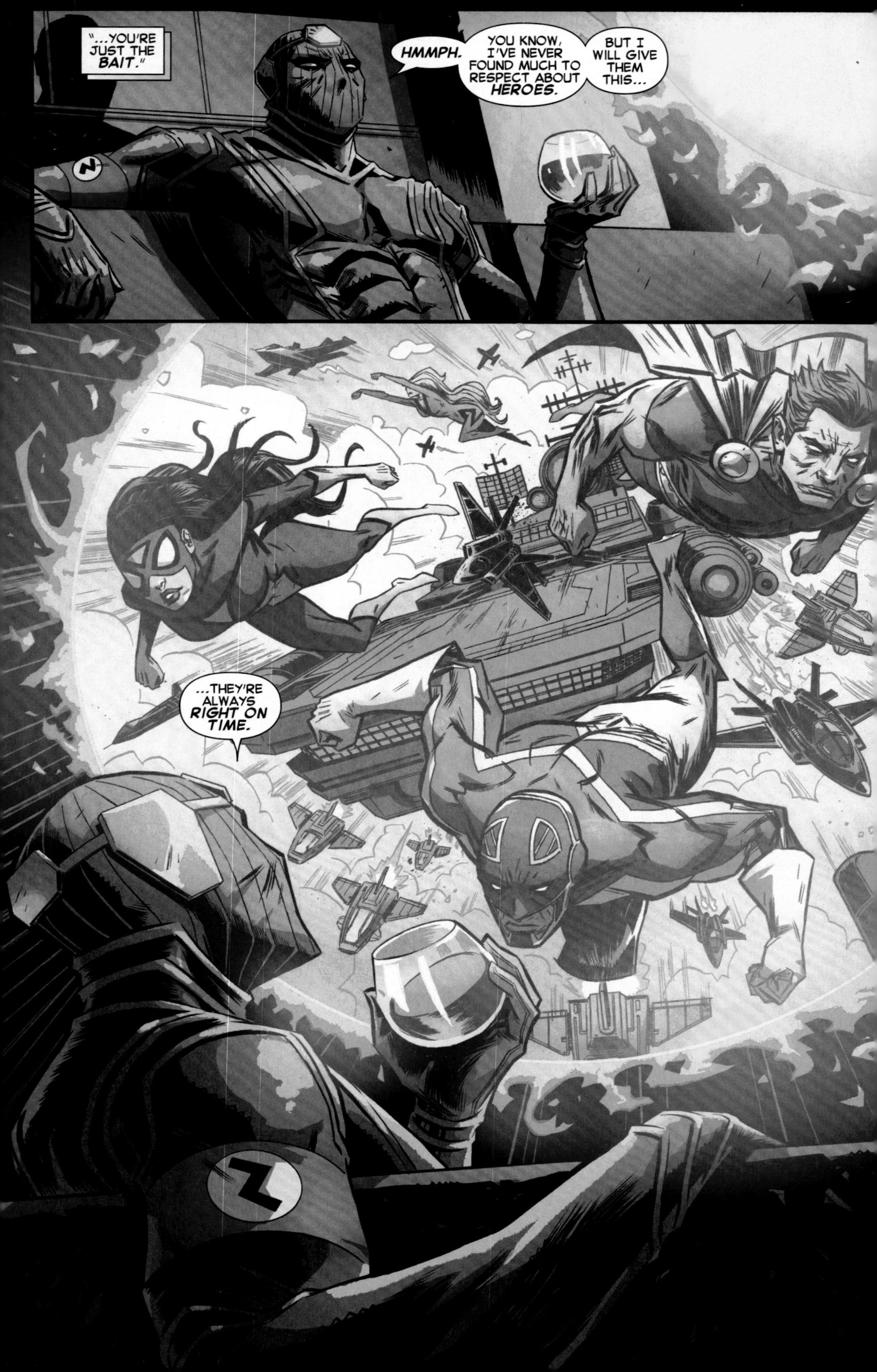
"...YOU'RE JUST THE BAIT."
HMMPH.
YOU KNOW, I'VE NEVER FOUND MUCH TO RESPECT ABOUT HEROES.
BUT I WILL GIVE THEM THIS...
...THEY'RE ALWAYS RIGHT ON TIME.

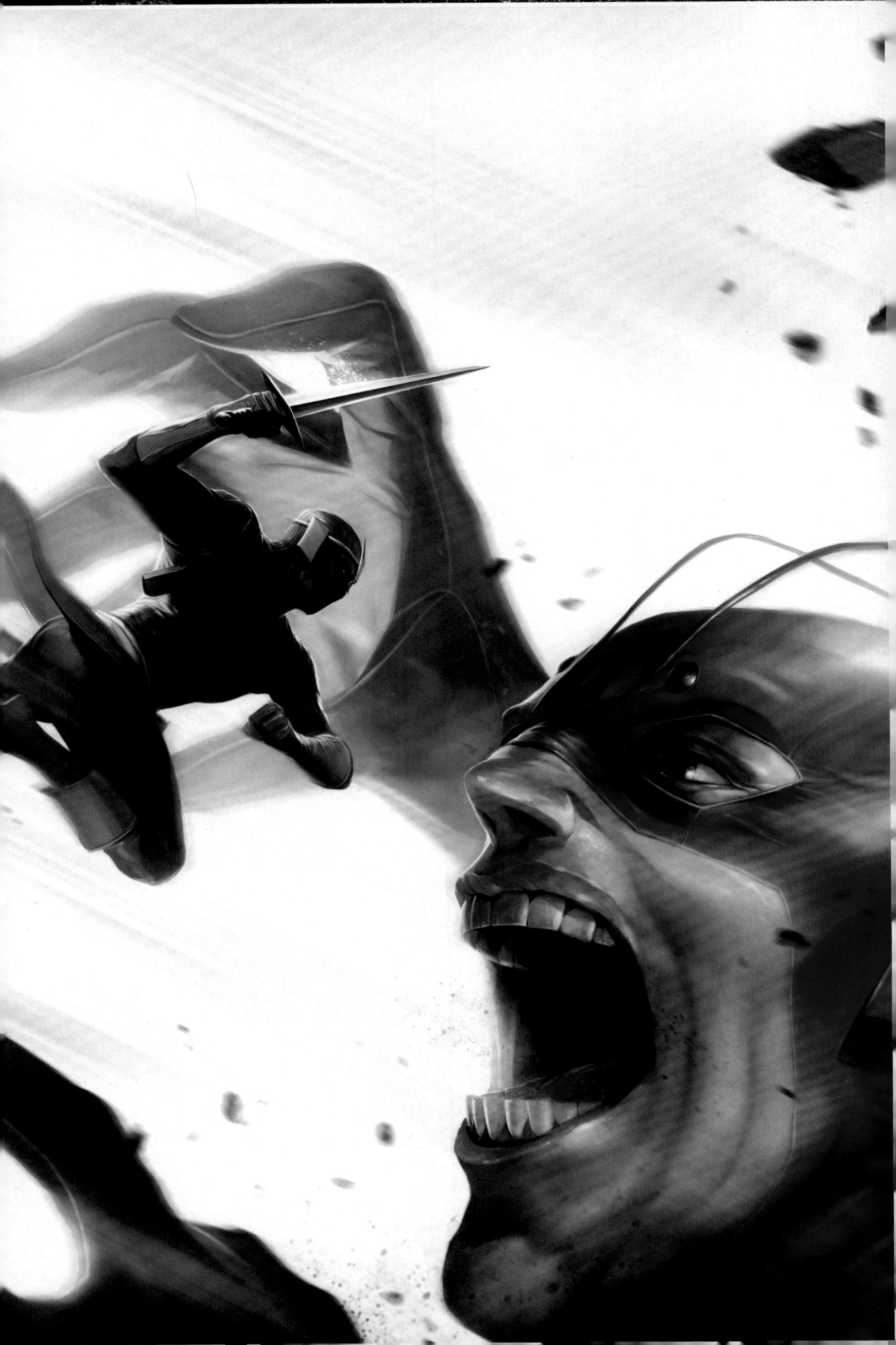

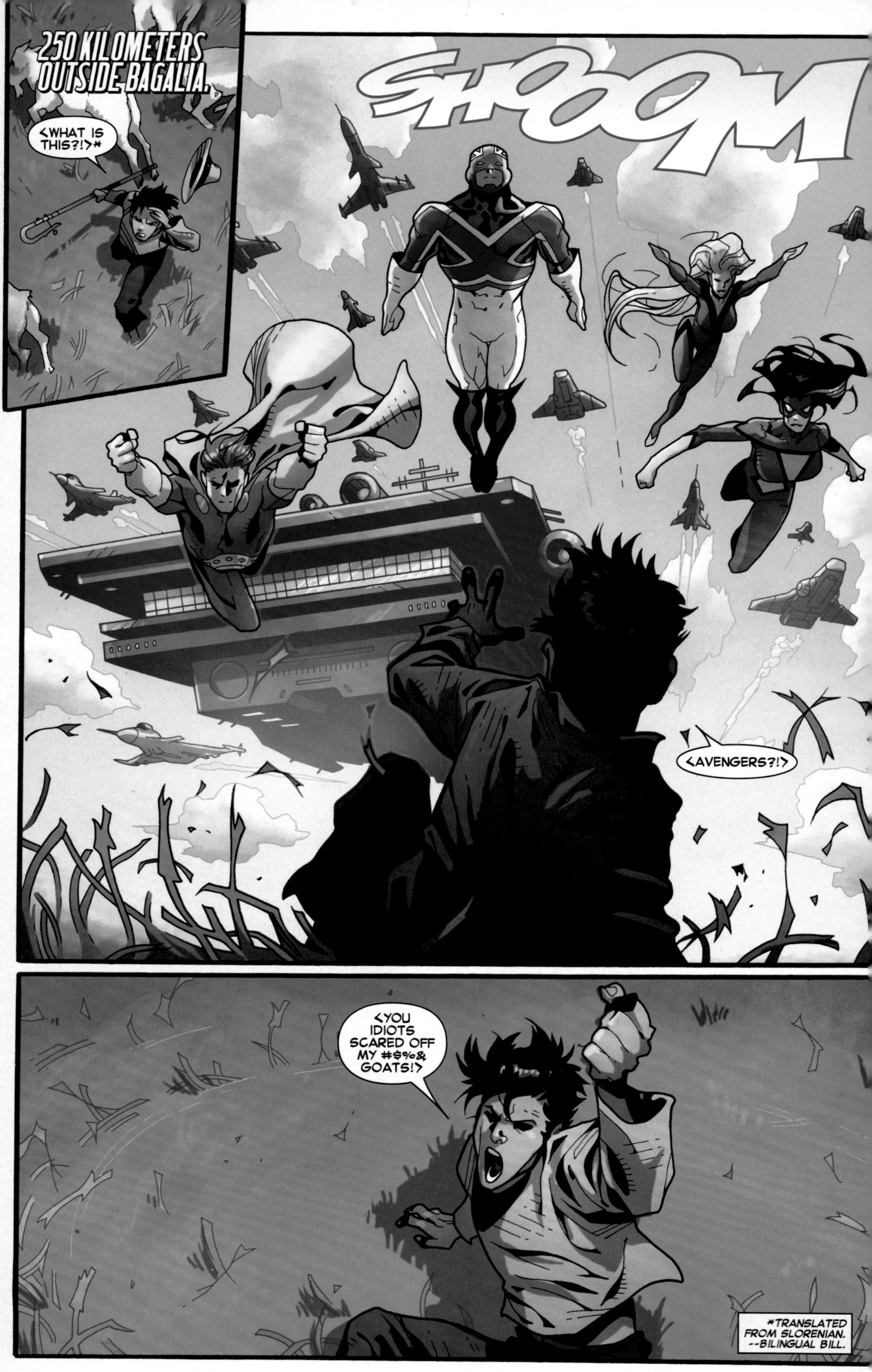
250 KILOMETERS OUTSIDE BAGALIA.
<WHAT IS THIS?!>*
SHOOOM
<AVENGERS?!>
<YOU IDIOTS SCARED OFF MY #$%& GOATS!>
*TRANSLATED FROM SLORENIAN. --BILINGUAL BILL.

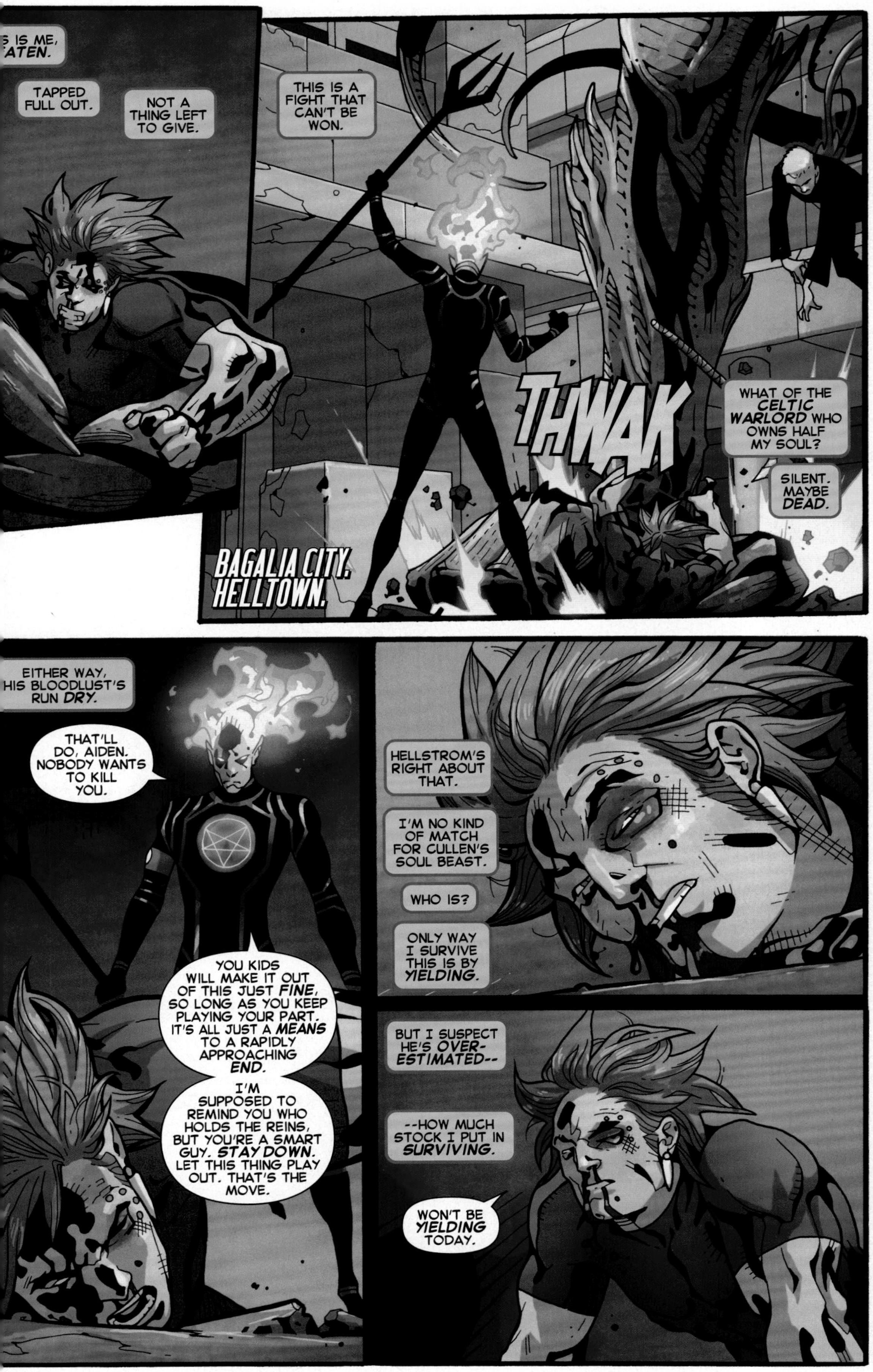
S IS ME, EATEN.
TAPPED FULL OUT.
NOT A THING LEFT TO GIVE.
THIS IS A FIGHT THAT CAN'T BE WON.
THWAK
WHAT OF THE CELTIC WARLORD WHO OWNS HALF MY SOUL?
SILENT. MAYBE DEAD.
BAGALIA CITY. HELLTOWN.
EITHER WAY, HIS BLOODLUST'S RUN DRY.
THAT'LL DO, AIDEN. NOBODY WANTS TO KILL YOU.
YOU KIDS WILL MAKE IT OUT OF THIS JUST FINE, SO LONG AS YOU KEEP PLAYING YOUR PART. IT'S ALL JUST A MEANS TO A RAPIDLY APPROACHING END.
I'M SUPPOSED TO REMIND YOU WHO HOLDS THE REINS, BUT YOU'RE A SMART GUY. STAY DOWN. LET THIS THING PLAY OUT. THAT'S THE MOVE.
HELLSTROM'S RIGHT ABOUT THAT.
I'M NO KIND OF MATCH FOR CULLEN'S SOUL BEAST.
WHO IS?
ONLY WAY I SURVIVE THIS IS BY YIELDING.
BUT I SUSPECT HE'S OVER-ESTIMATED--
--HOW MUCH STOCK I PUT IN SURVIVING.
WON'T BE YIELDING TODAY.

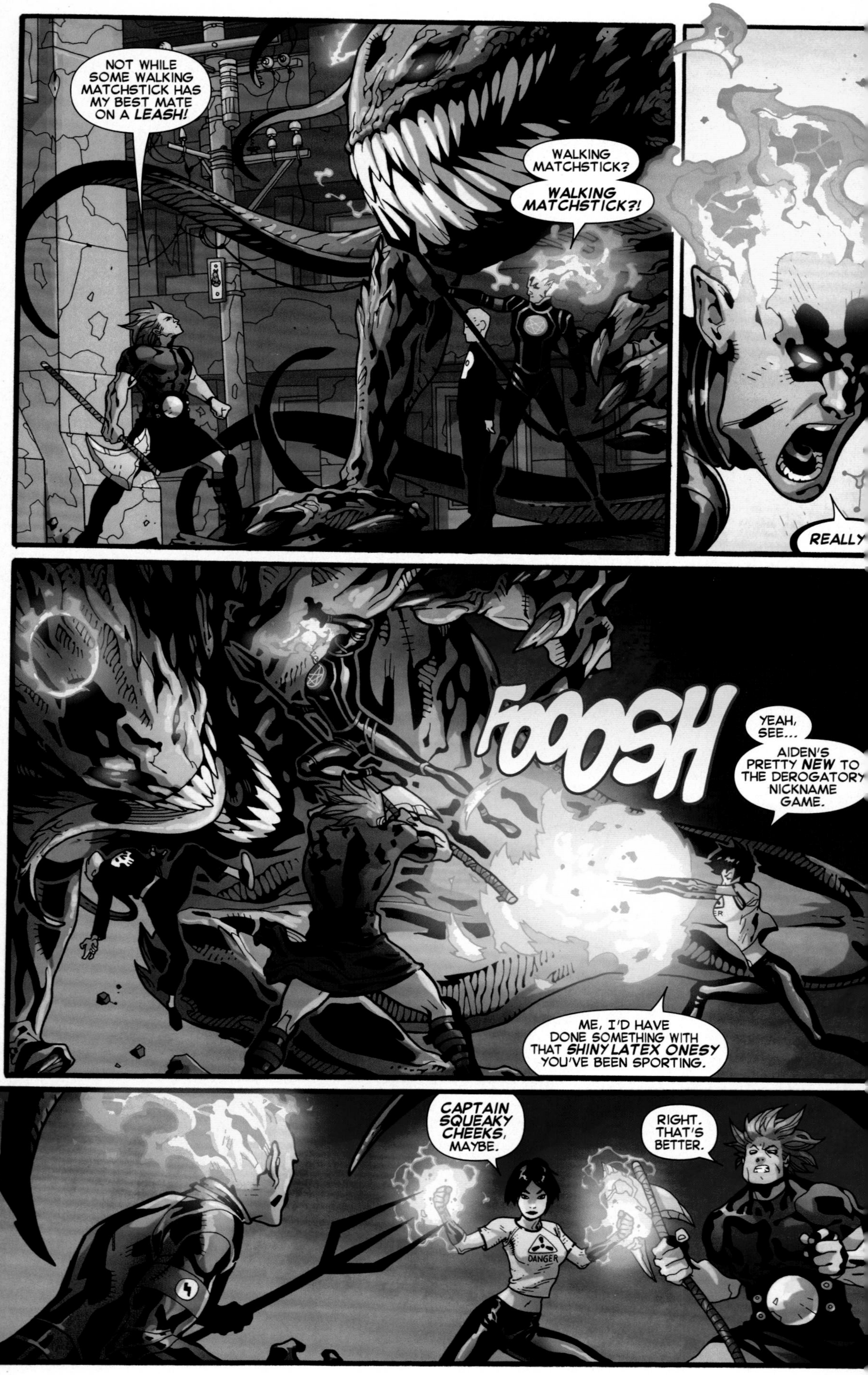

NOT WHILE SOME WALKING MATCHSTICK HAS MY BEST MATE ON A LEASH!
WALKING MATCHSTICK?
WALKING MATCHSTICK?!
REALLY
FOOOSH
YEAH, SEE... AIDEN'S PRETTY NEW TO THE DEROGATORY NICKNAME GAME.
ME, I'D HAVE DONE SOMETHING WITH THAT SHINY LATEX ONESY YOU'VE BEEN SPORTING.
CAPTAIN SQUEAKY CHEEKS, MAYBE.
RIGHT. THAT'S BETTER.
DANGER

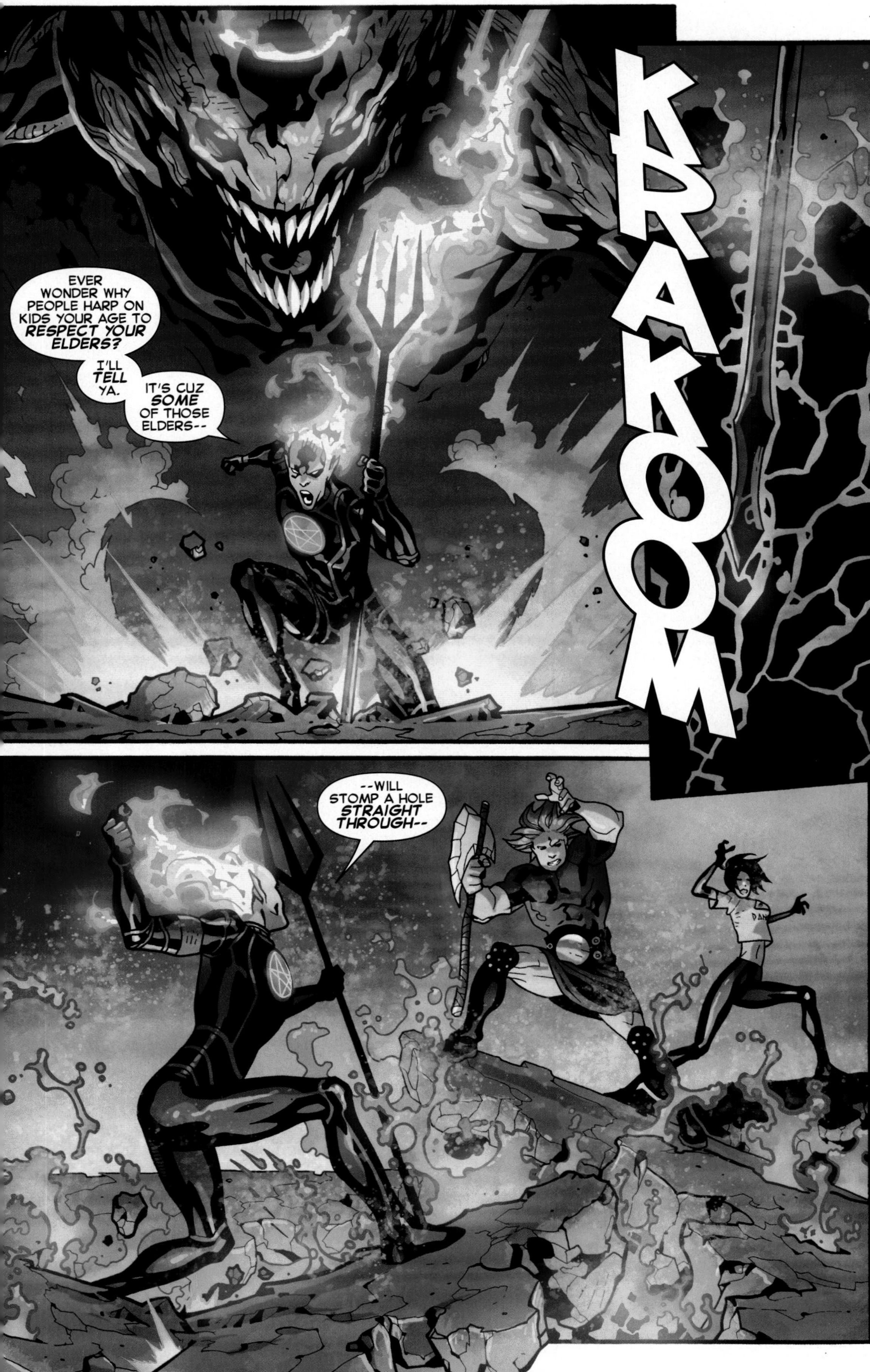
EVER WONDER WHY PEOPLE HARP ON KIDS YOUR AGE TO RESPECT YOUR ELDERS?
I'LL TELL YA.
IT'S CUZ SOME OF THOSE ELDERS--
KRAKOOM
--WILL STOMP A HOLE STRAIGHT THROUGH--

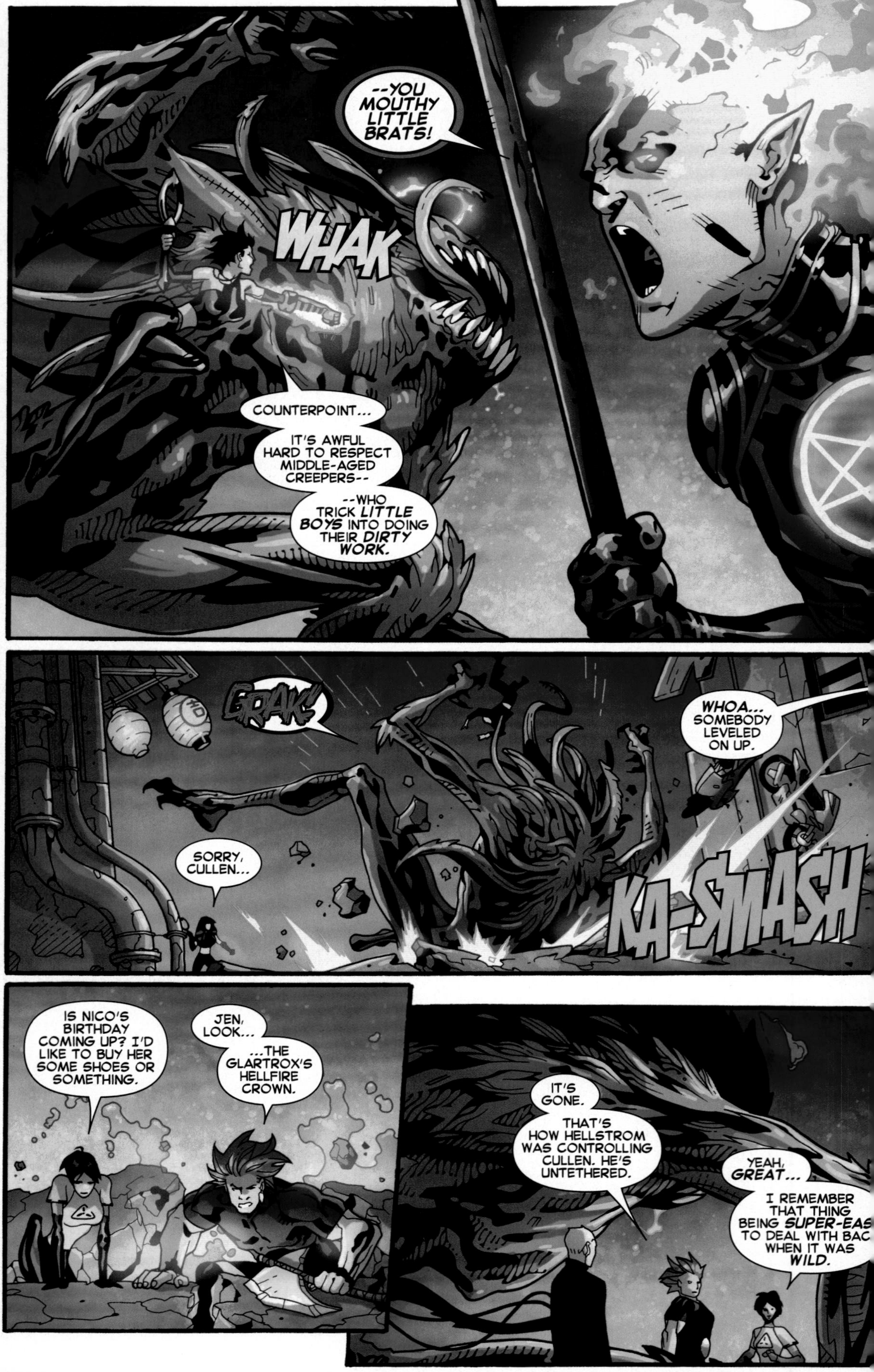
--YOU MOUTHY LITTLE BRATS!
WHAK
COUNTERPOINT...
IT'S AWFUL HARD TO RESPECT MIDDLE-AGED CREEPERS--
--WHO TRICK LITTLE BOYS INTO DOING THEIR DIRTY WORK.
GRAK!
WHOA... SOMEBODY LEVELED ON UP.
SORRY, CULLEN...
KA-SMASH
IS NICO'S BIRTHDAY COMING UP? I'D LIKE TO BUY HER SOME SHOES OR SOMETHING.
JEN, LOOK...
...THE GLARTROX'S HELLFIRE CROWN.
IT'S GONE.
THAT'S HOW HELLSTROM WAS CONTROLLING CULLEN. HE'S UNTETHERED.
YEAH, GREAT...
I REMEMBER THAT THING BEING SUPER-EAS TO DEAL WITH BAC WHEN IT WAS WILD.

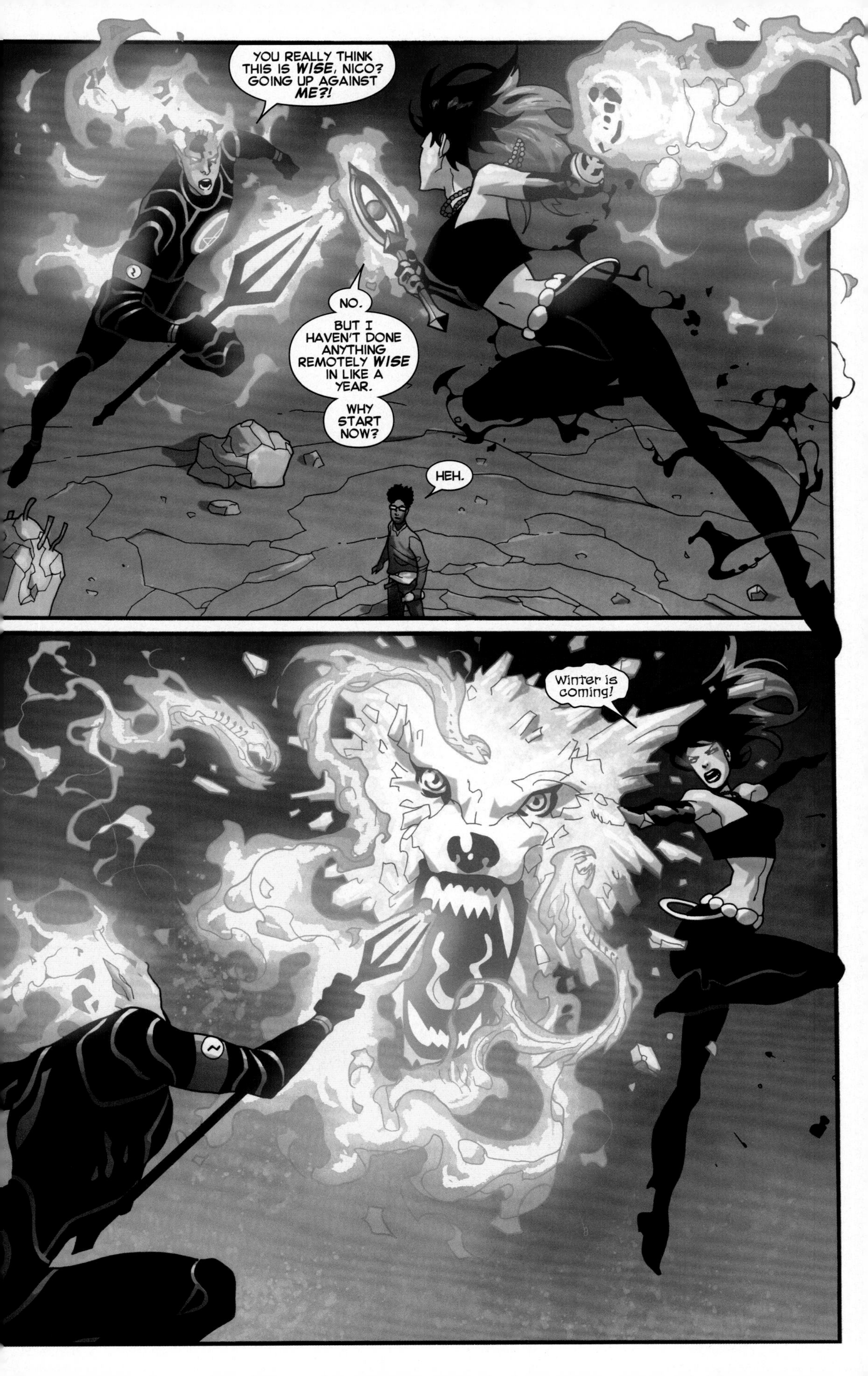
YOU REALLY THINK THIS IS WISE, NICO? GOING UP AGAINST ME?!
NO.
BUT I HAVEN'T DONE ANYTHING REMOTELY WISE IN LIKE A YEAR.
WHY START NOW?
HEH.
Winter is coming!

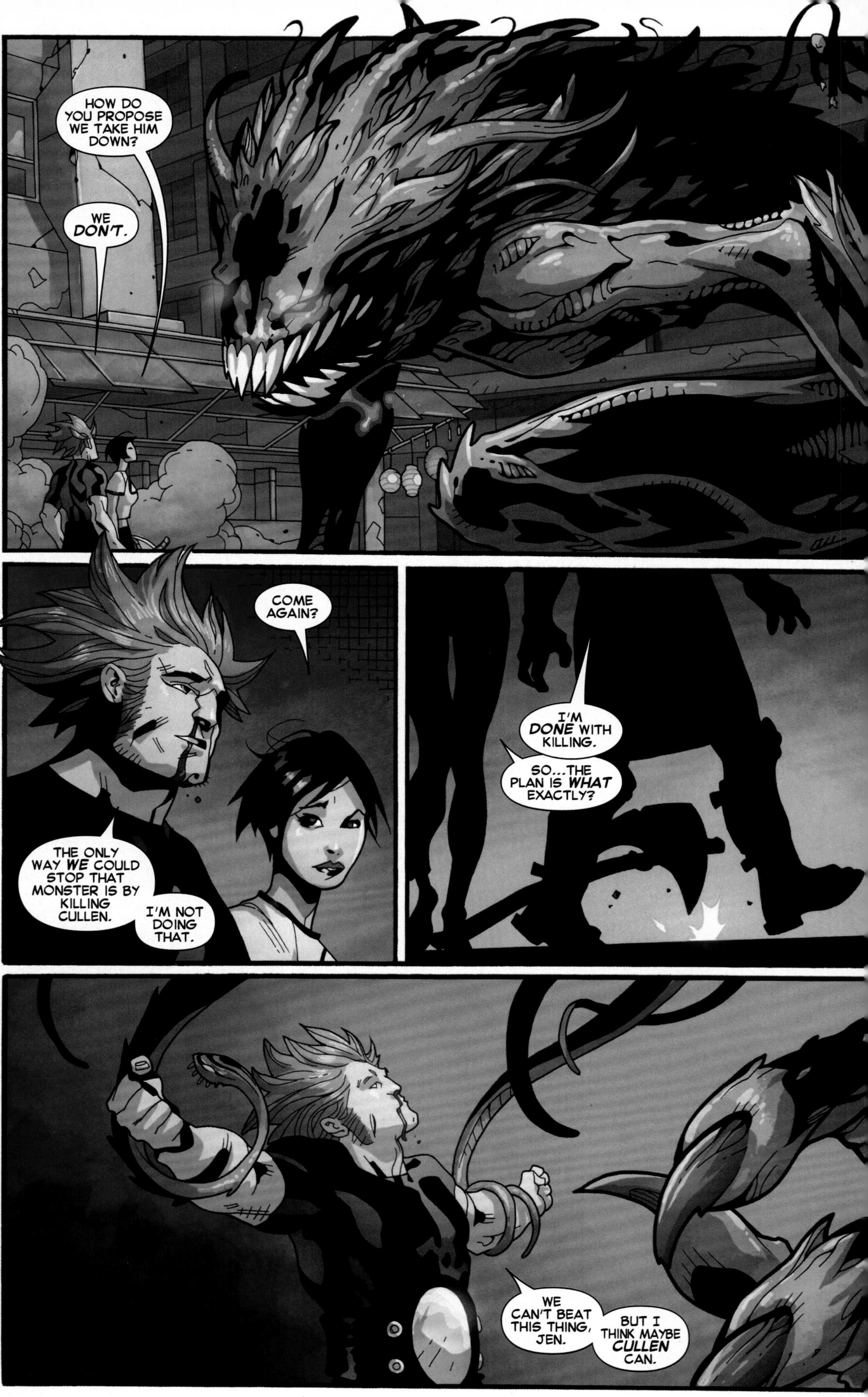
HOW DO YOU PROPOSE WE TAKE HIM DOWN?
WE *DON'T*.
COME AGAIN?
THE ONLY WAY *WE* COULD STOP THAT MONSTER IS BY KILLING CULLEN.
I'M NOT DOING THAT.
I'M *DONE* WITH KILLING.
SO...THE PLAN IS *WHAT* EXACTLY?
WE CAN'T BEAT THIS THING, JEN.
BUT I THINK MAYBE *CULLEN* CAN.

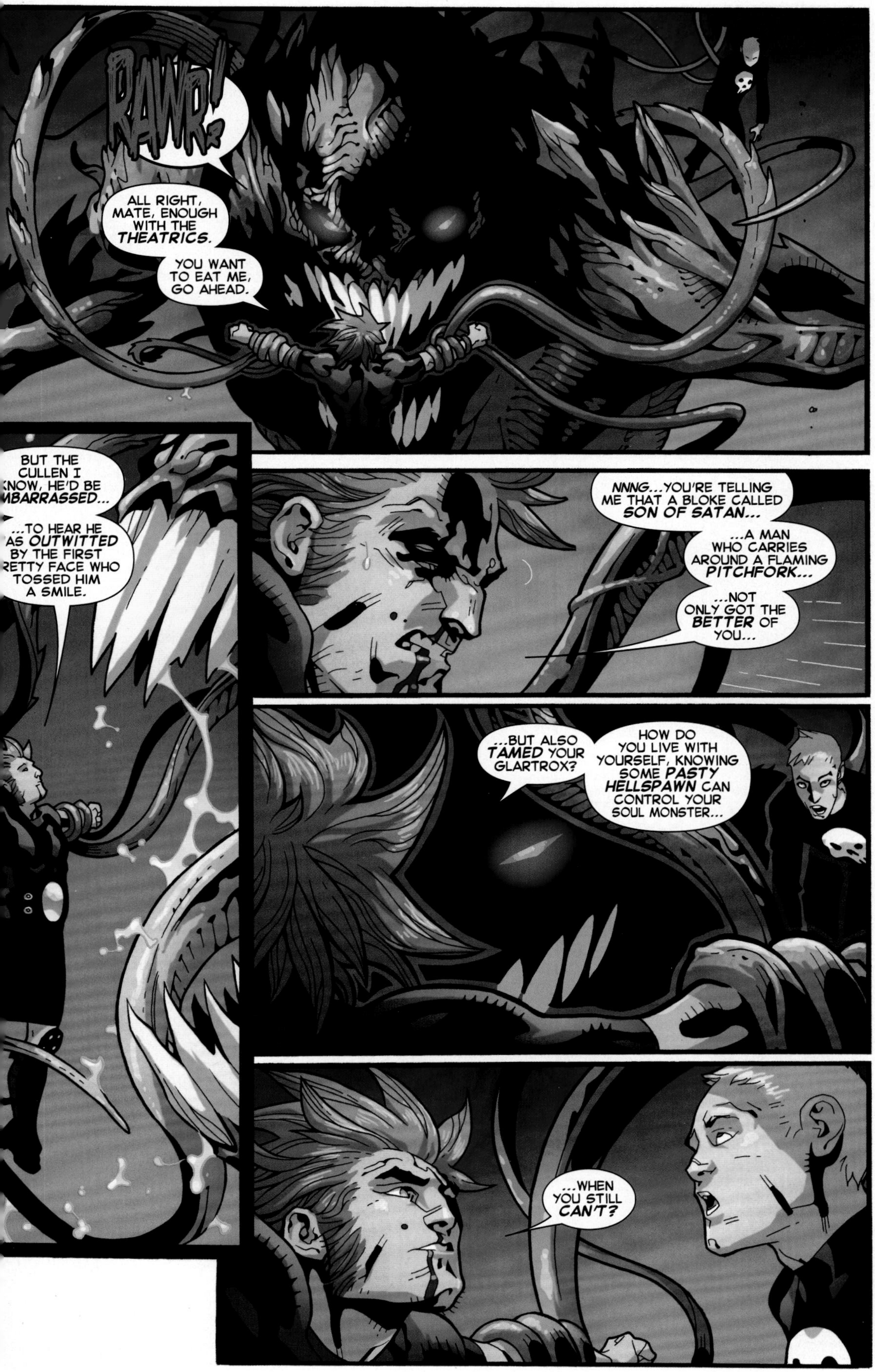

RAWR!!
ALL RIGHT, MATE, ENOUGH WITH THE THEATRICS.
YOU WANT TO EAT ME, GO AHEAD.
BUT THE CULLEN I KNOW, HE'D BE EMBARRASSED...
...TO HEAR HE WAS OUTWITTED BY THE FIRST PRETTY FACE WHO TOSSED HIM A SMILE.
NNNG...YOU'RE TELLING ME THAT A BLOKE CALLED SON OF SATAN...
...A MAN WHO CARRIES AROUND A FLAMING PITCHFORK...
...NOT ONLY GOT THE BETTER OF YOU...
...BUT ALSO TAMED YOUR GLARTROX?
HOW DO YOU LIVE WITH YOURSELF, KNOWING SOME PASTY HELLSPAWN CAN CONTROL YOUR SOUL MONSTER...
...WHEN YOU STILL CAN'T?

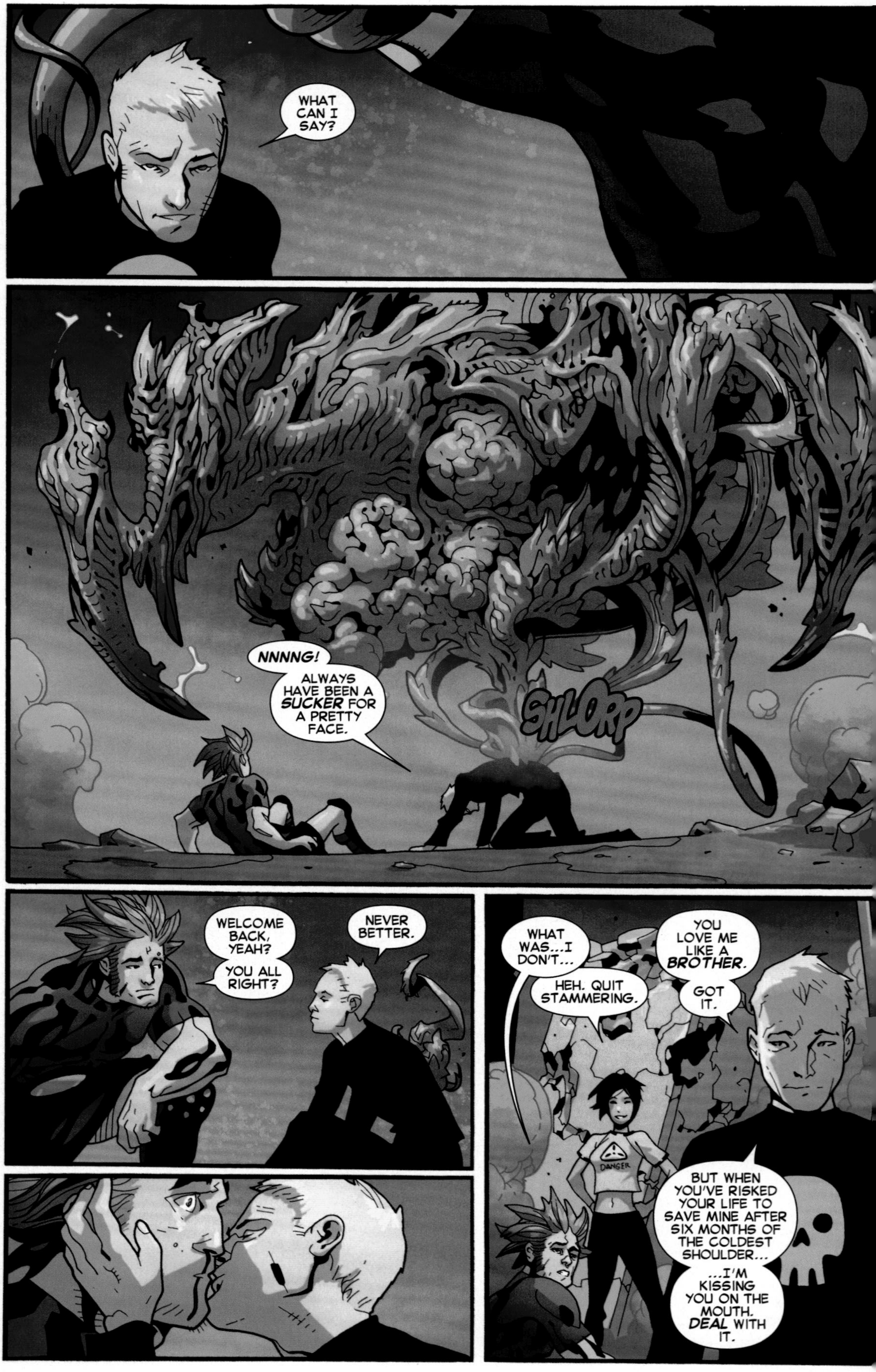

WHAT CAN I SAY?
NNNNG!
ALWAYS HAVE BEEN A SUCKER FOR A PRETTY FACE.
SHLORP
WELCOME BACK, YEAH?
YOU ALL RIGHT?
NEVER BETTER.
WHAT WAS...I DON'T...
HEH. QUIT STAMMERING.
YOU LOVE ME LIKE A BROTHER.
GOT IT.
BUT WHEN YOU'VE RISKED YOUR LIFE TO SAVE MINE AFTER SIX MONTHS OF THE COLDEST SHOULDER...
...I'M KISSING YOU ON THE MOUTH. DEAL WITH IT.
DANGER

DAMN, NICO. THAT WAS... DAMN.

THANKS. IT WON'T BE ENOUGH.

PROBABLY NOT, BUT STILL. SERIOUS PROPS.

THE KID'S RIGHT. YOU'RE THROWING NEXT-LEVEL STUFF OUT HERE. HELL OF A THING TO WATCH.

AS A TEACHER, I'M DAMNED PROUD OF YOU.

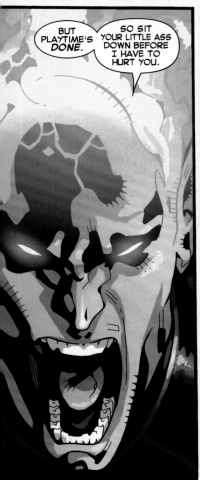

BUT PLAYTIME'S DONE.

SO SIT YOUR LITTLE ASS DOWN BEFORE I HAVE TO HURT YOU.

AWW... COME ON, MR. DAIMON.

JUST FIVE MORE MINUTES OF PLAYTIME?

BOOOM

HA!

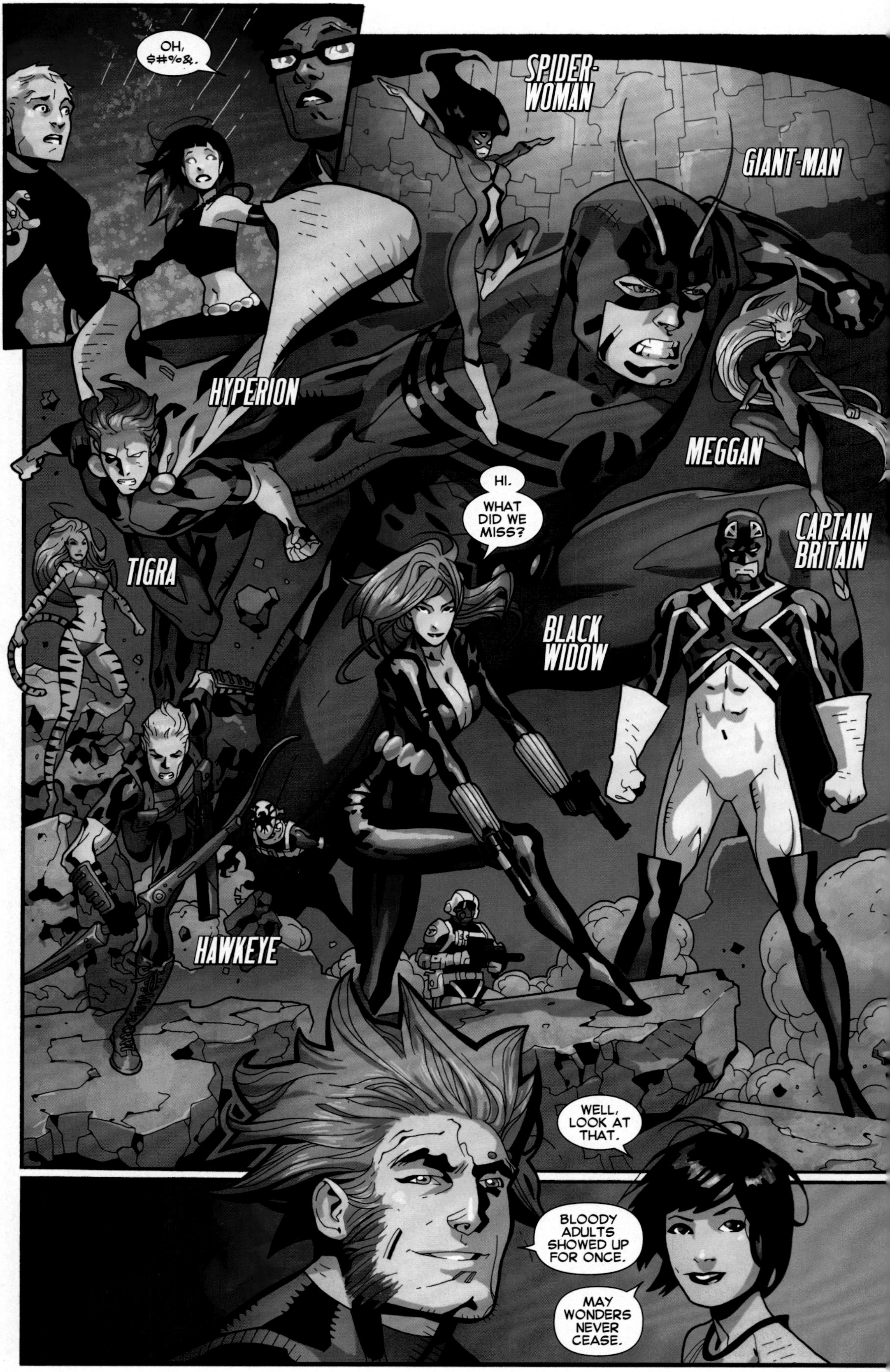
OH, $#%&.
SPIDER-WOMAN
GIANT-MAN
HYPERION
MEGGAN
HI.
WHAT DID WE MISS?
CAPTAIN BRITAIN
TIGRA
BLACK WIDOW
HAWKEYE
WELL, LOOK AT THAT.
BLOODY ADULTS SHOWED UP FOR ONCE.
MAY WONDERS NEVER CEASE.

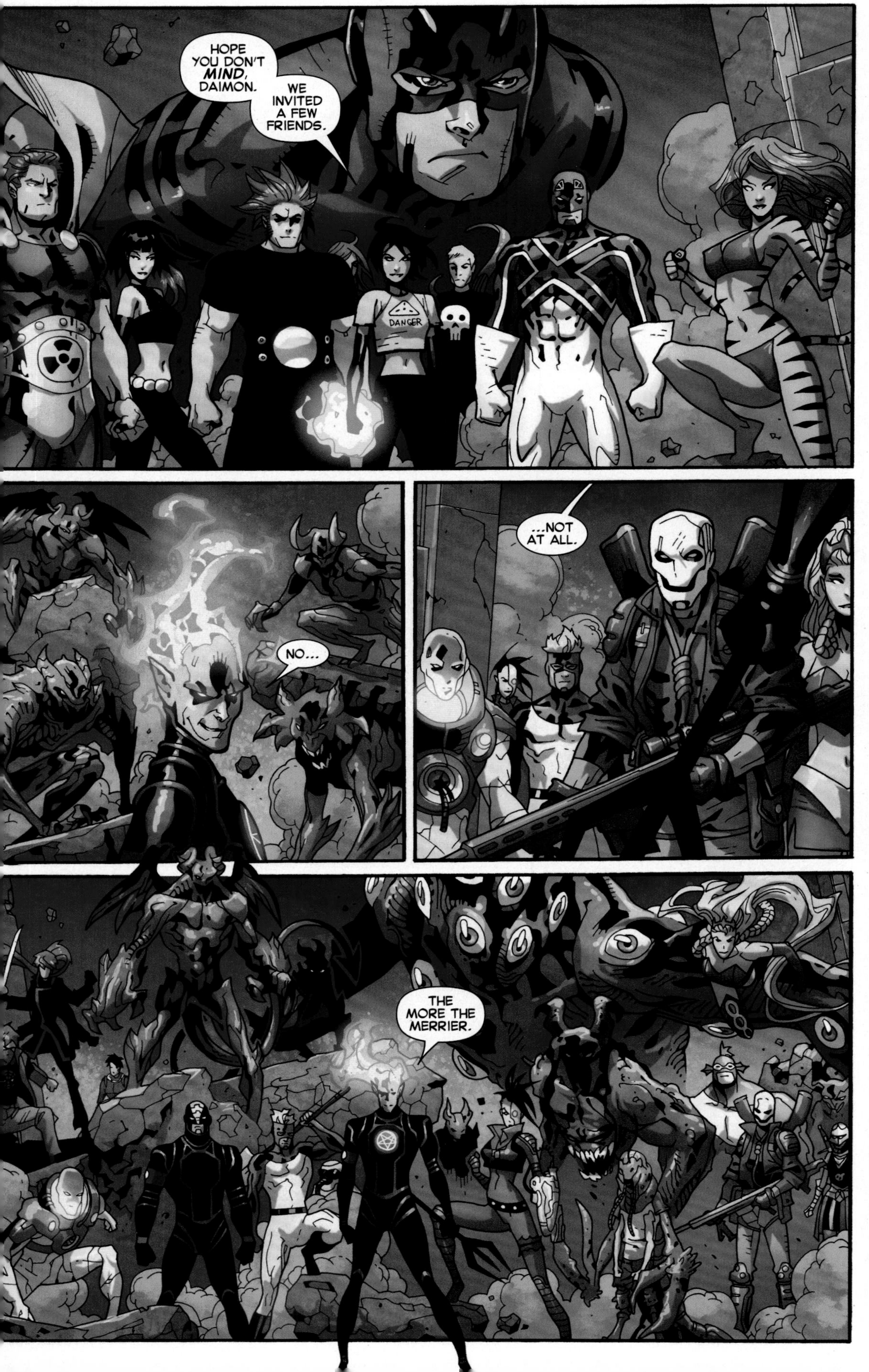
HOPE YOU DON'T *MIND*, DAIMON.
WE INVITED A FEW FRIENDS.
NO...
...NOT AT ALL.
THE MORE THE MERRIER.

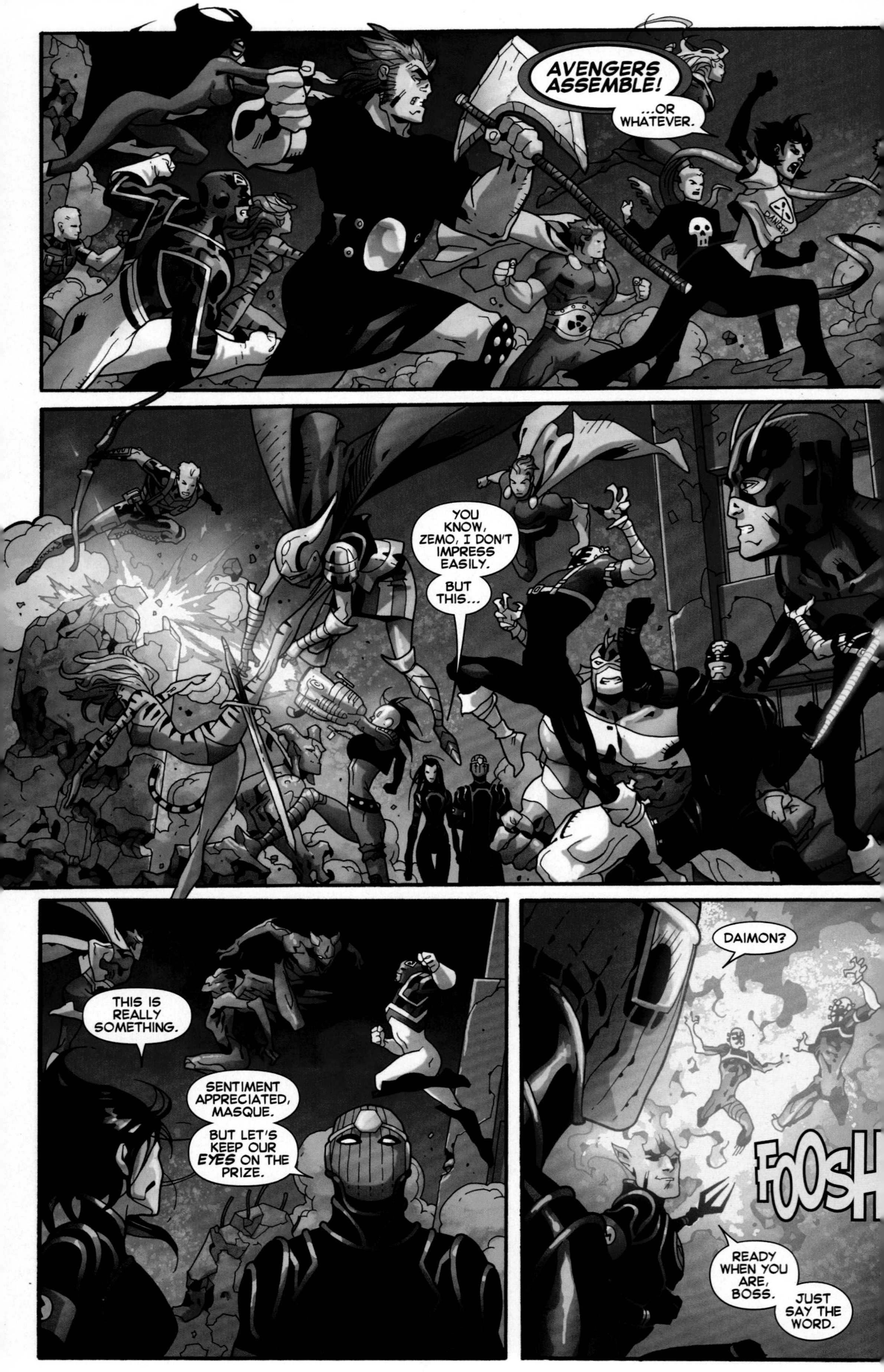
AVENGERS ASSEMBLE!
...OR WHATEVER.
YOU KNOW, ZEMO, I DON'T IMPRESS EASILY.
BUT THIS...
THIS IS REALLY SOMETHING.
SENTIMENT APPRECIATED, MASQUE.
BUT LET'S KEEP OUR *EYES* ON THE PRIZE.
DAIMON?
FOOSH
READY WHEN YOU ARE, BOSS.
JUST SAY THE WORD.

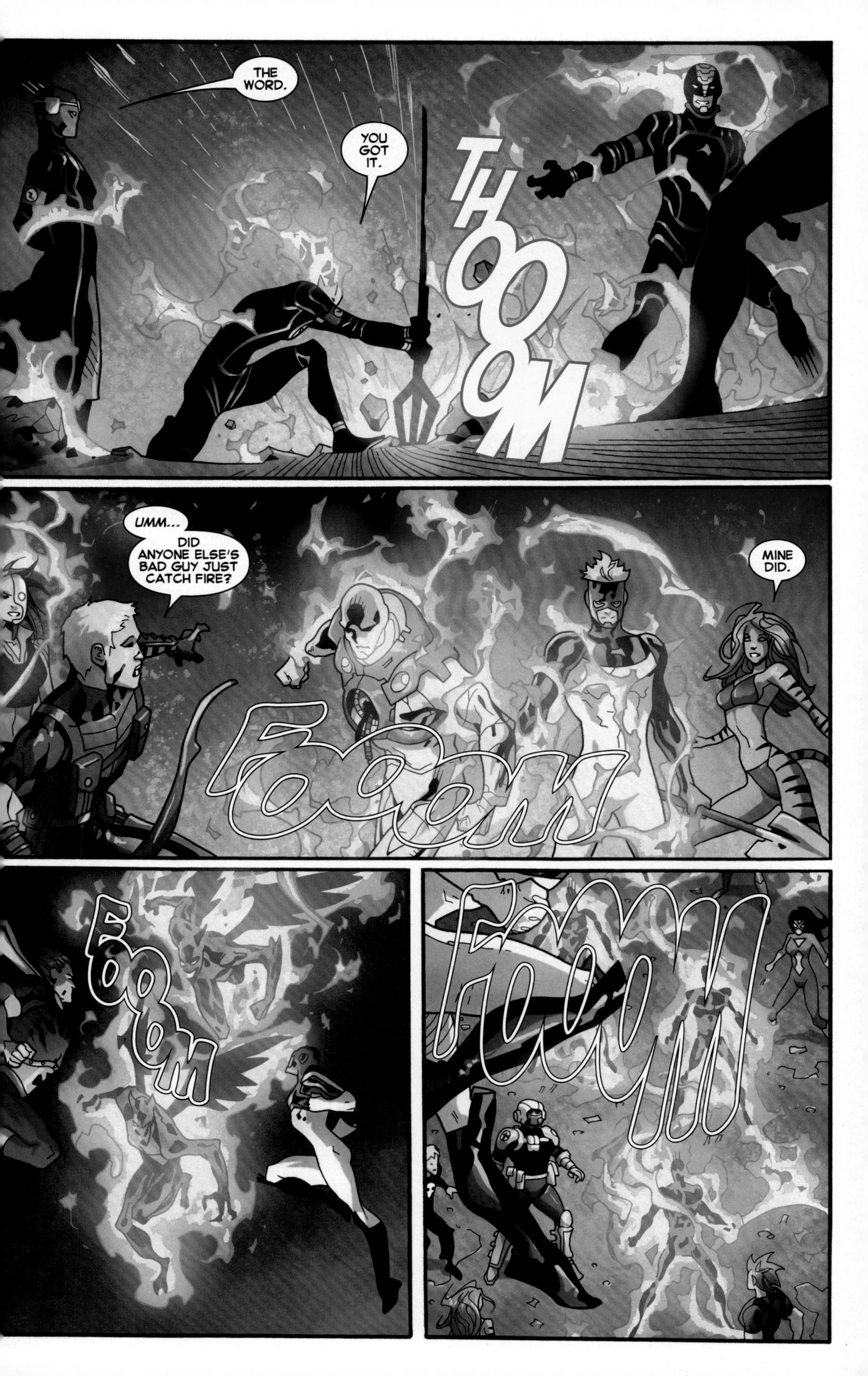
THE WORD.
YOU GOT IT.
THOOOM
UMM... DID ANYONE ELSE'S BAD GUY JUST CATCH FIRE?
MINE DID.
FOOOM
FOOOM
FOOOM

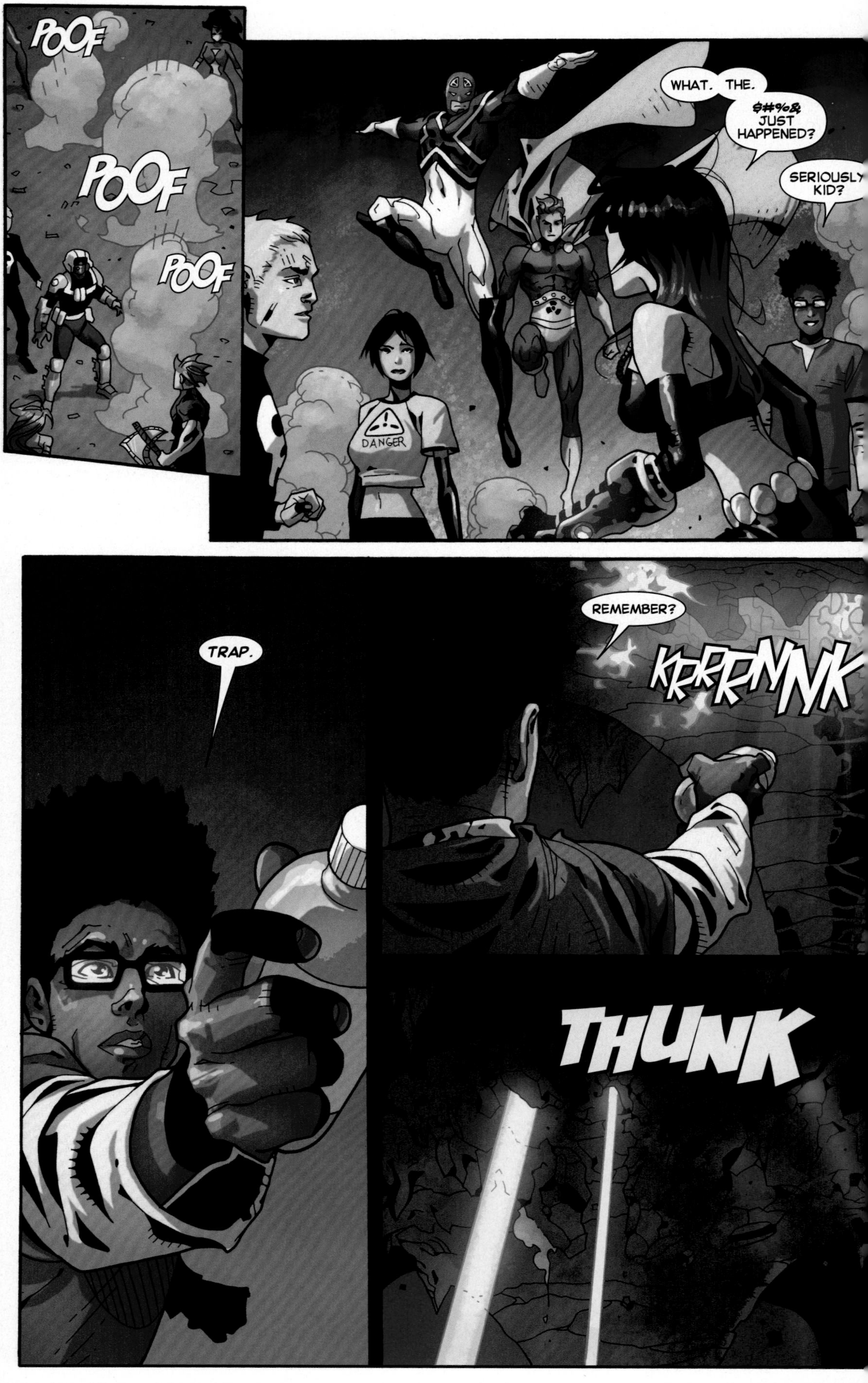
POOF
POOF
POOF
WHAT. THE.
$#%&
JUST
HAPPENED?
SERIOUSLY
KID?
DANGER
TRAP.
REMEMBER?
KRRRNNK
THUNK

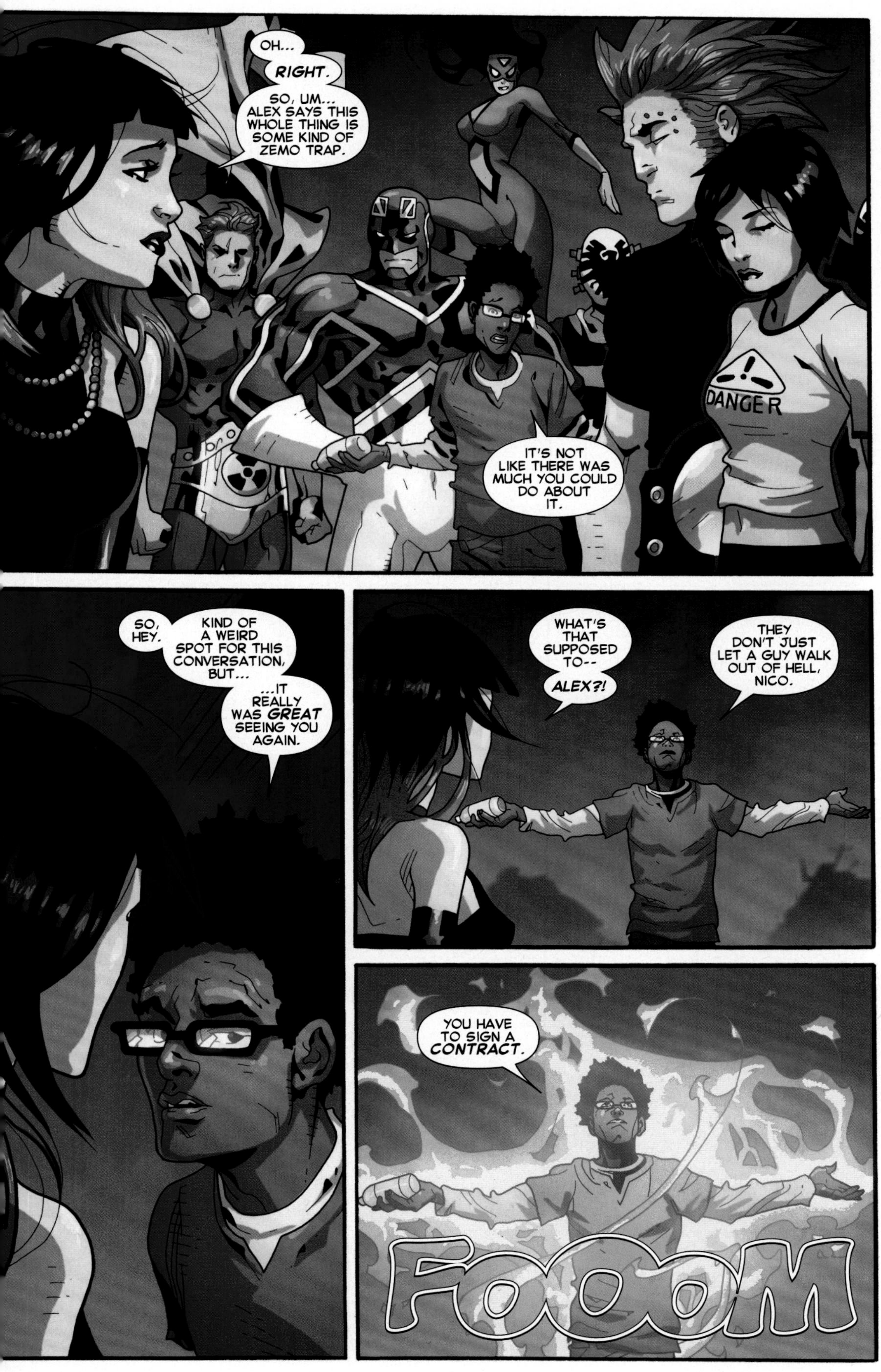
OH...
RIGHT.
SO, UM... ALEX SAYS THIS WHOLE THING IS SOME KIND OF ZEMO TRAP.
IT'S NOT LIKE THERE WAS MUCH YOU COULD DO ABOUT IT.
DANGER
SO, HEY.
KIND OF A WEIRD SPOT FOR THIS CONVERSATION, BUT...
...IT REALLY WAS GREAT SEEING YOU AGAIN.
WHAT'S THAT SUPPOSED TO--
ALEX?!
THEY DON'T JUST LET A GUY WALK OUT OF HELL, NICO.
YOU HAVE TO SIGN A CONTRACT.
FOOOM

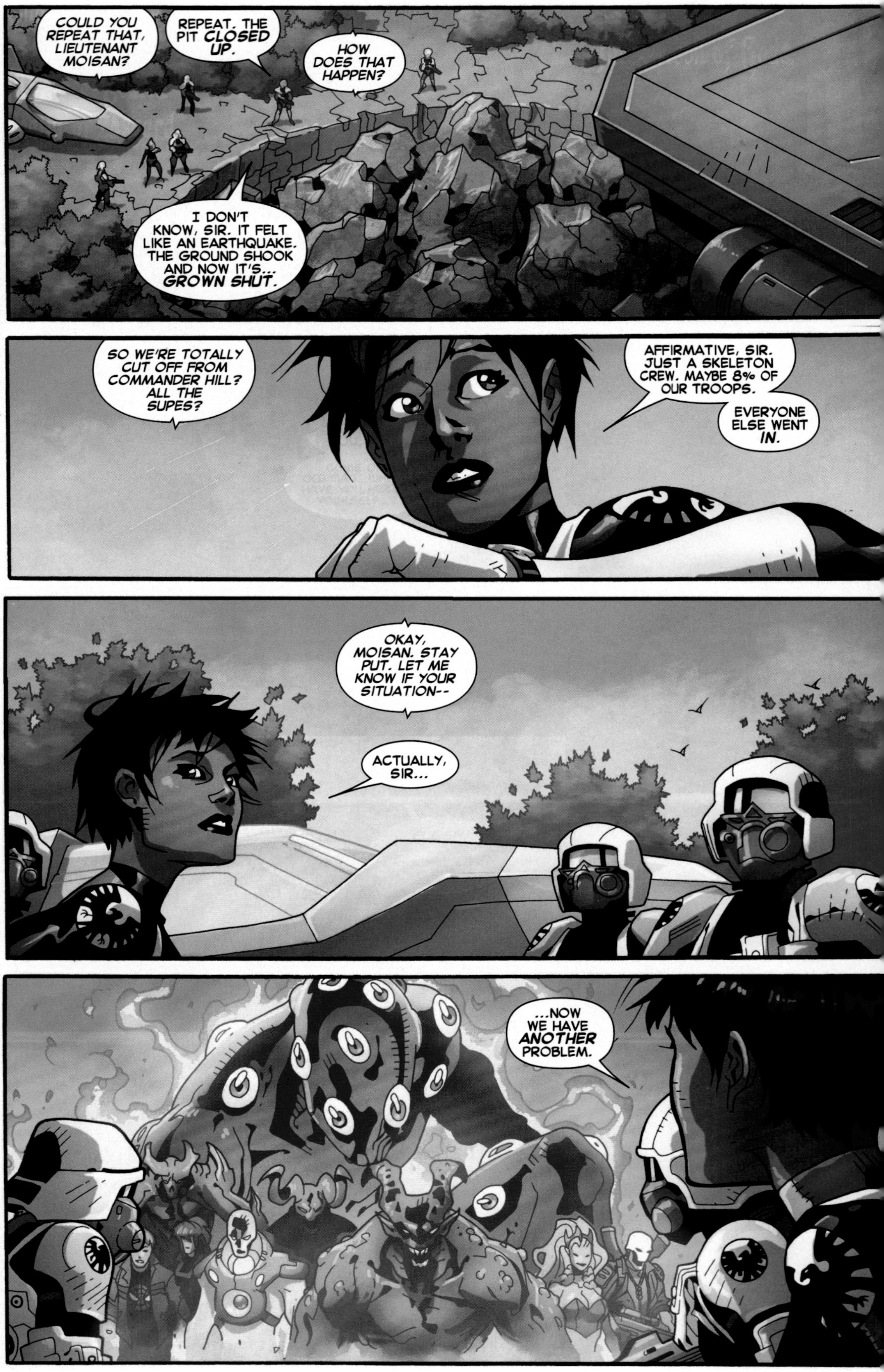
COULD YOU REPEAT THAT, LIEUTENANT MOISAN?
REPEAT. THE PIT CLOSED UP.
HOW DOES THAT HAPPEN?
I DON'T KNOW, SIR. IT FELT LIKE AN EARTHQUAKE. THE GROUND SHOOK AND NOW IT'S... GROWN SHUT.
SO WE'RE TOTALLY CUT OFF FROM COMMANDER HILL? ALL THE SUPES?
AFFIRMATIVE, SIR. JUST A SKELETON CREW. MAYBE 8% OF OUR TROOPS.
EVERYONE ELSE WENT IN.
OKAY, MOISAN. STAY PUT. LET ME KNOW IF YOUR SITUATION--
ACTUALLY, SIR...
...NOW WE HAVE ANOTHER PROBLEM.

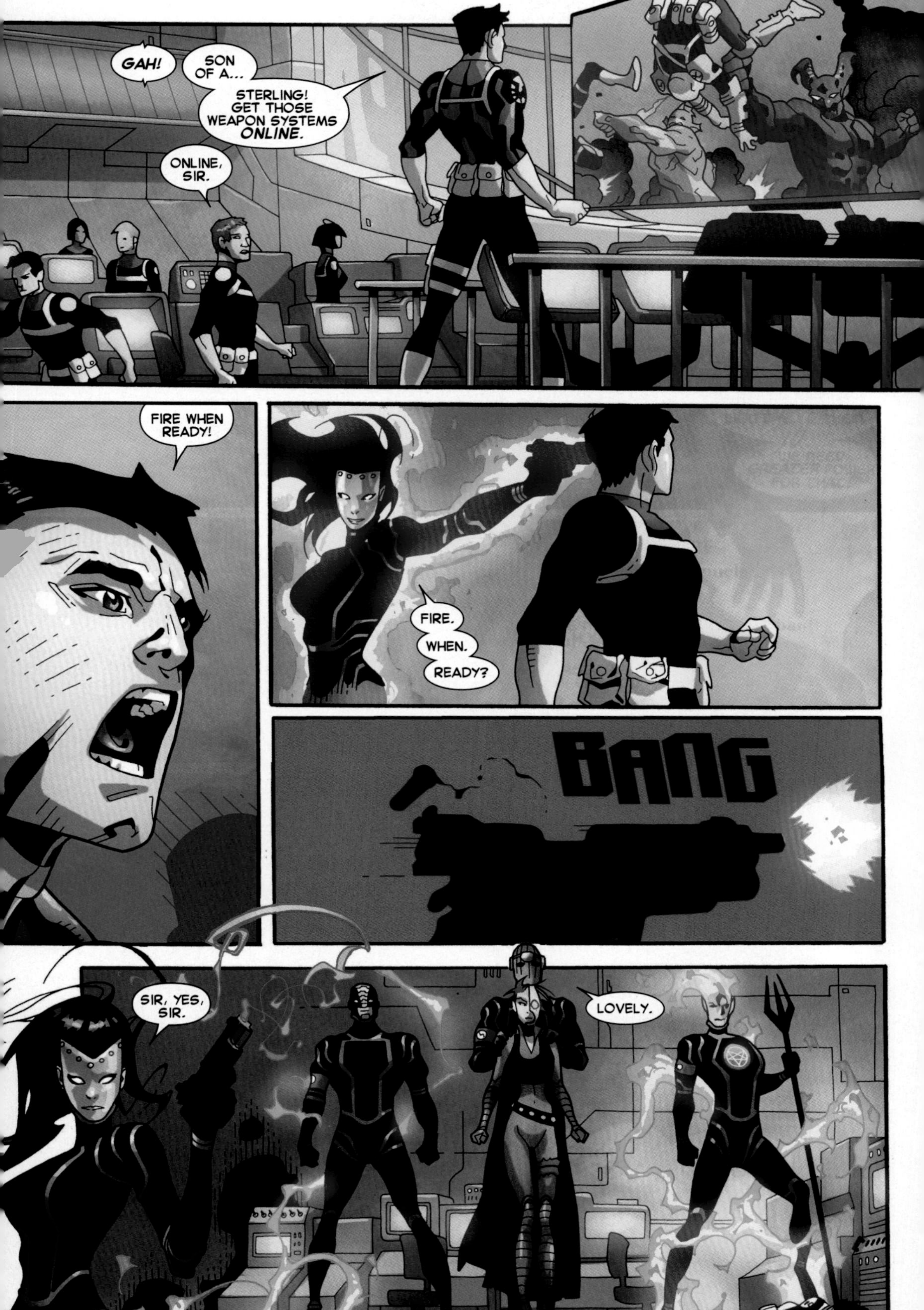
GAH!
SON OF A...
STERLING! GET THOSE WEAPON SYSTEMS ONLINE.
ONLINE, SIR.
FIRE WHEN READY!
FIRE.
WHEN.
READY?
BANG
SIR, YES, SIR.
LOVELY.

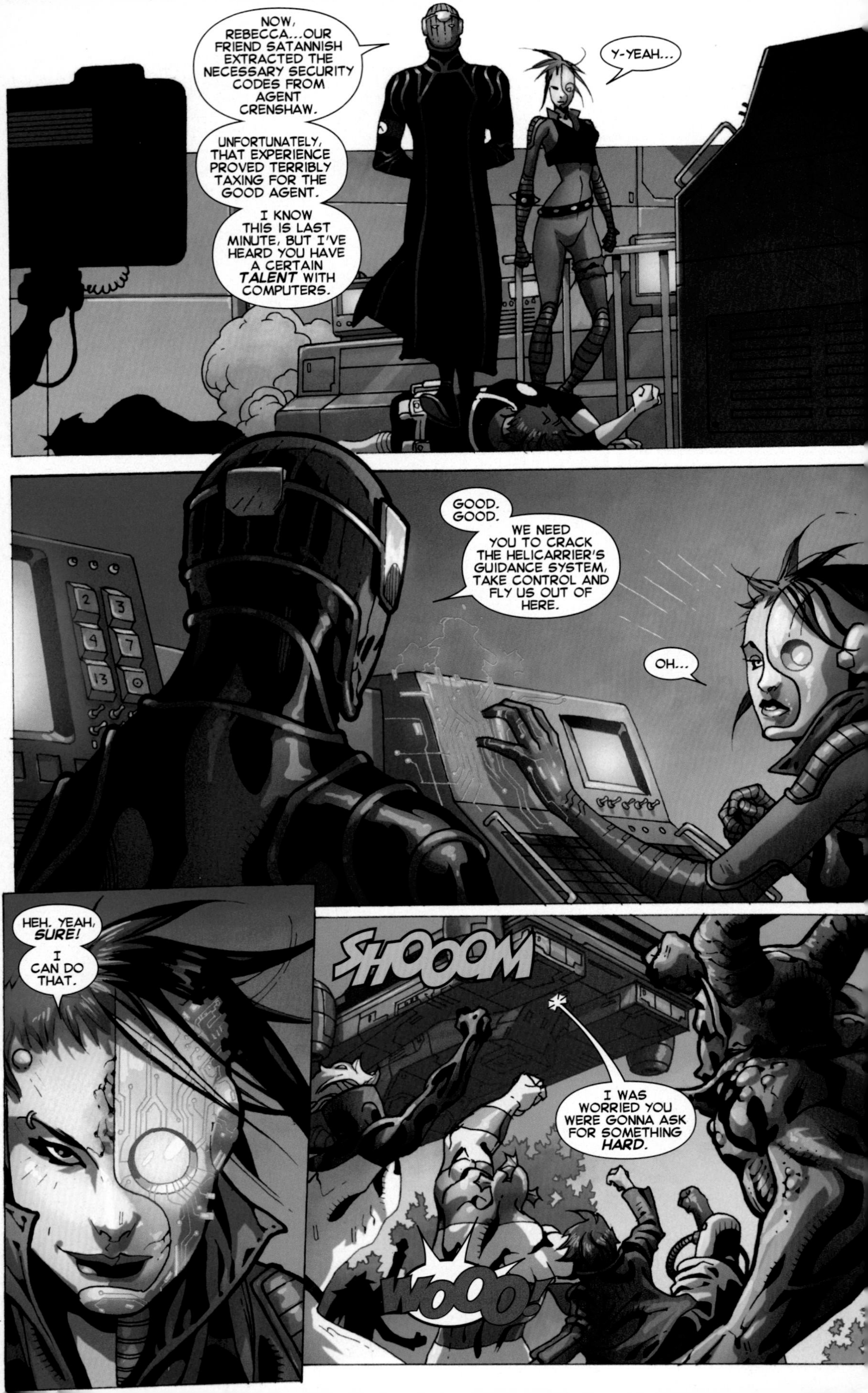
NOW, REBECCA...OUR FRIEND SATANNISH EXTRACTED THE NECESSARY SECURITY CODES FROM AGENT CRENSHAW.
UNFORTUNATELY, THAT EXPERIENCE PROVED TERRIBLY TAXING FOR THE GOOD AGENT.
I KNOW THIS IS LAST MINUTE, BUT I'VE HEARD YOU HAVE A CERTAIN *TALENT* WITH COMPUTERS.
Y-YEAH...
GOOD. GOOD. WE NEED YOU TO CRACK THE HELICARRIER'S GUIDANCE SYSTEM, TAKE CONTROL AND FLY US OUT OF HERE.
OH...
HEH. YEAH, *SURE!* I CAN DO THAT.
SHOOOM
I WAS WORRIED YOU WERE GONNA ASK FOR SOMETHING *HARD*.
WOOO

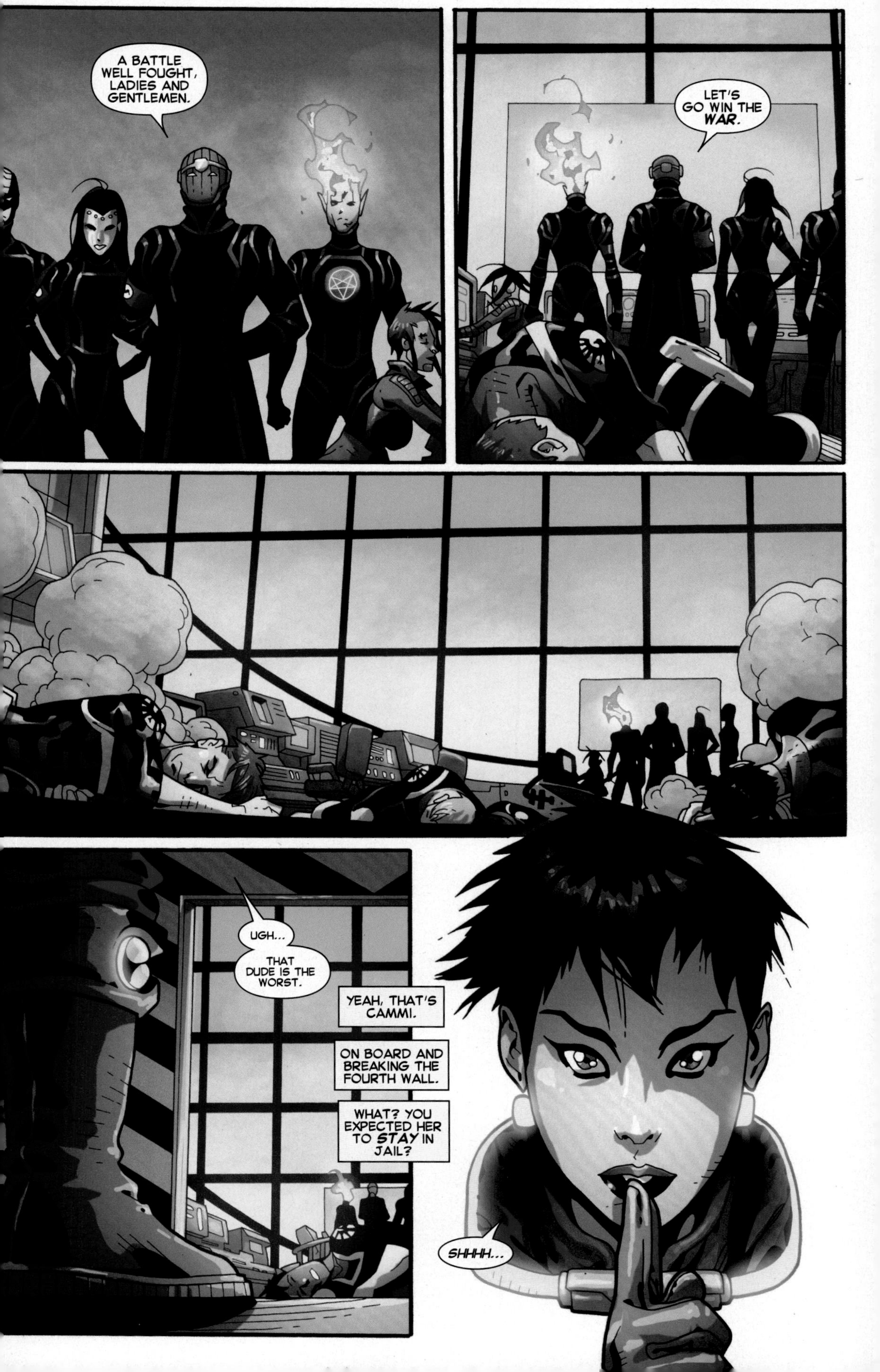
A BATTLE WELL FOUGHT, LADIES AND GENTLEMEN.
LET'S GO WIN THE WAR.
UGH...
THAT DUDE IS THE WORST.
YEAH, THAT'S CAMMI.
ON BOARD AND BREAKING THE FOURTH WALL.
WHAT? YOU EXPECTED HER TO STAY IN JAIL?
SHHHH...

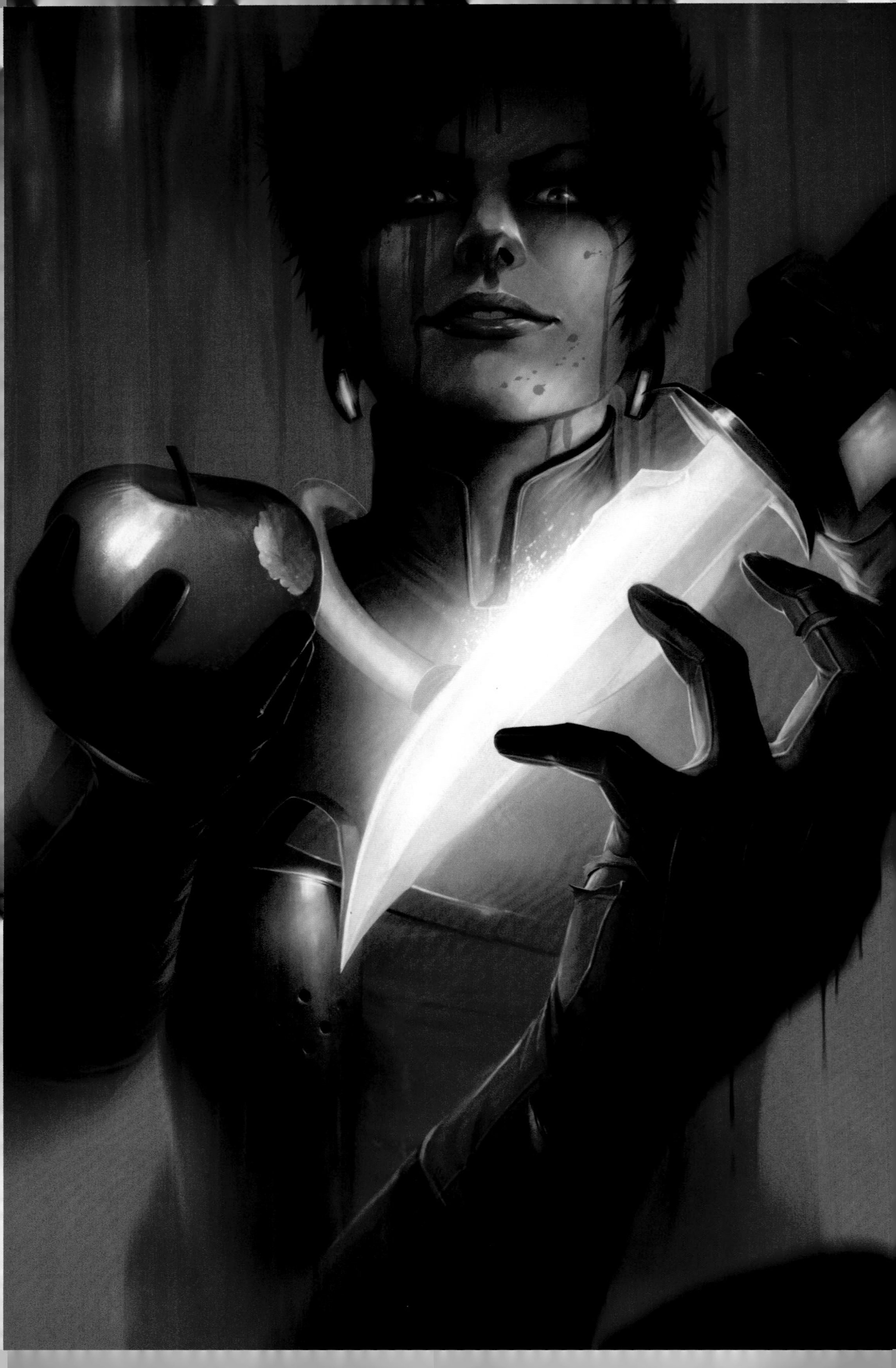

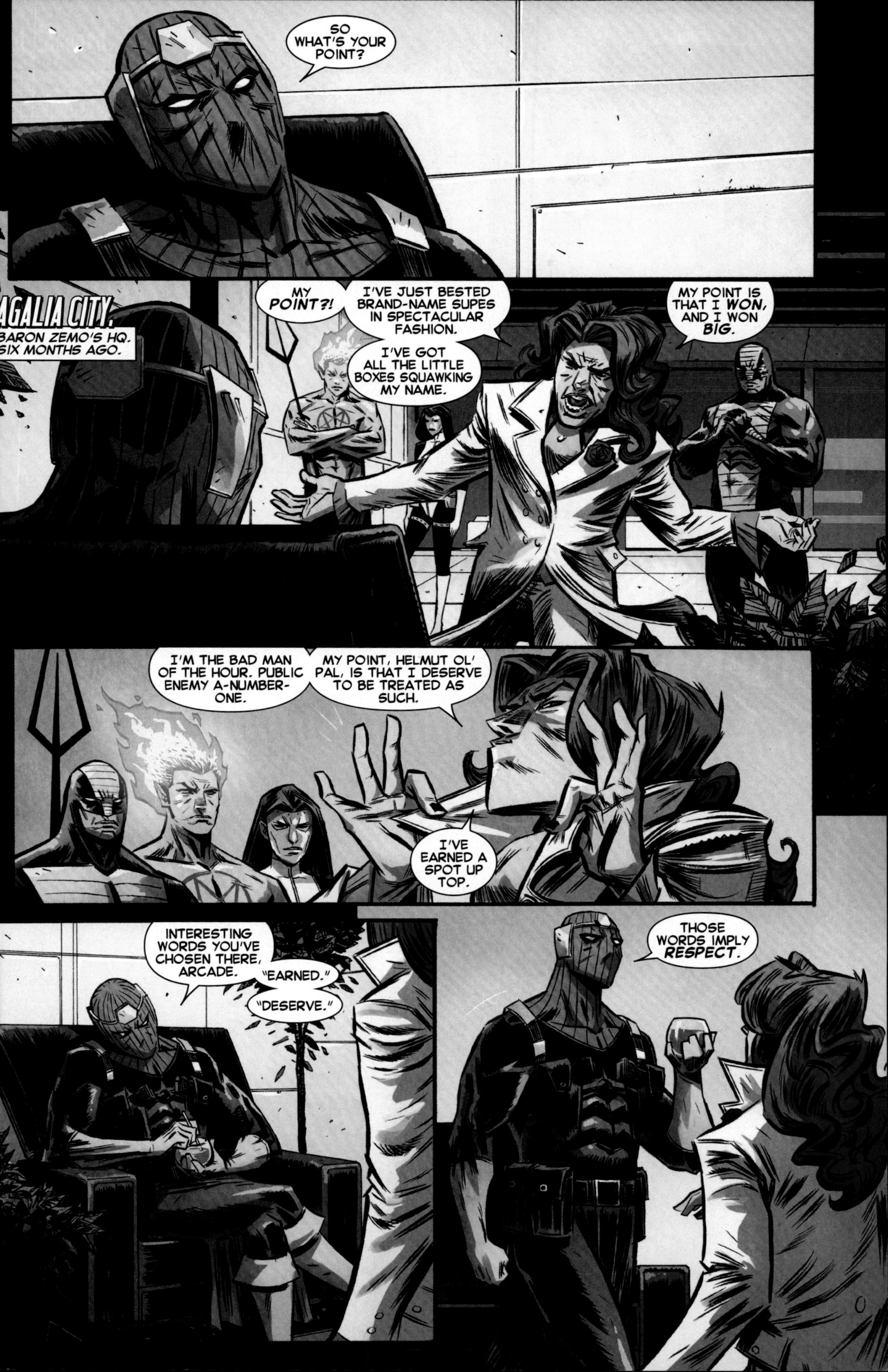
SO WHAT'S YOUR POINT?
...AGALIA CITY.
BARON ZEMO'S HQ. SIX MONTHS AGO.
MY POINT?!
I'VE JUST BESTED BRAND-NAME SUPES IN SPECTACULAR FASHION.
I'VE GOT ALL THE LITTLE BOXES SQUAWKING MY NAME.
MY POINT IS THAT I WON, AND I WON BIG.
I'M THE BAD MAN OF THE HOUR. PUBLIC ENEMY A-NUMBER-ONE.
MY POINT, HELMUT OL' PAL, IS THAT I DESERVE TO BE TREATED AS SUCH.
I'VE EARNED A SPOT UP TOP.
INTERESTING WORDS YOU'VE CHOSEN THERE, ARCADE.
"EARNED."
"DESERVE."
THOSE WORDS IMPLY RESPECT.

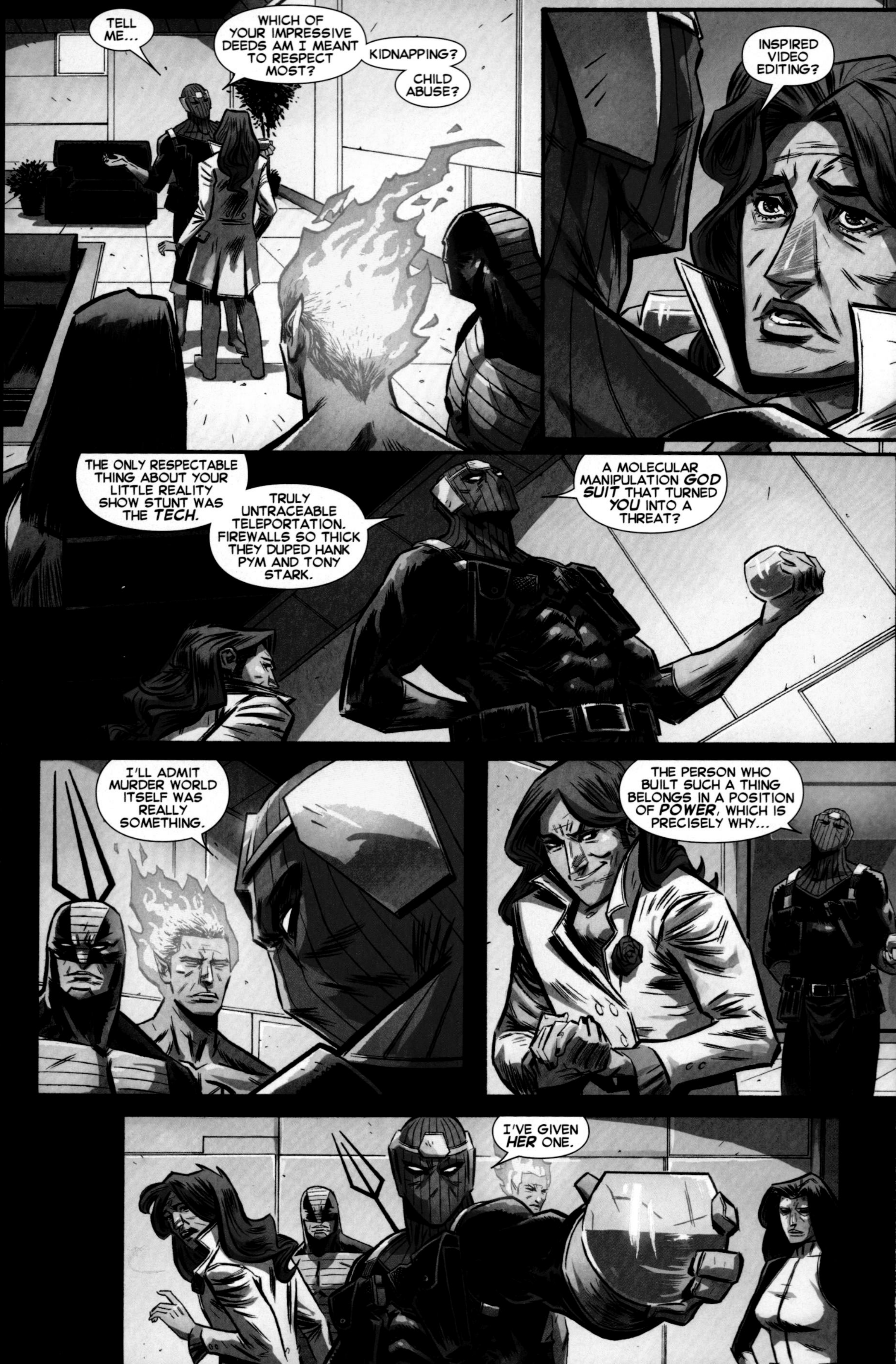
TELL ME...
WHICH OF YOUR IMPRESSIVE DEEDS AM I MEANT TO RESPECT MOST?
KIDNAPPING?
CHILD ABUSE?
INSPIRED VIDEO EDITING?
THE ONLY RESPECTABLE THING ABOUT YOUR LITTLE REALITY SHOW STUNT WAS THE TECH.
TRULY UNTRACEABLE TELEPORTATION. FIREWALLS SO THICK THEY DUPED HANK PYM AND TONY STARK.
A MOLECULAR MANIPULATION GOD SUIT THAT TURNED YOU INTO A THREAT?
I'LL ADMIT MURDER WORLD ITSELF WAS REALLY SOMETHING.
THE PERSON WHO BUILT SUCH A THING BELONGS IN A POSITION OF POWER, WHICH IS PRECISELY WHY...
I'VE GIVEN HER ONE.

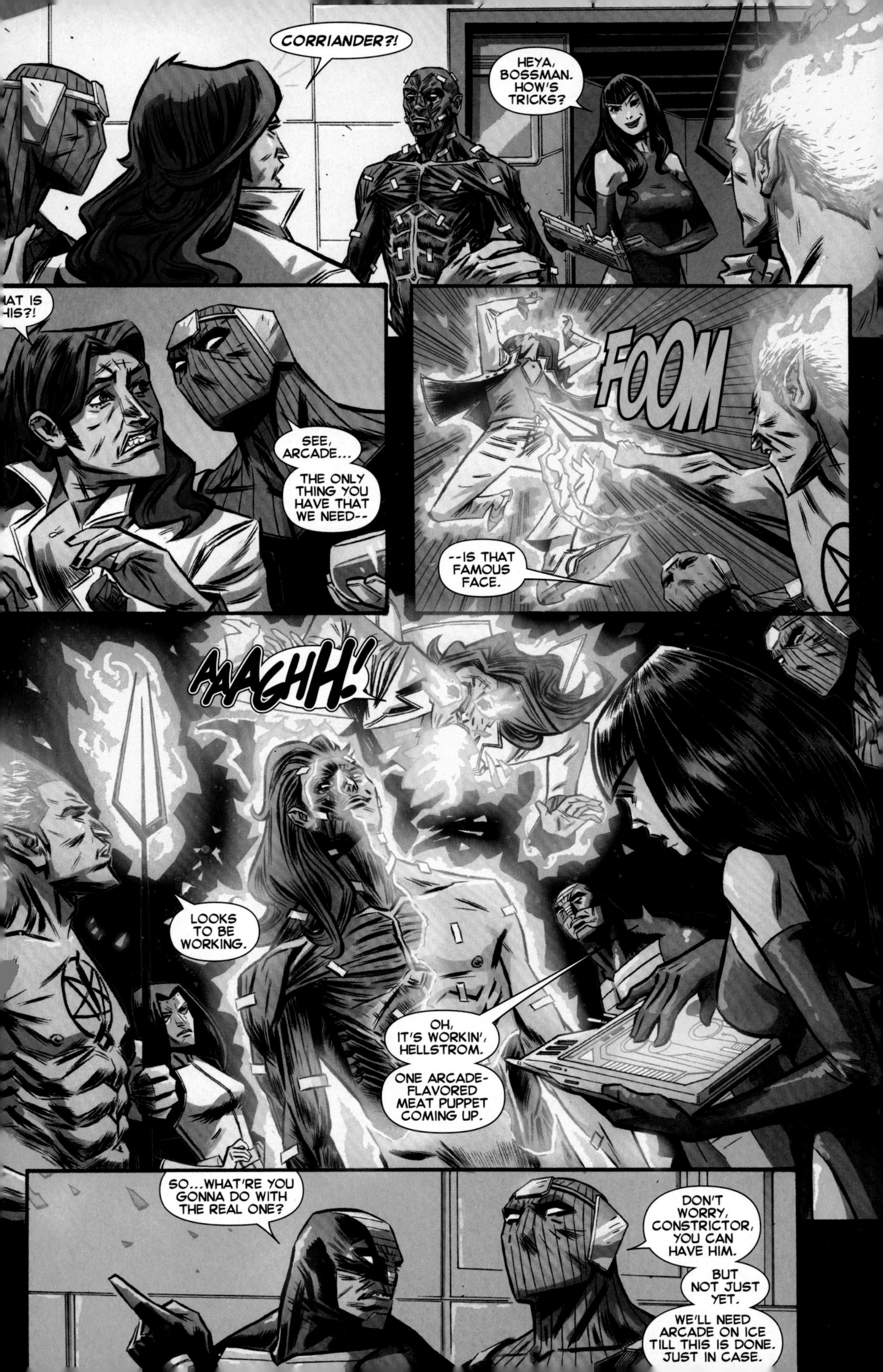
CORRIANDER?!
HEYA, BOSSMAN. HOW'S TRICKS?
...HAT IS ...HIS?!
SEE, ARCADE...
THE ONLY THING YOU HAVE THAT WE NEED--
FOOM
--IS THAT FAMOUS FACE.
AAAGHH!
LOOKS TO BE WORKING.
OH, IT'S WORKIN', HELLSTROM.
ONE ARCADE-FLAVORED MEAT PUPPET COMING UP.
SO...WHAT'RE YOU GONNA DO WITH THE REAL ONE?
DON'T WORRY, CONSTRICTOR, YOU CAN HAVE HIM.
BUT NOT JUST YET.
WE'LL NEED ARCADE ON ICE TILL THIS IS DONE. JUST IN CASE.

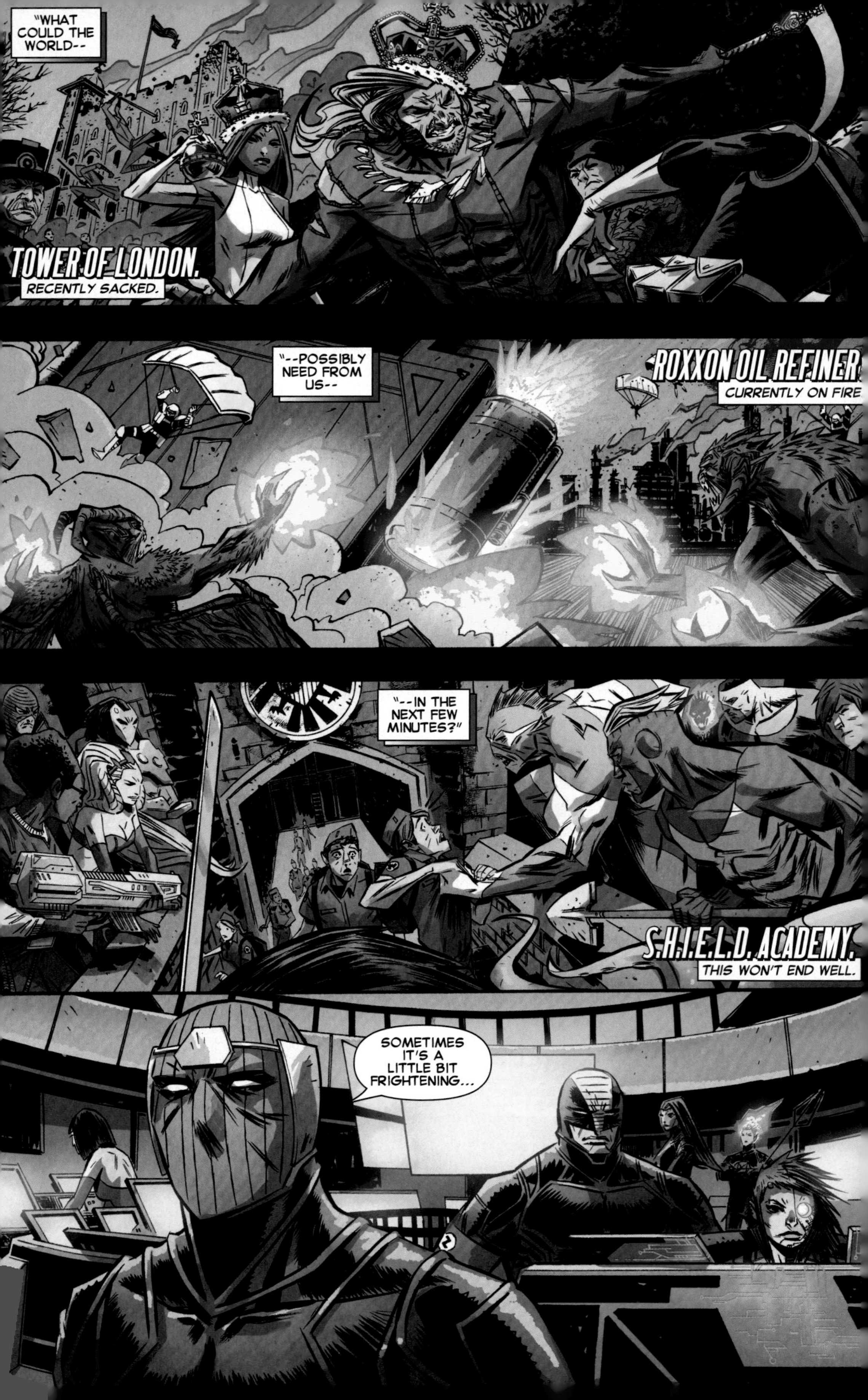
"WHAT COULD THE WORLD--
TOWER OF LONDON.
RECENTLY SACKED.
"--POSSIBLY NEED FROM US--
ROXXON OIL REFINER
CURRENTLY ON FIRE
"--IN THE NEXT FEW MINUTES?"
S.H.I.E.L.D. ACADEMY.
THIS WON'T END WELL.
SOMETIMES IT'S A LITTLE BIT FRIGHTENING...

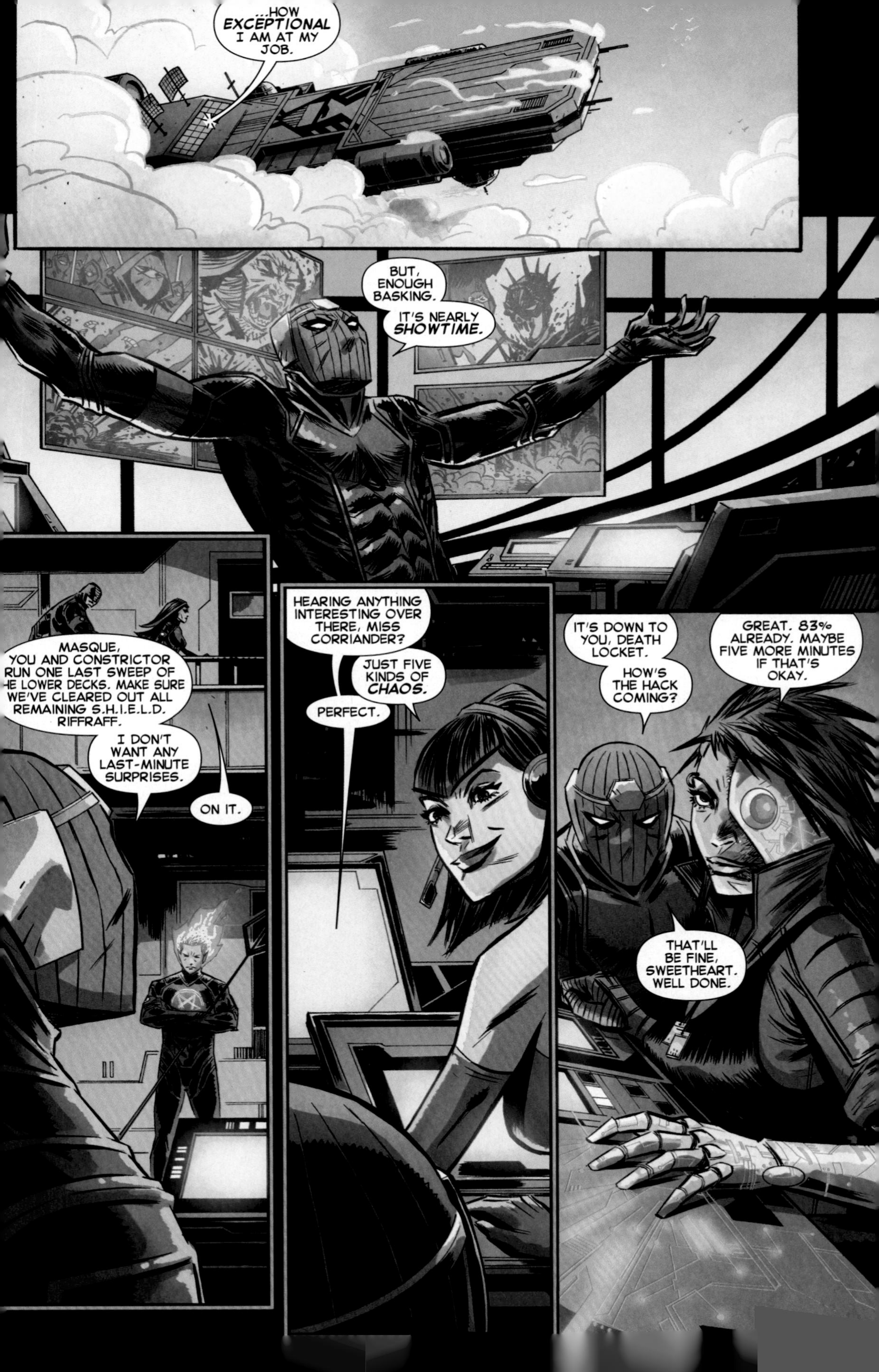
...HOW EXCEPTIONAL I AM AT MY JOB.
BUT, ENOUGH BASKING.
IT'S NEARLY SHOWTIME.
MASQUE, YOU AND CONSTRICTOR RUN ONE LAST SWEEP OF HE LOWER DECKS. MAKE SURE WE'VE CLEARED OUT ALL REMAINING S.H.I.E.L.D. RIFFRAFF.
I DON'T WANT ANY LAST-MINUTE SURPRISES.
ON IT.
HEARING ANYTHING INTERESTING OVER THERE, MISS CORRIANDER?
JUST FIVE KINDS OF CHAOS.
PERFECT.
IT'S DOWN TO YOU, DEATH LOCKET.
HOW'S THE HACK COMING?
GREAT. 83% ALREADY. MAYBE FIVE MORE MINUTES IF THAT'S OKAY.
THAT'LL BE FINE, SWEETHEART. WELL DONE.

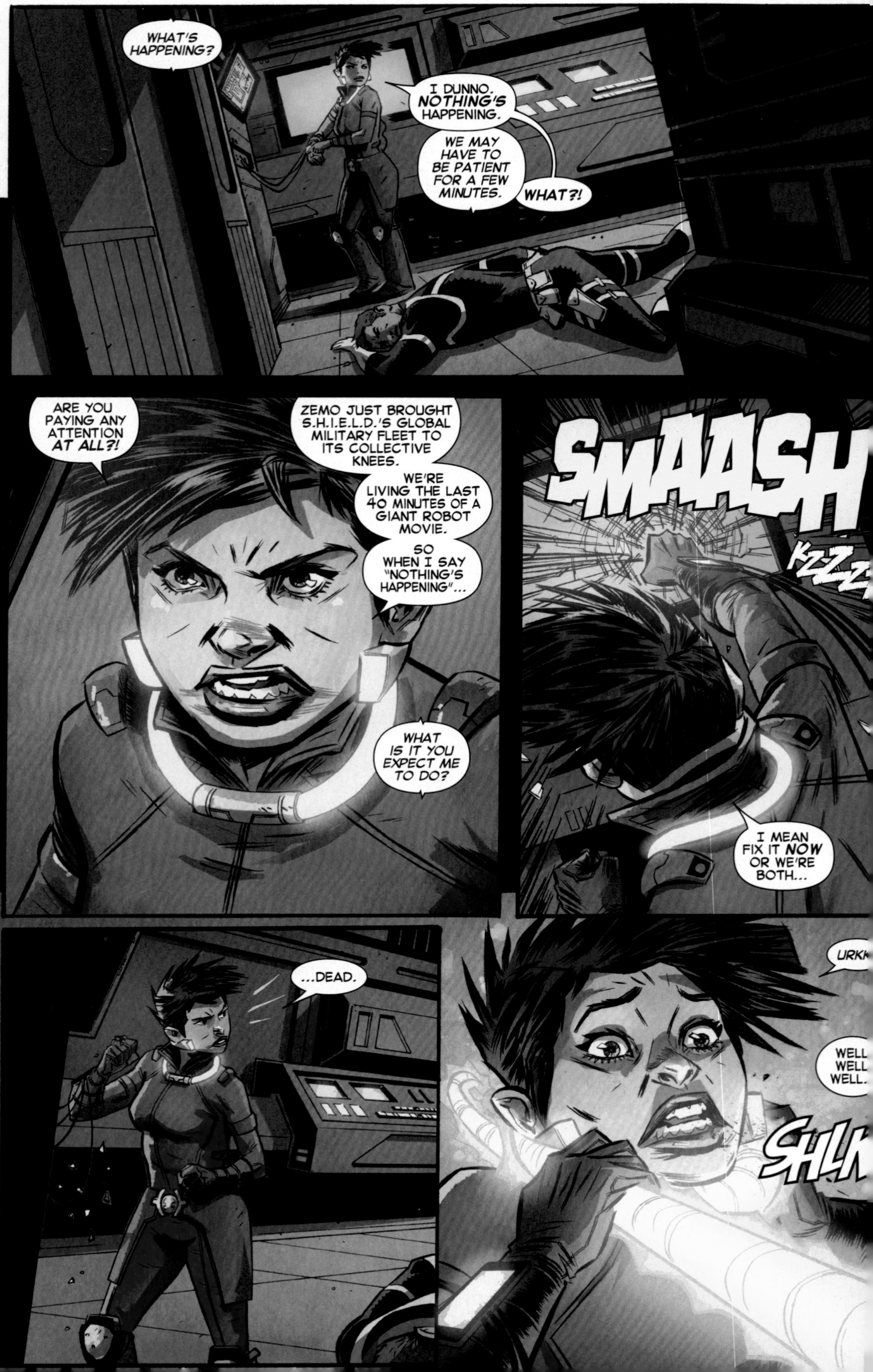
WHAT'S HAPPENING?
I DUNNO. NOTHING'S HAPPENING.
WE MAY HAVE TO BE PATIENT FOR A FEW MINUTES.
WHAT?!
ARE YOU PAYING ANY ATTENTION AT ALL?!
ZEMO JUST BROUGHT S.H.I.E.L.D.'S GLOBAL MILITARY FLEET TO ITS COLLECTIVE KNEES.
WE'RE LIVING THE LAST 40 MINUTES OF A GIANT ROBOT MOVIE.
SO WHEN I SAY "NOTHING'S HAPPENING"...
WHAT IS IT YOU EXPECT ME TO DO?
SMAASH
I MEAN FIX IT NOW OR WE'RE BOTH...
...DEAD.
WELL WELL WELL.

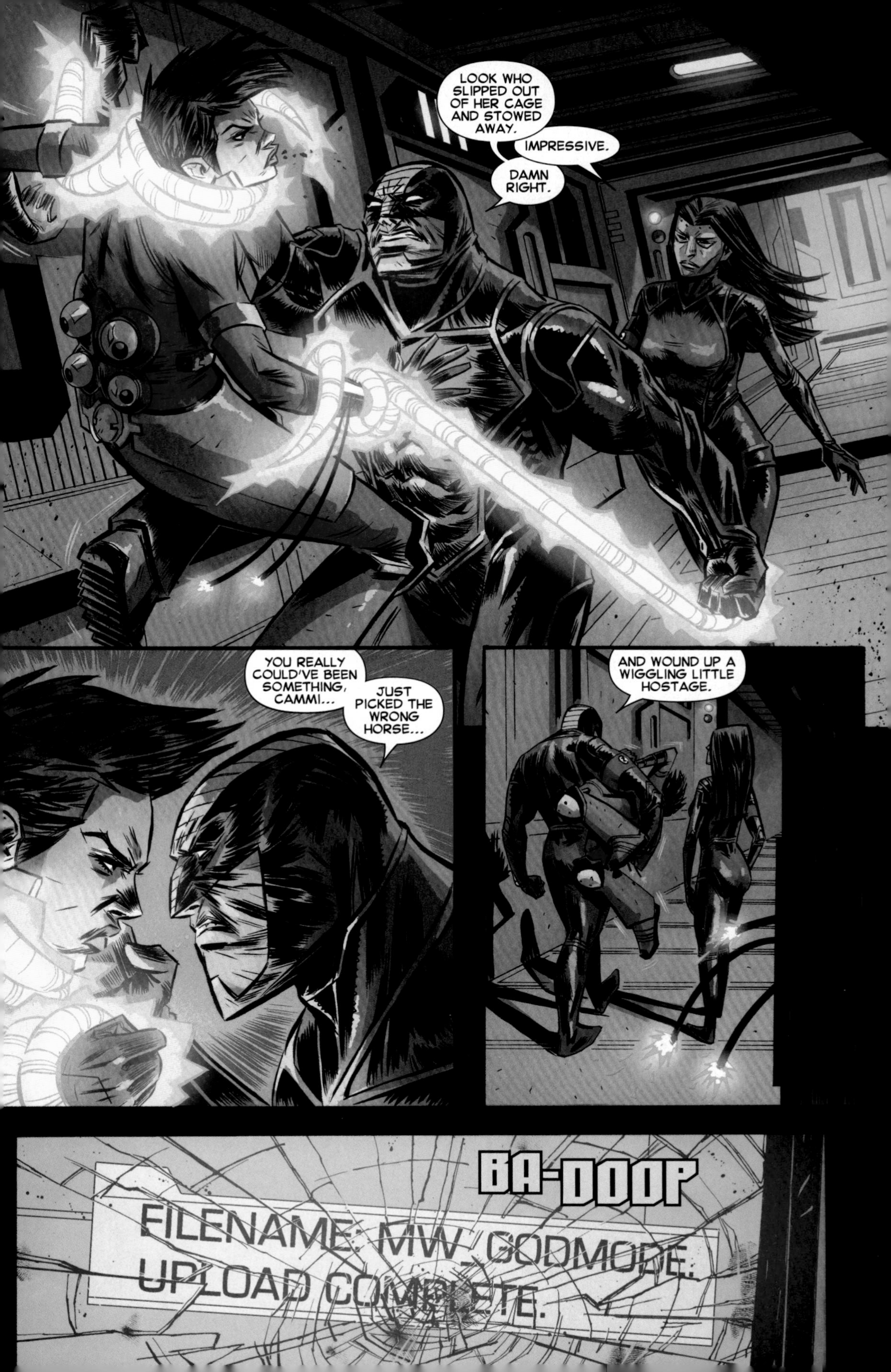
LOOK WHO SLIPPED OUT OF HER CAGE AND STOWED AWAY.
IMPRESSIVE.
DAMN RIGHT.
YOU REALLY COULD'VE BEEN SOMETHING, CAMMI...
JUST PICKED THE WRONG HORSE...
AND WOUND UP A WIGGLING LITTLE HOSTAGE.
BA-DOOP
FILENAME: MW_GODMODE.
UPLOAD COMPLETE.

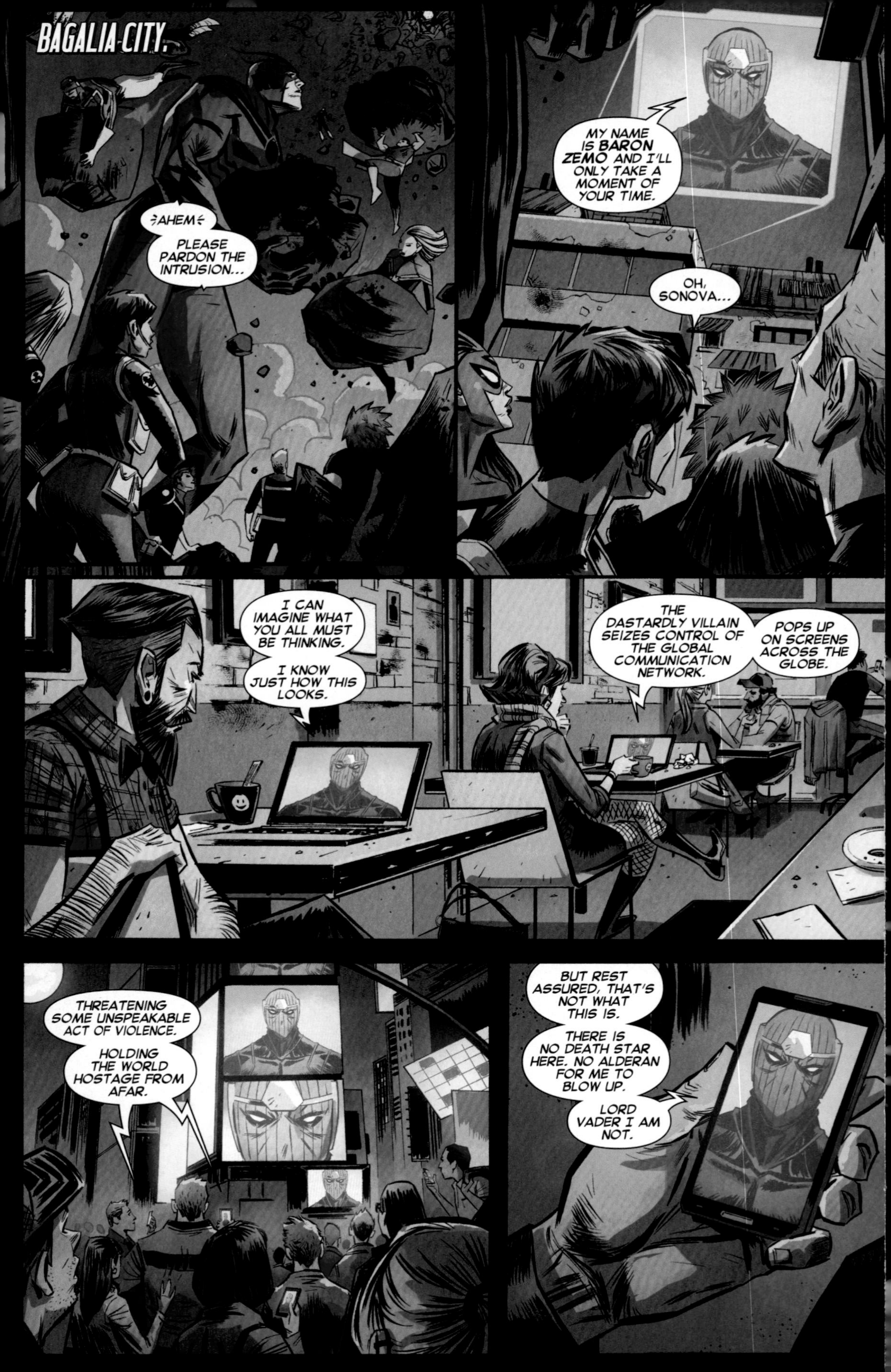
BAGALIA CITY.
≠AHEM≠
PLEASE PARDON THE INTRUSION...
MY NAME IS BARON ZEMO AND I'LL ONLY TAKE A MOMENT OF YOUR TIME.
OH, SONOVA...
I CAN IMAGINE WHAT YOU ALL MUST BE THINKING.
I KNOW JUST HOW THIS LOOKS.
THE DASTARDLY VILLAIN SEIZES CONTROL OF THE GLOBAL COMMUNICATION NETWORK.
POPS UP ON SCREENS ACROSS THE GLOBE.
THREATENING SOME UNSPEAKABLE ACT OF VIOLENCE.
HOLDING THE WORLD HOSTAGE FROM AFAR.
BUT REST ASSURED, THAT'S NOT WHAT THIS IS.
THERE IS NO DEATH STAR HERE. NO ALDERAN FOR ME TO BLOW UP.
LORD VADER I AM NOT.

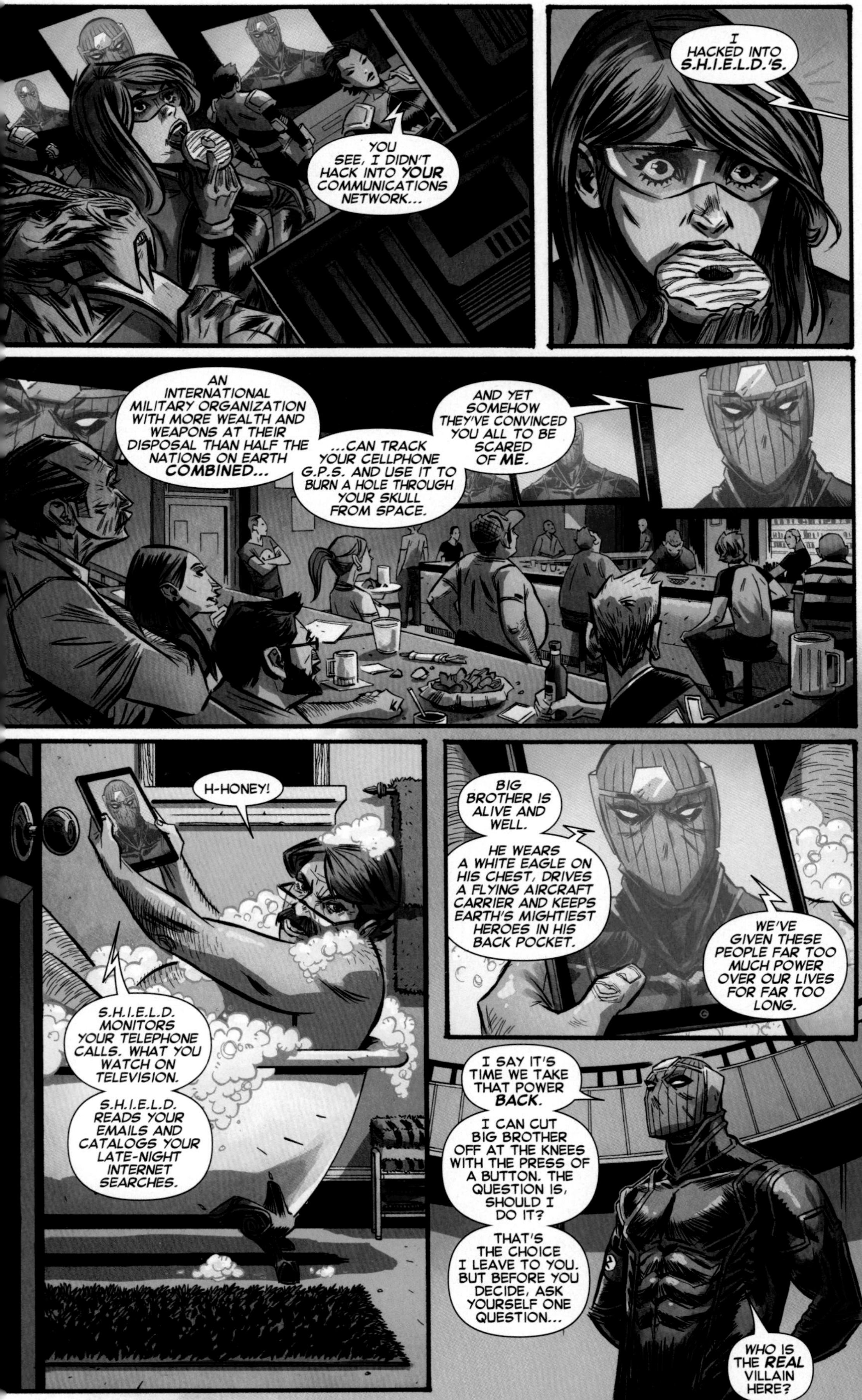
YOU SEE, I DIDN'T HACK INTO YOUR COMMUNICATIONS NETWORK...
I HACKED INTO S.H.I.E.L.D.'S.
AN INTERNATIONAL MILITARY ORGANIZATION WITH MORE WEALTH AND WEAPONS AT THEIR DISPOSAL THAN HALF THE NATIONS ON EARTH COMBINED...
...CAN TRACK YOUR CELLPHONE G.P.S. AND USE IT TO BURN A HOLE THROUGH YOUR SKULL FROM SPACE.
AND YET SOMEHOW THEY'VE CONVINCED YOU ALL TO BE SCARED OF ME.
H-HONEY!
S.H.I.E.L.D. MONITORS YOUR TELEPHONE CALLS. WHAT YOU WATCH ON TELEVISION.
S.H.I.E.L.D. READS YOUR EMAILS AND CATALOGS YOUR LATE-NIGHT INTERNET SEARCHES.
BIG BROTHER IS ALIVE AND WELL.
HE WEARS A WHITE EAGLE ON HIS CHEST, DRIVES A FLYING AIRCRAFT CARRIER AND KEEPS EARTH'S MIGHTIEST HEROES IN HIS BACK POCKET.
WE'VE GIVEN THESE PEOPLE FAR TOO MUCH POWER OVER OUR LIVES FOR FAR TOO LONG.
I SAY IT'S TIME WE TAKE THAT POWER BACK.
I CAN CUT BIG BROTHER OFF AT THE KNEES WITH THE PRESS OF A BUTTON. THE QUESTION IS, SHOULD I DO IT?
THAT'S THE CHOICE I LEAVE TO YOU. BUT BEFORE YOU DECIDE, ASK YOURSELF ONE QUESTION...
WHO IS THE REAL VILLAIN HERE?

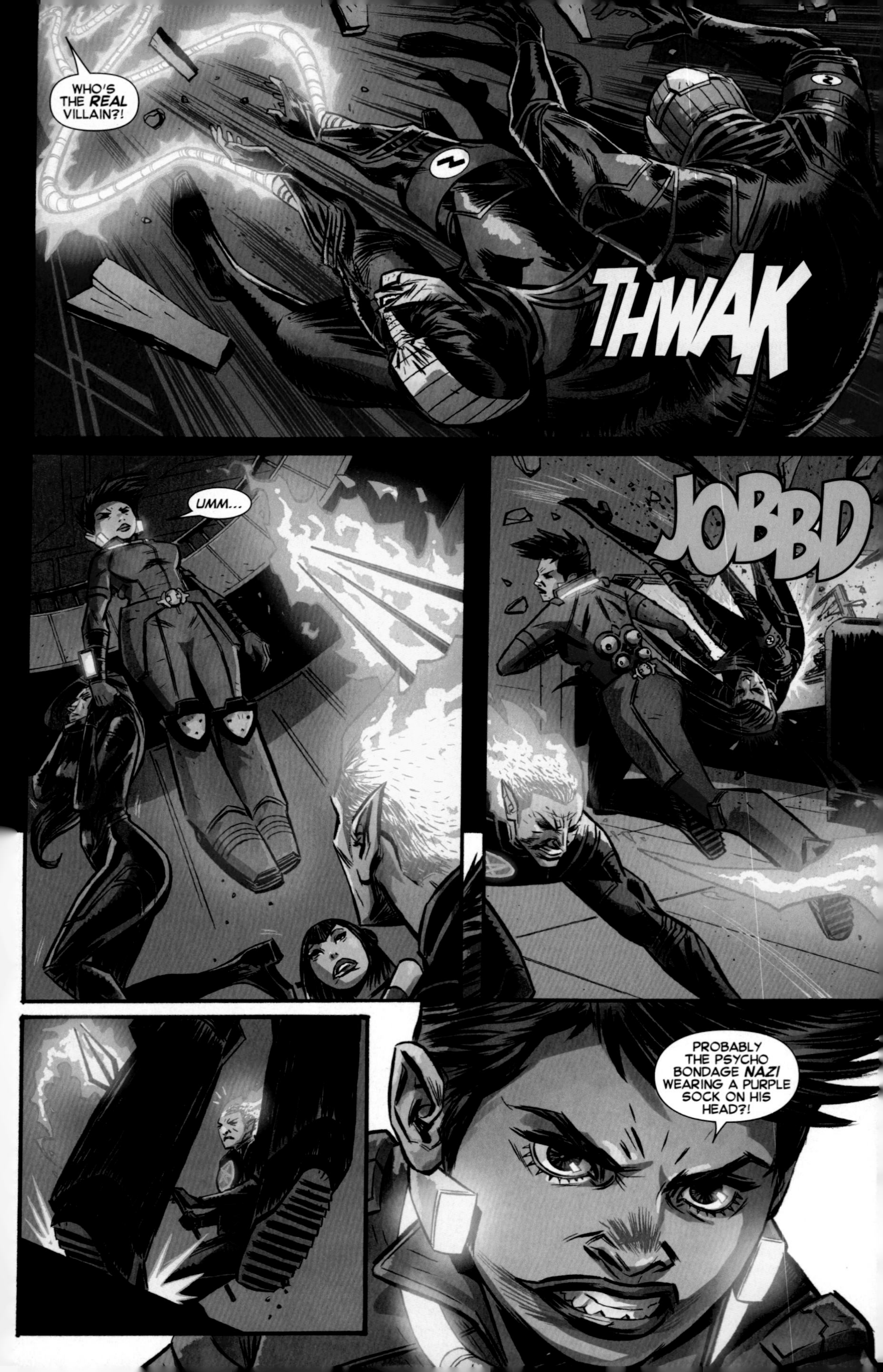
WHO'S THE *REAL* VILLAIN?!
THWAK
UMM...
JOBBD
PROBABLY THE PSYCHO BONDAGE *NAZI* WEARING A PURPLE SOCK ON HIS HEAD?!

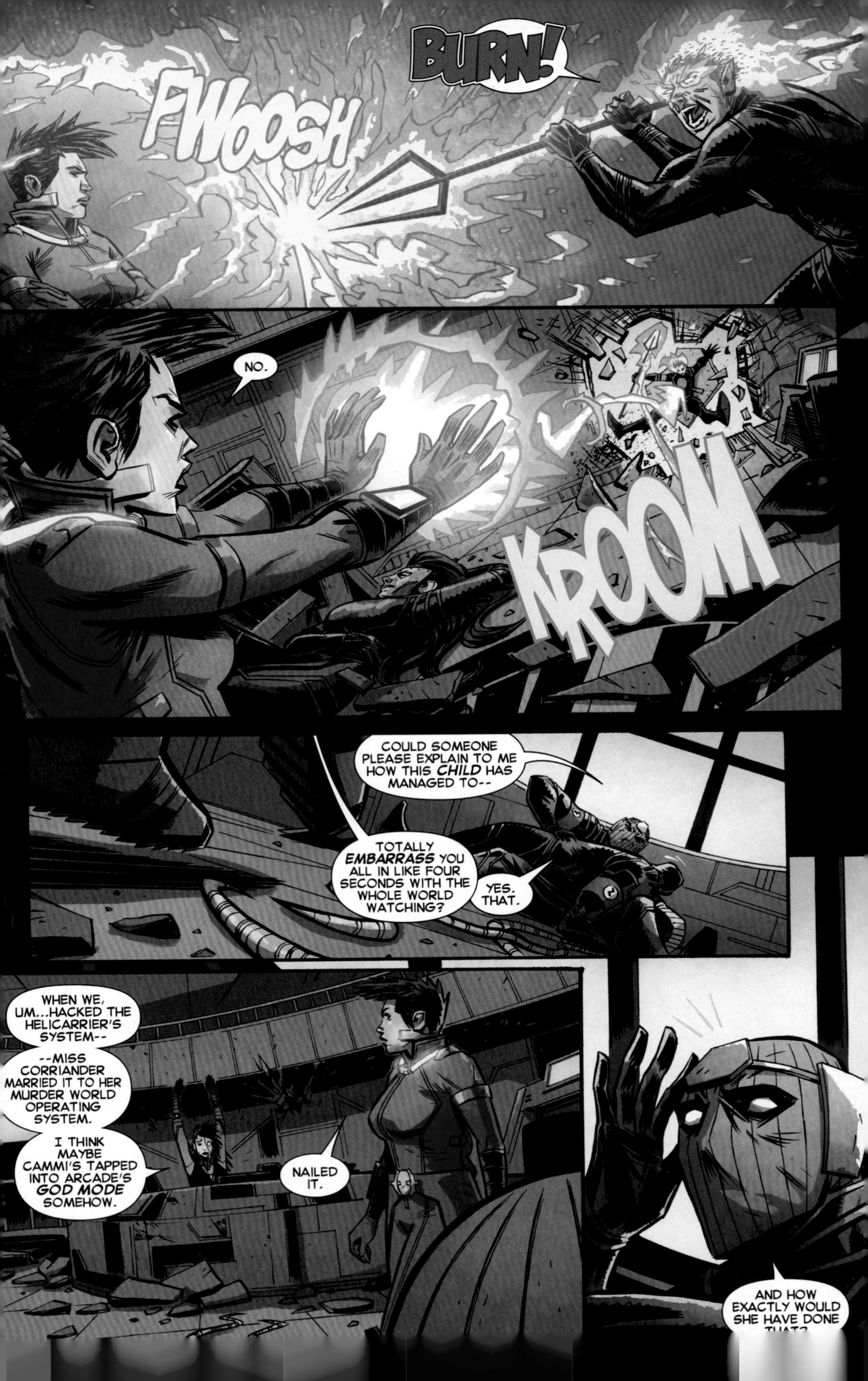
FWOOSH
BURN!
NO.
KROOM
COULD SOMEONE PLEASE EXPLAIN TO ME HOW THIS CHILD HAS MANAGED TO--
TOTALLY EMBARRASS YOU ALL IN LIKE FOUR SECONDS WITH THE WHOLE WORLD WATCHING?
YES. THAT.
WHEN WE, UM...HACKED THE HELICARRIER'S SYSTEM--
--MISS CORRIANDER MARRIED IT TO HER MURDER WORLD OPERATING SYSTEM.
I THINK MAYBE CAMMI'S TAPPED INTO ARCADE'S GOD MODE SOMEHOW.
NAILED IT.
AND HOW EXACTLY WOULD SHE HAVE DONE

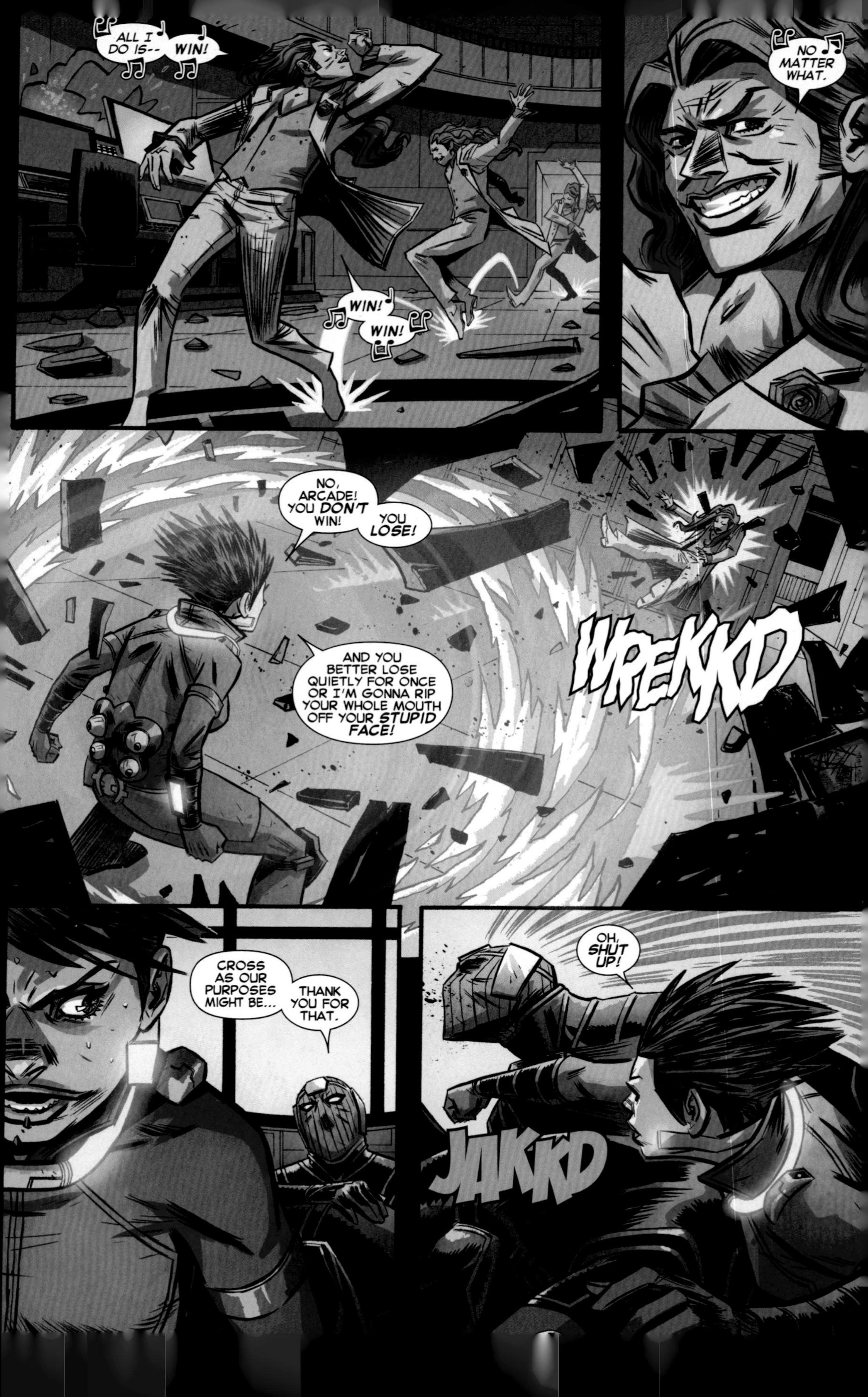
ALL I DO IS--
WIN!
NO MATTER WHAT.
WIN!
WIN!
NO, ARCADE! YOU DON'T WIN!
YOU LOSE!
AND YOU BETTER LOSE QUIETLY FOR ONCE OR I'M GONNA RIP YOUR WHOLE MOUTH OFF YOUR STUPID FACE!
WREKKD
CROSS AS OUR PURPOSES MIGHT BE...
THANK YOU FOR THAT.
OH, SHUT UP!
JAKKD

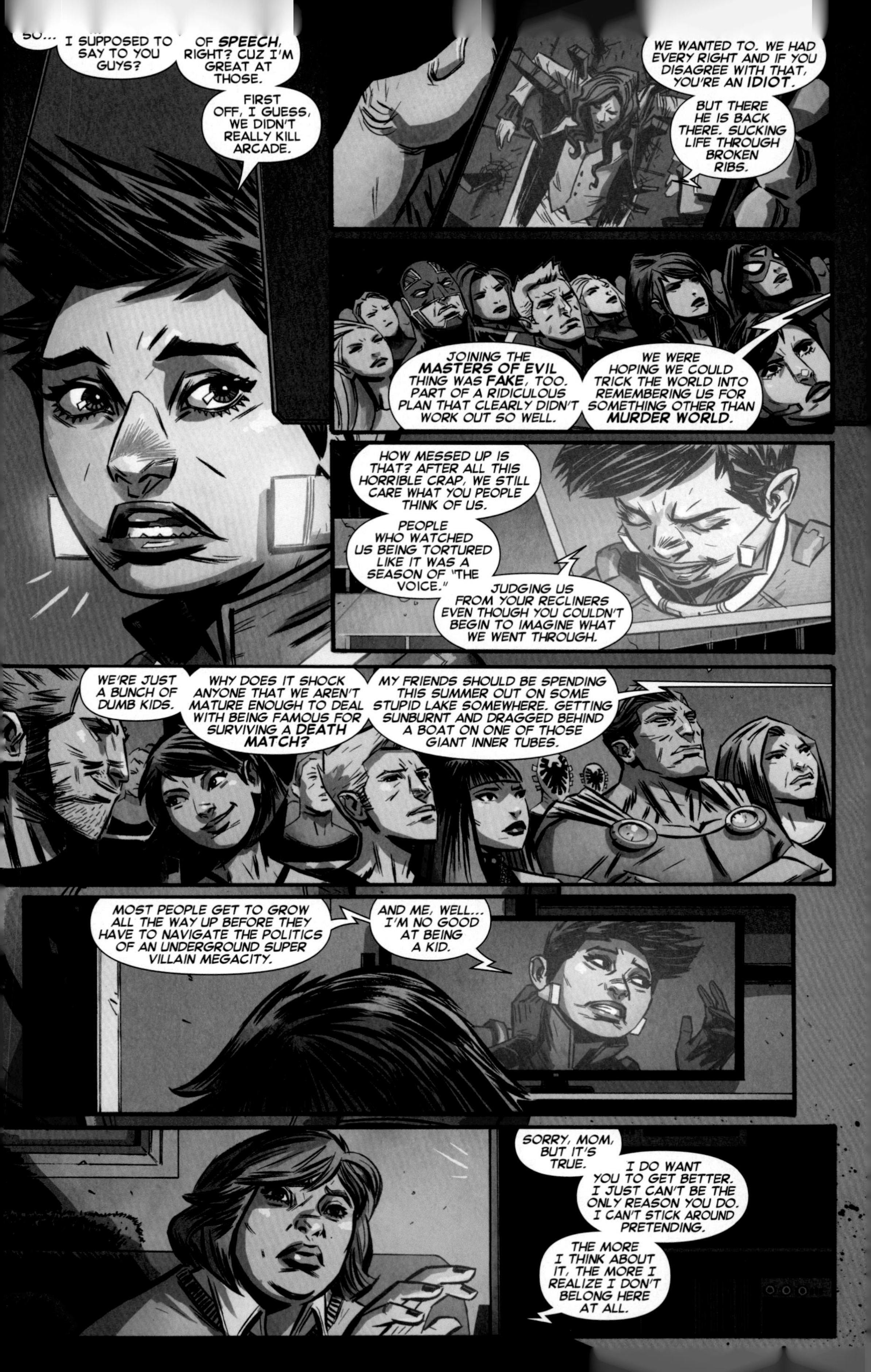
I SUPPOSED TO SAY TO YOU GUYS?
OF SPEECH, RIGHT? CUZ I'M GREAT AT THOSE.
FIRST OFF, I GUESS, WE DIDN'T REALLY KILL ARCADE.
WE WANTED TO. WE HAD EVERY RIGHT AND IF YOU DISAGREE WITH THAT, YOU'RE AN IDIOT.
BUT THERE HE IS BACK THERE. SUCKING LIFE THROUGH BROKEN RIBS.
JOINING THE MASTERS OF EVIL THING WAS FAKE, TOO. PART OF A RIDICULOUS PLAN THAT CLEARLY DIDN'T WORK OUT SO WELL.
WE WERE HOPING WE COULD TRICK THE WORLD INTO REMEMBERING US FOR SOMETHING OTHER THAN MURDER WORLD.
HOW MESSED UP IS THAT? AFTER ALL THIS HORRIBLE CRAP, WE STILL CARE WHAT YOU PEOPLE THINK OF US.
PEOPLE WHO WATCHED US BEING TORTURED LIKE IT WAS A SEASON OF "THE VOICE."
JUDGING US FROM YOUR RECLINERS EVEN THOUGH YOU COULDN'T BEGIN TO IMAGINE WHAT WE WENT THROUGH.
WE'RE JUST A BUNCH OF DUMB KIDS.
WHY DOES IT SHOCK ANYONE THAT WE AREN'T MATURE ENOUGH TO DEAL WITH BEING FAMOUS FOR SURVIVING A DEATH MATCH?
MY FRIENDS SHOULD BE SPENDING THIS SUMMER OUT ON SOME STUPID LAKE SOMEWHERE. GETTING SUNBURNT AND DRAGGED BEHIND A BOAT ON ONE OF THOSE GIANT INNER TUBES.
MOST PEOPLE GET TO GROW ALL THE WAY UP BEFORE THEY HAVE TO NAVIGATE THE POLITICS OF AN UNDERGROUND SUPER VILLAIN MEGACITY.
AND ME, WELL... I'M NO GOOD AT BEING A KID.
SORRY, MOM, BUT IT'S TRUE.
I DO WANT YOU TO GET BETTER. I JUST CAN'T BE THE ONLY REASON YOU DO. I CAN'T STICK AROUND PRETENDING.
THE MORE I THINK ABOUT IT, THE MORE I REALIZE I DON'T BELONG HERE AT ALL.

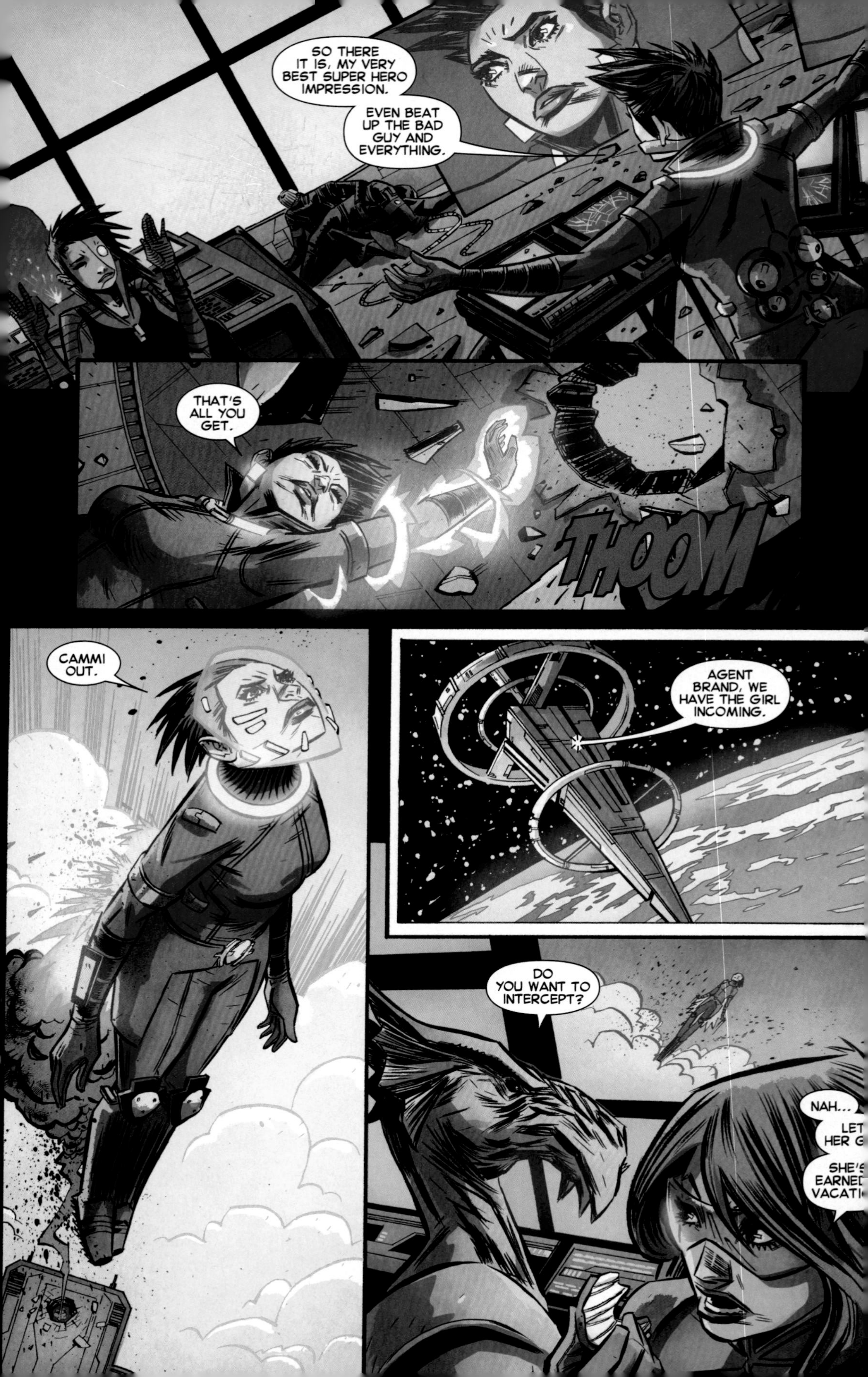
SO THERE IT IS, MY VERY BEST SUPER HERO IMPRESSION.
EVEN BEAT UP THE BAD GUY AND EVERYTHING.
THAT'S ALL YOU GET.
THOOM
CAMMI OUT.
AGENT BRAND, WE HAVE THE GIRL INCOMING.
DO YOU WANT TO INTERCEPT?
NAH...

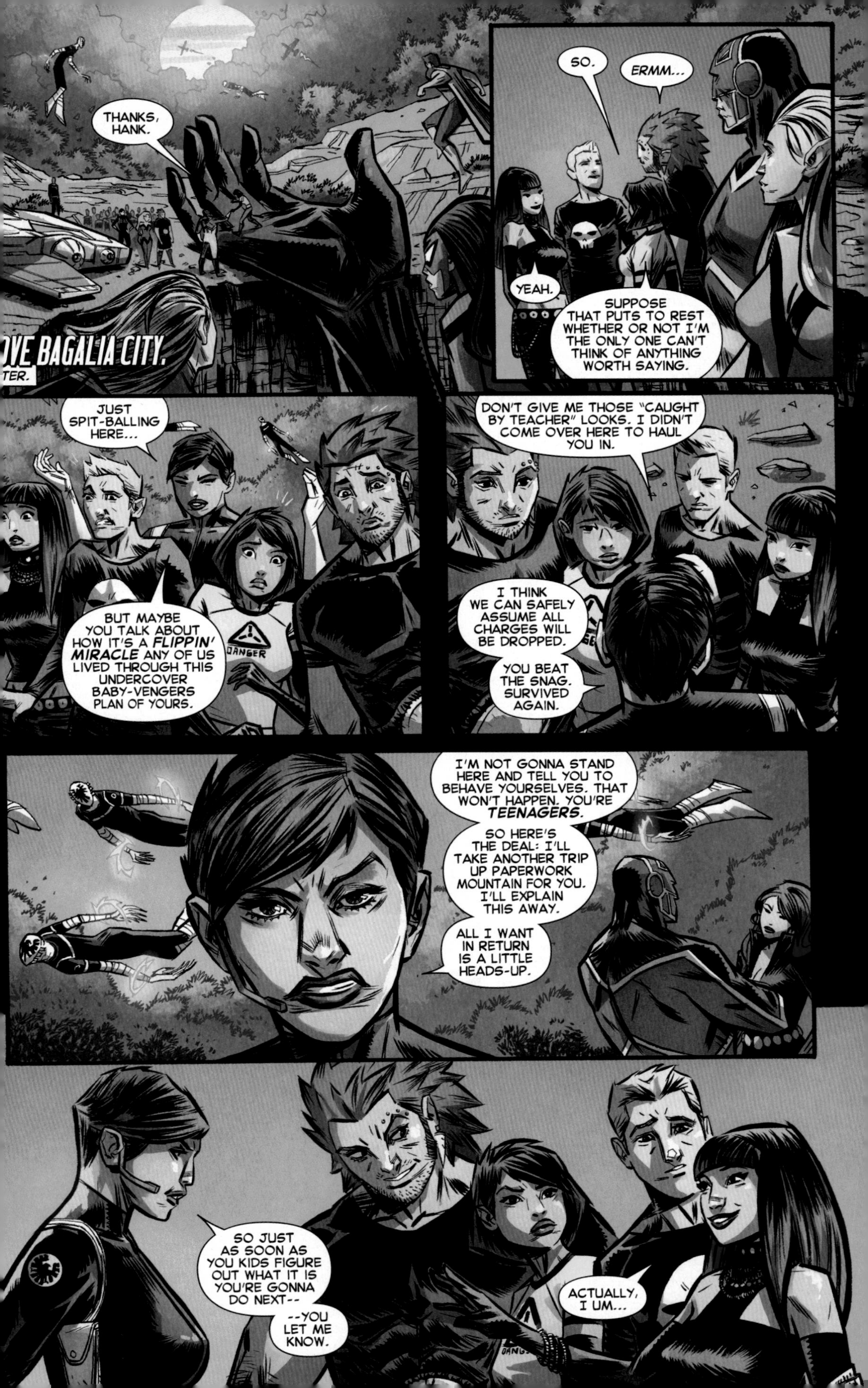

THANKS, HANK.
OVE BAGALIA CITY.
TER.
SO.
ERMM...
YEAH.
SUPPOSE THAT PUTS TO REST WHETHER OR NOT I'M THE ONLY ONE CAN'T THINK OF ANYTHING WORTH SAYING.
JUST SPIT-BALLING HERE...
BUT MAYBE YOU TALK ABOUT HOW IT'S A FLIPPIN' MIRACLE ANY OF US LIVED THROUGH THIS UNDERCOVER BABY-VENGERS PLAN OF YOURS.
DANGER
DON'T GIVE ME THOSE "CAUGHT BY TEACHER" LOOKS. I DIDN'T COME OVER HERE TO HAUL YOU IN.
I THINK WE CAN SAFELY ASSUME ALL CHARGES WILL BE DROPPED.
YOU BEAT THE SNAG. SURVIVED AGAIN.
I'M NOT GONNA STAND HERE AND TELL YOU TO BEHAVE YOURSELVES. THAT WON'T HAPPEN. YOU'RE TEENAGERS.
SO HERE'S THE DEAL: I'LL TAKE ANOTHER TRIP UP PAPERWORK MOUNTAIN FOR YOU. I'LL EXPLAIN THIS AWAY.
ALL I WANT IN RETURN IS A LITTLE HEADS-UP.
SO JUST AS SOON AS YOU KIDS FIGURE OUT WHAT IT IS YOU'RE GONNA DO NEXT--
--YOU LET ME KNOW.
ACTUALLY, I UM...

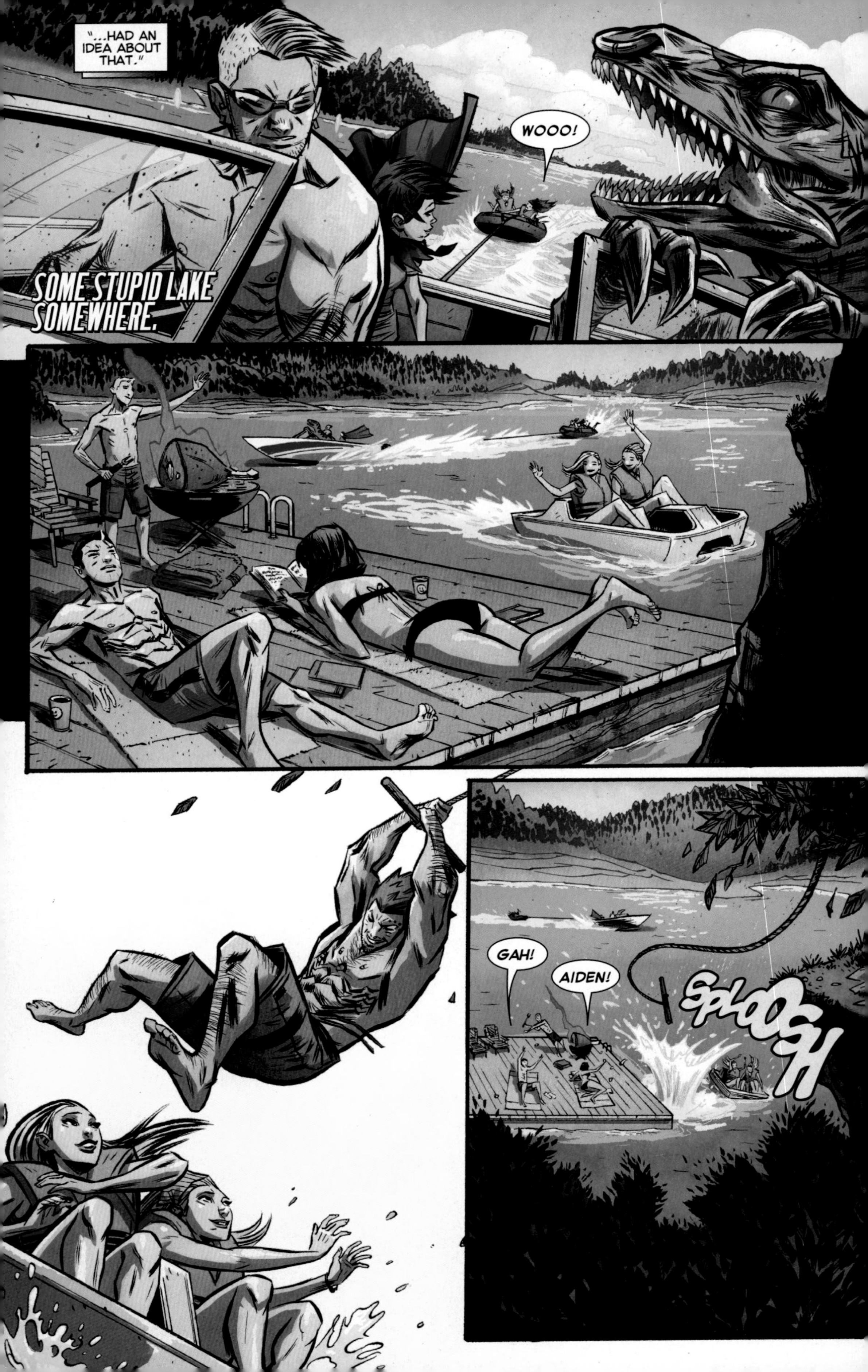
"...HAD AN IDEA ABOUT THAT."
WOOO!
SOME STUPID LAKE SOMEWHERE.
GAH!
AIDEN!
SPLOOSH

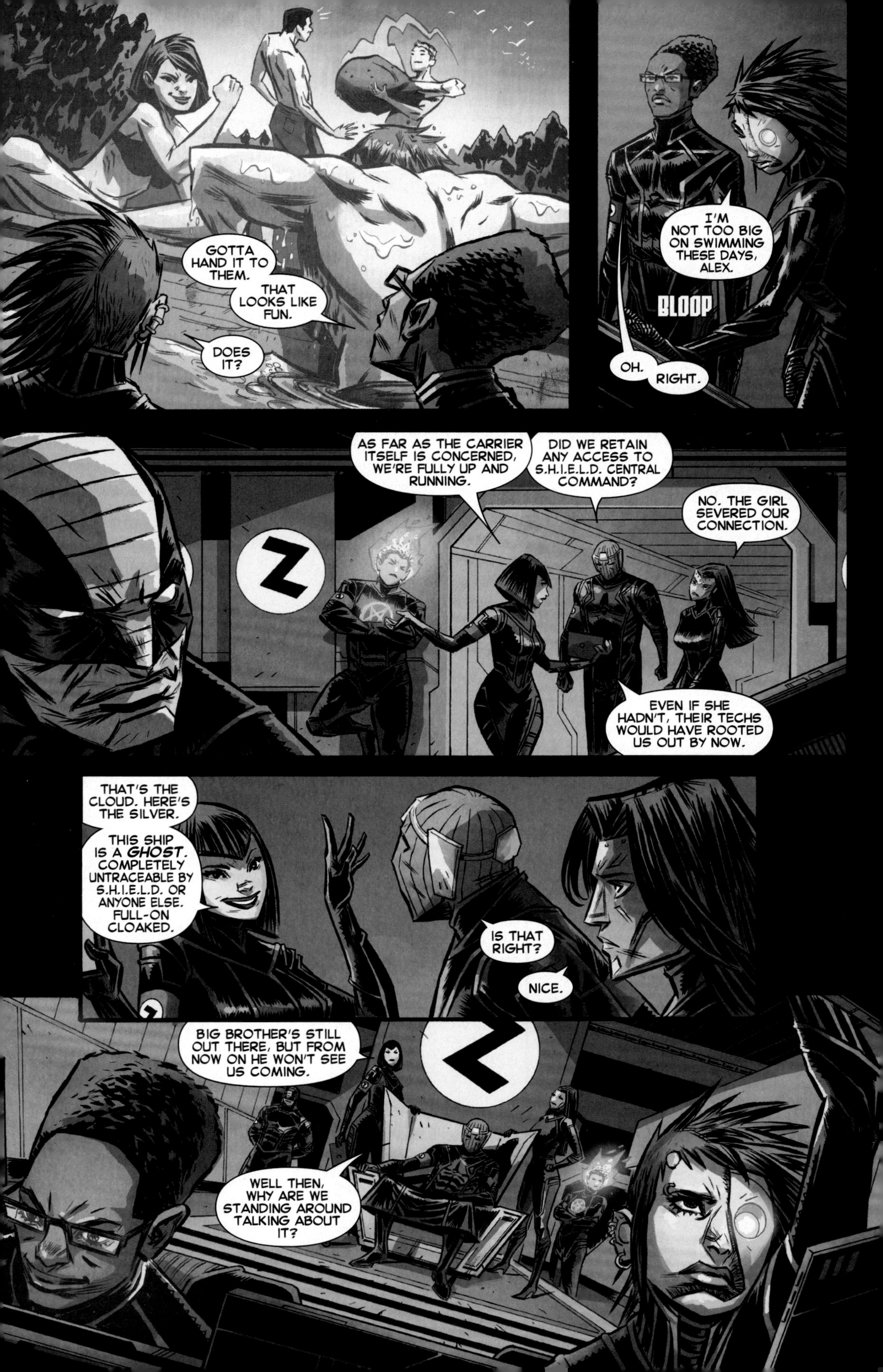

GOTTA HAND IT TO THEM.
THAT LOOKS LIKE FUN.
DOES IT?
I'M NOT TOO BIG ON SWIMMING THESE DAYS, ALEX.
BLOOP
OH.
RIGHT.
AS FAR AS THE CARRIER ITSELF IS CONCERNED, WE'RE FULLY UP AND RUNNING.
DID WE RETAIN ANY ACCESS TO S.H.I.E.L.D. CENTRAL COMMAND?
NO. THE GIRL SEVERED OUR CONNECTION.
EVEN IF SHE HADN'T, THEIR TECHS WOULD HAVE ROOTED US OUT BY NOW.
THAT'S THE CLOUD. HERE'S THE SILVER.
THIS SHIP IS A GHOST. COMPLETELY UNTRACEABLE BY S.H.I.E.L.D. OR ANYONE ELSE. FULL-ON CLOAKED.
IS THAT RIGHT?
NICE.
BIG BROTHER'S STILL OUT THERE, BUT FROM NOW ON HE WON'T SEE US COMING.
WELL THEN, WHY ARE WE STANDING AROUND TALKING ABOUT IT?

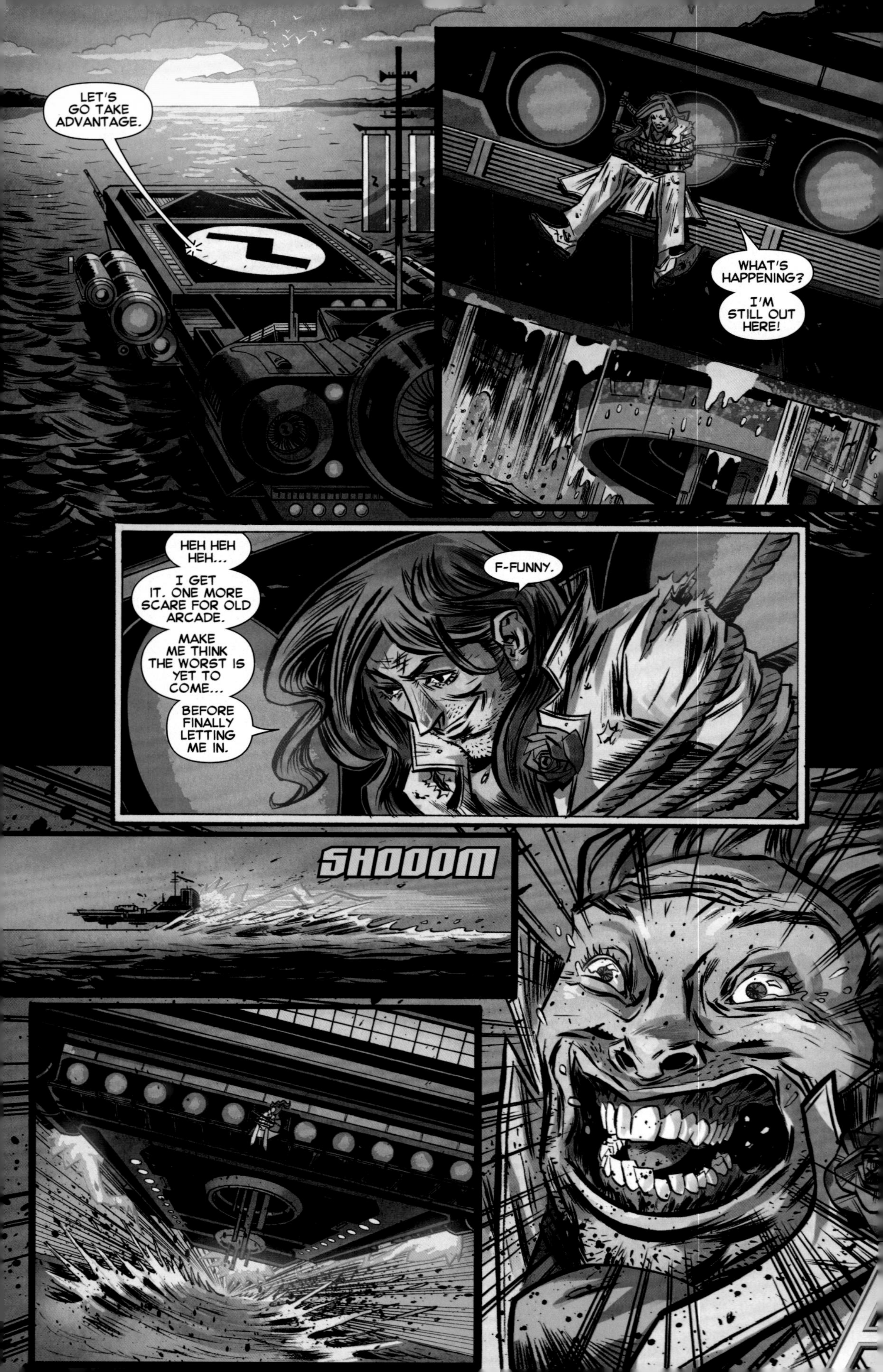
LET'S GO TAKE ADVANTAGE.
WHAT'S HAPPENING?
I'M STILL OUT HERE!
HEH HEH HEH...
I GET IT. ONE MORE SCARE FOR OLD ARCADE.
MAKE ME THINK THE WORST IS YET TO COME...
BEFORE FINALLY LETTING ME IN.
F-FUNNY.
SHOOOM

#8 LAYOUTS BY TIGH WALKER

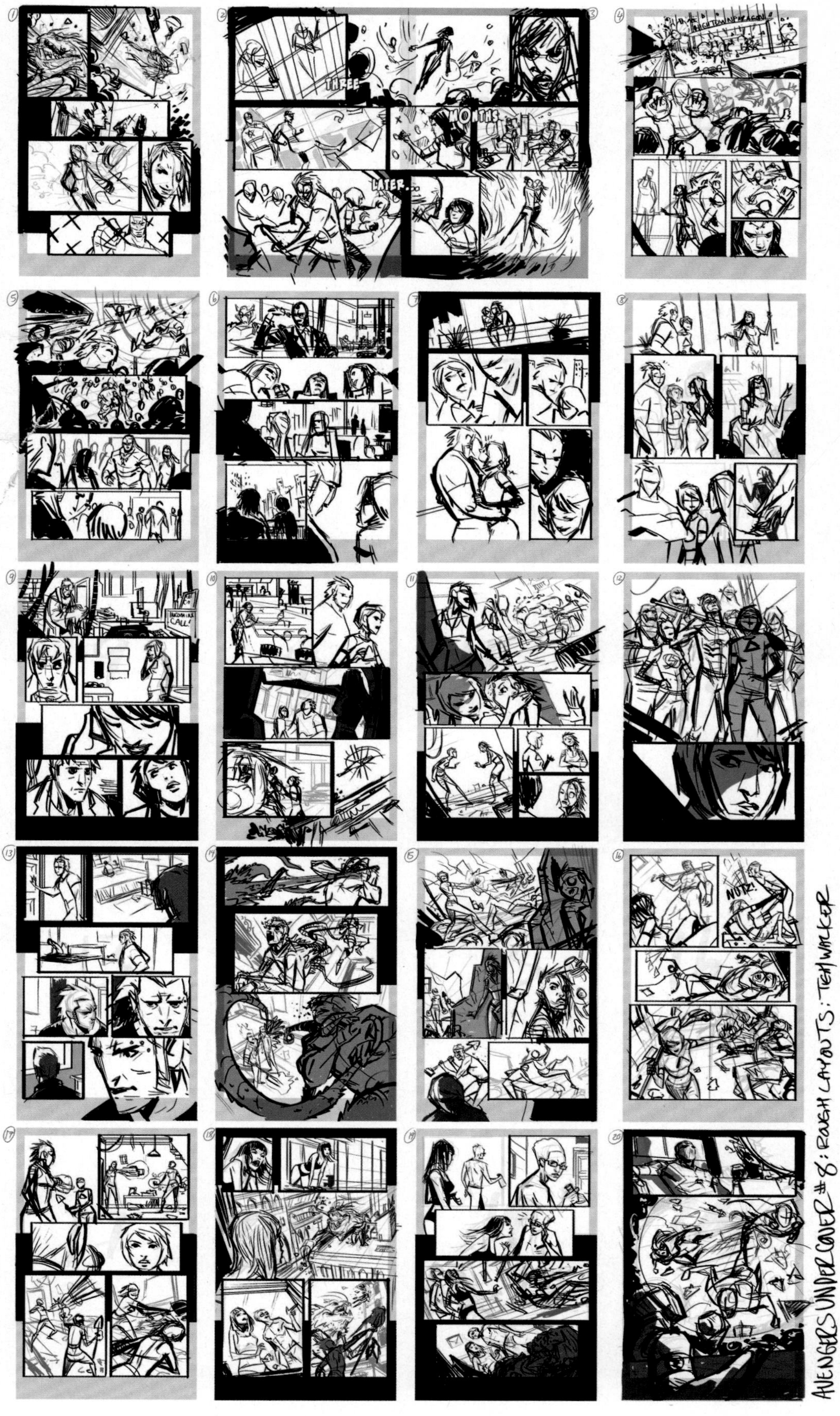
THREE
MONTHS
LATER...
NUTZ!
AVENGERS UNDERCOVER #8: ROUGH LAYOUTS: TIGH WALKER

#8 PAGE 11 AND 15 PENCILS AND INKS BY TIGH WALKER

AVENGERS UNDERCOVER #8 PG. 11

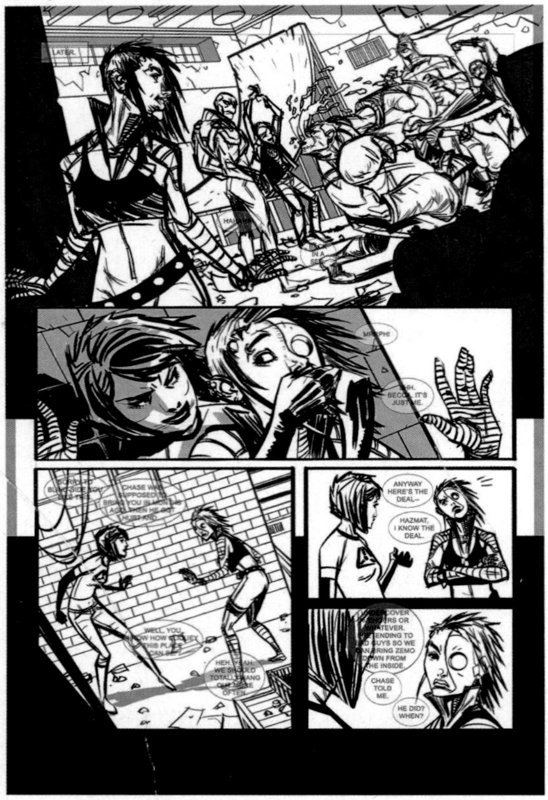
LATER.
MRRPH!
ANYWAY HERE'S THE DEAL--
HAZMAT, I KNOW THE DEAL.
CHASE TOLD ME.
HE DID? WHEN?

AVENGERS UNDERCOVER #8 PG. 15

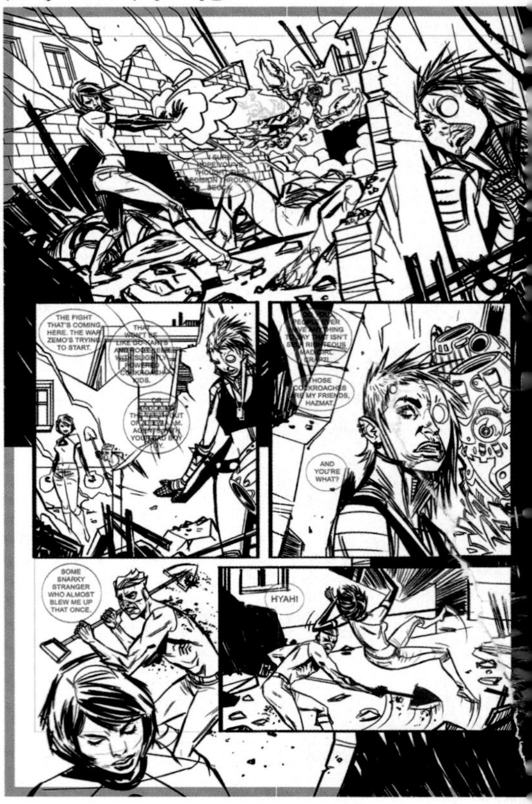
THE FIGHT THAT'S COMING. HERE. THE WAR ZEMO'S TRYING TO START.
AND YOU'RE WHAT?
SOME SNARKY STRANGER WHO ALMOST BLEW ME UP THAT ONCE.
HYAH!

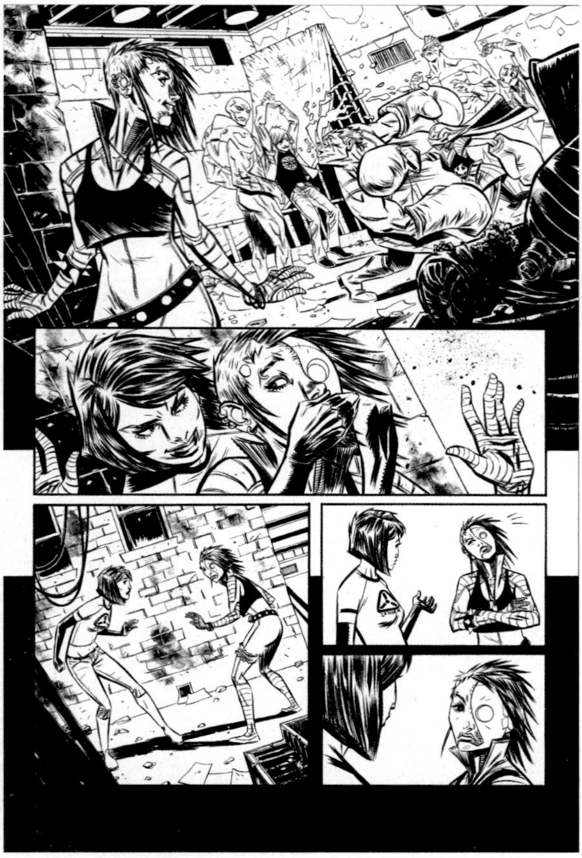

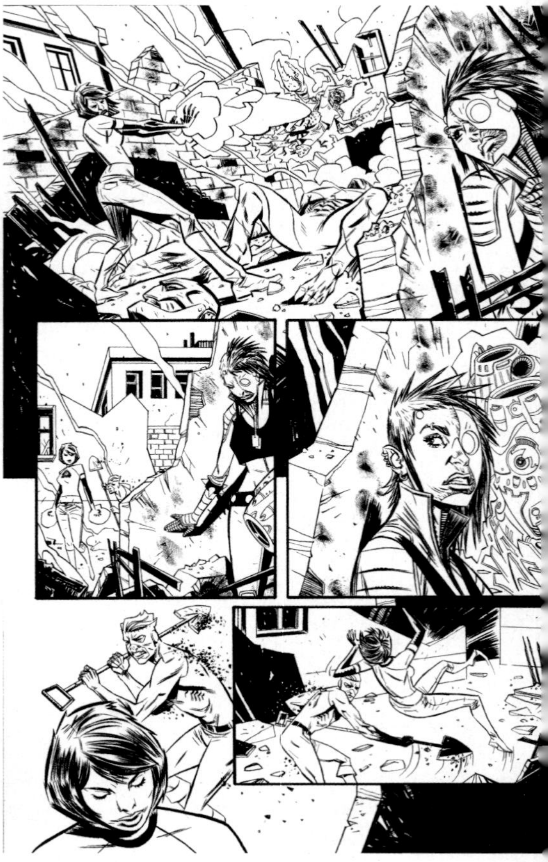